the VALLEY

CHRIS CLEMENT-GREEN

Mirror Books

Published by Mirror Books,
an imprint of Trinity Mirror plc,
1 Canada Square,
London E14 5AP, England

www.mirrorbooks.com
twitter.com/themirrorbooks

ISBN 978-1-907324-72-7

First paperback edition

**Names, dates and identifying details have been changed to
protect the privacy of individuals**

Printed and bound in Great Britain
by CPI Group (UK) Ltd, Croydon, CR0 4YY

Contents

1	New Beginnings	01
2	Once a Rebel...	09
3	It's a Man's World	16
4	The Importance of Being Spoofed	25
5	'Yer Doona Wanna Do That'	41
6	Taking the Rough With the Rough	54
7	Black Man's Wheels	64
8	Domestic Bliss	70
9	Life's a Riot	88
10	Angel Dust Andy	98
11	Driving, Drinking and Discretion	106
12	On Death and Dying	121
13	Big Thief, Little Thief	131
14	All In A Day's Work	146
15	The Ins and Outs of Sex	157
16	Baby Sitters	168
17	Sons and Daughters	184
18	Breaking Patterns - Not Bones	190
19	Guns and Teddy Bears	201
20	More Domestics, More Disputes	219
21	Life's Still a Riot	229
22	Face Off	249
23	Not All Gay Men Mince	265
24	Fallout (The Saga of Henley Regatta)	276
25	Dungeons and Pendragons	292
	Epilogue	299

This memoir is dedicated to the memory
of Kathleen May Clements – a mother
whose guidance is much missed

I'd also like to thank Mirror Books for their belief in
non-celebratory memoirs

CHAPTER 1

New Beginnings

In 1984 I had sleep-walked into a life of marriage and unfulfilling routine that paid the bills but did not challenge me. Climbing up the narrow wooden stairs to the staffroom, I pushed thirty-pence into the drinks machine and received a watery hot chocolate that matched the beige of the thin plastic cup it came in. Collapsing onto the steel-framed chair with the fewest dubious stains, I picked up an abandoned copy of the Oxford Mail and came across a half-page recruitment advert for Thames Valley Police:

Are you over 18? I was 24.

Do you have at least four O-levels? I had nine.

Are you over 5'8" if male, or 5'6" if female? I was 5'10" and female.

Are you looking for exciting challenges? Depends.

Would you like to earn £8,000 a year? Do bears shit in the woods – I was currently earning £3,500 for my nine-to-five and alternate Saturdays job, as a sales assistant in the famous Blackwell's bookshop.

Unashamedly motivated by the last question, I tore out and filled in the request for an application form. Pat, the shop's resident pessimist, walked in and glanced over my shoulder,

'You do know the police have the second highest rate of divorce?'

I was fully aware of this fact. I was secretly hoping that it might become the cherry on top of a double-my-income cake.

'You've done what!' Brian was apoplectic.

'I've applied to join the police.'

'In God's name, why?'

'So we can get out of this poxy flat and into a police house. So we can afford a decent car and nice holidays and, most importantly, I can look forward to getting out of bed in the morning!'

'But it won't just be mornings will it? You'll be doing shifts – we'll never see each other!'

'Yeah, Brian, I get that you hate shift work – it's why you left Cowley – and why we're stuck living here.' I swept an accusing arm around the cramped galley kitchen.

I knew I was being bitchy but, since posting off that application, I was growing more and more excited by the prospect of a different life; I was sick of stacking shelves – even if it was books and not cornflakes. There was no challenge, no chance to use my brain or initiative; my only decisions revolved around what to eat for lunch. I wasn't about to let my husband's rut-riven expectations rain on my parade. However, guilt made me try a more conciliatory tone. 'I probably won't get in.'

'If you do, you won't be there long – you'll never take the discipline.' Brian drained his mug, wiped the back of a still-oily hand across his salt and pepper moustache. Getting up from the table with a shake of his head, he went back outside to work on the diarrhoea-coloured Austin Princess he'd just bought.

The sergeant in charge of shuffling potential recruits from pillar to post imparted one piece of advice. 'If you're asked if you mind where you're posted, say no – even if you do. They're unlikely to go to the expense of moving you too far from home, but you need to appear flexible.'

I was both amused and alarmed at being asked to start my police career with a lie, however small and white, but I was prepared to do whatever it took.

I was also confident enough in my B-plus looks to remain unperturbed as I watched my passport photo travel between the three middle-aged men sitting behind the large, highly polished table. Each stared at the photo, glanced at me and stared at the photo again before passing it on. It ended up back with the man in the middle, the assistant chief constable.

'You're not nearly as ugly in real life,' he observed.

He wasn't wrong. My face in the photo resembled the surface of the moon.

'No, Sir. I had an allergic reaction to some new biological washing powder when that was taken, but I wanted to get my application in before the closing date.'

He nodded and slipped the offending image back under the paperclip, which held together the rest of my paperwork. I sensed a palpable relief that they would not have to employ a truly ugly woman police constable.

'So, Mrs Foster, what does your husband think of you becoming a WPC?'

'He's very supportive, Sir.'

'What about children?'

'Children?'

'Do you have any children?'

'No, Sir.'

'How long before you intend starting a family?'

'I've never wanted children, Sir not my thing.'

'And your husband's okay with that?' The question held a tone of mild disbelief.

'Yes, Sir. He's 13 years older than me and has a son from his first marriage.'

'Do you look after the boy?'

'God no!' The three men looked offended by this reaction and I quickly added, 'What I mean, Sir, is that the lad lives with his mother.'

One of the two divisional superintendents then asked if my husband would be prepared to move and, despite being tied into a fairly new six-month tenancy agreement, I lied,

'Yes Sir, we've discussed all the implications.'

It was a warm morning in mid-April when I stood to attention with 39 other recruits in the lecture theatre of Sulhamstead Park near Reading. With my right hand raised and a serious-ness of purpose I'd never experienced before, not even on my wedding day, I swore allegiance to Her Majesty the Queen.

I swear by almighty God that I will well and truly serve the Queen in the office of constable, with fairness, integrity, diligence and impartiality. I will, to the best of my power, cause the peace to be kept and preserve and prevent all offences against people and property; and that while I continue to hold the said office I will, to the best of my skill and knowledge, dis-charge all the duties thereof faithfully according to law.

Although I didn't believe in God, I meant every other word.

Thirty minutes later my lungs and legs were burning; I could feel sweat dripping into eyes scrunched against such unknown exertion. The fitness test consisted of a one-and-a-half mile run, followed by a minute each of press-ups, burpees, sit-ups, thrust-jumps and star-jumps. It finished with a flexi-bility test which, thank God, involved sitting down and stretching forward to touch upturned toes. The WPCs had thirteen-and-a-half minutes to complete the run; the men were allowed only ten.

My efforts were rewarded by a new force record, which, as far as I'm aware, has never been beaten. No one in the illustrious history of Thames Valley Police recruit training has ever taken 26 minutes to complete that run – exactly twice the allotted time – and I didn't stop once. I was in perpetual motion, with one of the physical training instructors walking alongside my jogging frame yelling encouragement, 'Come on WPC Foster – make a fucking effort!'

That night in the bar I was approached by a pack of alpha males. David Blythe BEM was their natural leader.

'You're the 26-minuter aren't you?'

I nodded acknowledgement, embarrassed by such early notoriety.

'Most of us,' Dave indicated the pack, 'are doing it in under seven.'

'Bully for you.'

Dave ignored the sarcasm. 'We're each prepared to sponsor you ten pence per minute over the first ten that you can keep the run going.' I must have looked confused because he added, 'The longer we have to recover from the run the more we can put into our gym reps – we got records of our own to break.'

Dave was shorter than most of the pack but seemed to carry more authority. His British Empire Medal was awarded for bomb-disposal duties in Northern Ireland and, when another recruit observed, 'Britain's no longer got an Empire, mate – they should rename it the Isle of White Badge!' Dave's response had been swift and silent – the observer landing on his arse with a bloodied nose.

I counted the pack and did a quick mental calculation; it could work out at over a tenner a test. I shook hands on my pact with the pack.

After a week's initiation at Sulhamstead, I arrived at Ryton-on-Dunsmore regional training centre at six on a Sunday evening. We were sent to the gym where a row of ten desks lined the far wall. Behind each desk sat a bored-looking sergeant, and as I waited to be called forward to have my details ticked off, I saw Alpha Dave looking business-like in a dark blue suit.

As we headed off towards the two red-brick accommodation blocks, we were each hauling a suitcase and carrying five hangers holding pressed shirts.

'How come the difference?' I waved my white shirts at Dave.

'Well now, there are two theories. One is that you whoopsie [as we WPCs were affectionately called] won't be getting down and dirty like us lads and can therefore afford to wear white, and the other runs along the lines that if a whoopsie does find herself in a bundle, the white shirt will make her easier to identify and rescue.' Dave grinned at me and slung his blue shirts over his shoulder.

'Bollocks!' I retorted.

'Well what's your theory?' When I couldn't think of one he shouted, 'See you in the bar' as he peeled off towards the male block.

My room was magnolia and adequate. It contained a single bed with a duvet and one pillow (both had hard white cotton covers emblazoned with the centre's logo), a plywood wardrobe with three drawers, a basin, a desk and a chair. I quickly unpacked and was sitting on the edge of the bed wondering what to do next when a female voice boomed up the stairs,

'Ladies! Rec room, five minutes!'

We emerged from our rooms smiling nervously and headed downstairs to the lounge. We were all wearing dresses or skirts as instructed by our joining papers. When not in uniform or gym kit, men had to wear suits, collars and ties and women dresses or skirts – no trousers, not even as a trouser-suit, for the girlies. This had pissed me off – I'd had to go out and buy a skirt – but I was prepared to play the game if only to show Brian I could.

He'd been generous in his praise at my getting through the interview process, but remained quietly sceptical about me making it through basic training.

In the lounge, WPS Redman went through the centre's rules. Two were reinforced: no males in the female accommodation block, not even the lounge; and everyone must be in the bar between eight and ten every night, no exceptions!

A rather bookish-looking girl raised her hand, 'But sergeant, shouldn't we be studying in the evening?'

'Yes, WPC King, you will indeed need to study every evening. The Monday morning exam has a pass mark of eighty-five percent and if you fail it you'll have to re-sit it on Friday afternoon, when everyone else is buggering off home. And, as your class instructors will no doubt remind you, three fails and you're out! But,' she sighed, this was obviously a conversation she had every fourteen weeks, 'you'll still need to be in the bar between eight and ten. Working relationships are as important as exam marks – this is not a job you can do on your own and your socialising skills, like everything else you do here, will be monitored and reported on.'

'But definitely no socialising in here with the lads?' I couldn't help myself. Except for the sergeant I was the oldest female there and already feeling patronised.

'No, WPC Foster – *no socialising in here with the lads* – not that you'll be wanting to being *a married* woman.' She raised an over-plucked eyebrow.

I was one of only two married women in the whole intake, and as I looked around at my fellow recruits I realised that the younger girls would probably want to fly below the sergeant's radar. They didn't strike me as potential fellow rebels and, in fairness, policing was not a job you joined to break the rules. But Brian was right about me, I've never been big on rules, especially if they seemed petty or perverse; like the 'two-item rule'.

'Your rooms will be inspected every morning before eight o'clock parade and you can only have two items on show; if your toothbrush and toothpaste are left out they will be considered your two items.'

I was already thinking that my giant orange and chocolate-brown teddy bear and a pig poster stating *Shit Happens* would brighten up the magnolia no end.

CHAPTER 2

Once a Rebel...

My teenage friends would have been horrified that I joined the police at all. They would have condemned me for going over to the 'dark side'. They were a great group of cider-drinking, bike-riding, pretend Hells Angels, who head-banged to Lynyrd Skynyrd and grew their own marijuana from seeds collected from packets of budgie food.

I am secretly proud to say that I cultivated a number of plants to a respectable height, although they never reached the maturity required for use. I was sixteen and studying hard for my O-levels when I recall my mum walking into my bedroom with an armful of ironing and a cup of tea. She noticed the three small tomato-like plants on the windowsill, which I'd moved from behind the normally half-closed curtains,

"They're nice, love, what are they?"

'Pot plants,' I replied without looking up.

'Lovely.' She closed the door, leaving me to my studies.

Everyone in the gang possessed cannabis plants at varying stages of maturity. Weevil (so named because he once ate a live maggot for a bet), was the only one of us with a car and for some reason – he never satisfactorily explained – he even kept a small seed-tray in his glove compartment.

I also smoked commercially grown weed and by fifteen could roll a good tight joint. Our gang was based in a small cottage at the foot of Cheddar Gorge and we would spend milder nights sitting around a small fire in one of the shallow caves near the top of the gorge, drinking scrumpy, sharing joints and arguing the merits of Lynyrd Skynyrd and Deep Purple, versus the newly arrived Meat Loaf.

At seventeen I left home to study A-levels at Chippenham Tech, together with a riding instructor's exam. Horses were a lifelong passion that had been joined by heavy-metal bikers. I still came home each weekend, and one Saturday night was sitting with the gang in our local, when two strangers walked in. Like a bad cowboy movie a short hush followed their progress to the bar and when the noise resumed, it carried whispered warnings that they were drug squad from Weston-super-Mare.

'How can you tell?' I asked Tiny (who was ironically named).

'Look at their shoes,' he replied, his right hand shoving a recently purchased eighth of Moroccan-black down the back of the soiled padded seating.

I laughed out loud when I saw the polished loafers peeping out from the men's shrink-to-fit jeans. Nevertheless, their presence in the midst of our tight-knit biking community resulted in quite a few people hurrying out, to return a few minutes later with a look of relieved defiance on their faces.

Clarence (so named because of his slight squint; like the famous cross-eyed lion) rushed over to our table.

'They've asked Barry about the cottage. We're going to get raided!'

'I doubt it – not tonight anyway.' My confidence was based on the arrogance of youth and an addiction to documentaries – odd for a seventeen-year-old, I know. 'They don't do raids without uniform in tow. They're just sussing things out.'

'Well, we need to get rid of the plants. They're too big to

hide.' Clarence, whose name was on the rent-book, had the most to lose. We nodded agreement.

Then I had what I thought was a brilliant idea. 'Wait until later tonight. I've got a plan.'

It wasn't a 'cunning plan' (Blackadder belonged to the future), but it appealed to both the Buddhist and the rebel in me. When I outlined my idea to the gang, it divided them. The ones with jobs or at college were all for it, the ones who still wore black and gold T-shirts declaring 'Ride Hard – Die Young' were more cautious. As with all split decisions we held a vote. We had always been democratic bikers, but while most decisions revolved around available money and/or transport, this one was based on guts – who had them and who didn't.

Peer pressure paid off and at two in the morning we reconvened at the cottage with our respective pot plants. There were twenty-seven in all.

It was the Buddha in me that hated the idea of killing anything living. I was the teenager who would insist on rescuing the spider rather than have someone stamp on it, and when the cottage was invaded by a mouse it was me who insisted on a humane trap.

At three, the famous four (Weevil, Tiny, Clarence and me) walked the six hundred yards to the local bobby's house, which also acted as a part-time police station. Amongst hushed giggles, brought on by the joint we had shared for luck, we set about rehoming our little collection of plants in the front garden of the police station.

Fortunately it was the plants that vanished quickly, rather than the local bobby.

By the time I joined the police, I hadn't smoked pot since college. My adult friends thought the whole idea of me joining was hilarious and, like my husband, assumed I'd never take the discipline. They were all convinced that I'd be chucked out in a matter of weeks, if not days.

The first week of training passed quickly with the majority of it taking place behind desks, where we learnt law by reading books and asking endless 'what if' questions. We fell silent and stood whenever a sergeant or inspector entered the classroom and saluted all inspectors or above whenever we saw them. In addition to law we learnt: first-aid, self-defence, life-saving, drill and radio procedure. We also got fit, (in my case fit enough to complete the last run in just under twelve minutes), and we travelled between classroom, pool, gym and parade square as a marching squad. Alpha Dave became the class drill-pig – in charge of class turnout and marching – and he took this responsibility as seriously as his fitness tests.

Monday morning of week two saw a giant teddy sitting smartly on my bed, while the pig poster had been blu-tacked to the wall above my desk. Sergeant Redman's outrage was satisfying in its predictability,

'What are those monstrosities, WPC Foster?'

'My two items, Sergeant.'

She threw a look of pure malice at me before storming back down the corridor. When the outer door banged shut, the other recruits who, like me, had been standing to attention outside our open bedroom doors, burst into tense laughter. They took bets on WPC Foster getting 'nine-o'clockers' for the remaining thirteen weeks.

These unpopular evening sessions meant getting changed out of civvies and into your best uniform for inspection by the duty sergeant at 9pm, followed by changing back into civvies to help clear up the bar at ten; before re-pressing and re-polishing of said uniform ready for the next day's parade.

I closed my door and was preparing for class when the female inspector knocked and walked straight in. She found it hard to conceal a smile but left with a straight face and without saying a word or looking at me. Running to the door I was in time to hear,

'Yes, sergeant, rules are rules, but she doesn't appear to be actually breaking any.'

Sergeant Redman took her revenge the following morning when she awarded me a nine o'clock parade for 'tramlines' in my tunic sleeve. No one else could see these imaginary double lines where only one pressed crease should be, but I remained surprisingly philosophical about the whole thing. I quickly realised that no recruit was likely to leave Ryton without at least one late-night punishment parade – who else would clear up the bar each night?

I thought *eat your heart out Brian* as I marched around the parade square revelling in all the shouting and stomping to stirring military music. It was the least useful part of basic training, but I was surprised to find it the most enjoyable. Dave was determined our class would win the coveted Drill Cup, so most lunchtimes found us on the parade square for extra practice. Then, in the fifth week of our fourteen weeks of training, Metpol arrived.

The night before, we'd all gathered around our respective accommodation-block TVs to watch the evening news and the pitched battle between police and miners outside Orgreave colliery. Metropolitan Police officers had been drafted in as reinforcements and were suddenly billeted at the centre, in some unused Nissan huts at the far end of the Parade Square. They'd lounge around the bar before starting out for a night on the picket lines, and their experience attracted other recruits like moths to a flame. I think this was the first time that Metpol officers had been deployed in any numbers outside London and they strutted around like urban knights, brought in to help out the carrot-crunching peasants.

Their self-absorbed arrogance got right up my nose – as did the strike tie-pins they were all wearing. The small enamelled circles had the initials ASPOM (Arthur Scargill Pays Our Mortgage – thanks to the excessive overtime) curved around a crossed pick-axe and truncheon. I later learned that Thames Valley officers were selling their spare blue shirts to Nottinghamshire and Leicestershire officers who, like Metpol, wore white. The miners hated all coppers, but they hated Metpol with an admirable intensity, and they were giving any officer in a white shirt as much shit as possible – quite literally in some cases.

The day after Metpol descended on Ryton like a hoard of disruptive locusts, Dave was conducting another lunchtime drill practice. As usual he was balling instructions at the top of his very powerful lungs, when two Metpol officers approached him from the Nissan huts.

'What the fuck do you think you're playing at?' they yelled

Dave was standing too far away for us to hear his reply, but we all heard the two officers clearly outline what they would do to Dave if he didn't *desist from all the fucking stamping and shouting.* They then returned, muttering further profanities, to their cooling beds.

Dave was not a man easily distracted; and five minutes later the class returned to the square, still in full uniform but now sporting trainers and radios, over which Dave gave his commands. The night we won the drill cup was a serious celebration which, to everyone's surprise, not least of all Dave's, ended with a full-on kiss from the married WPC

Foster. I'd grown to like Dave but I certainly didn't fancy him. I was simply swept up by the moment and a little drunk.

Metpol were gone from the centre in under a week. It was rumoured they'd stolen the commandant's car and sold it at the local auction for beer money.

Brian was suitably impressed at the passing-out parade. He swept me into his arms as the parade was dismissed for the final time.

'I've got to hand it to you, darling, you did it!'

I'm not sure if he could feel my reluctance to be kissed in front of my classmates, but his smile was one of genuine pride and I suddenly felt guilty. At the time I brushed aside the feeling as connected to the kiss I'd given Dave but, looking back on it, I think I was feeling guilty about the (still subconscious) embarrassment of Brian's lack of career. I certainly felt guilty about cherries on cakes – my motive for joining being divorce. So I clung on to my husband's arm, smiled, and forced a feeling that things would be okay now.

CHAPTER 3

It's a Man's World

We had survived fourteen weeks of basic training and (with one exception) we were all still standing. After passing out, we had a week's holiday before returning to Sulhamstead for a further two weeks of training in local procedures and policies.

As probationers bursting with knowledge and (often misplaced) confidence, we were desperate to be out in the real world. Although these two weeks passed quickly enough, I had a further two days to wait, as my new shift had that weekend off. It was not until 10pm the following Monday that I officially started as the newest member of 'C' Shift at St Aldates Police Station in the centre of Oxford. My first tour of duty was nights – the most exciting time for a probationer. Night-time equalled 'crime-time'.

When Inspector Cooper walked into the parade room of St Aldates, the twelve PCs, three WPCs and two sergeants scraped back their plywood chairs and stood to attention. He seated himself at the head of the table, but it was PS Brown, the patrol sergeant, who conducted the pre-shift parade. He assigned car and foot beats and briefed us on local crime trends.

Coops (as the shift referred to him once he retreated to his office, with its habitually closed door) sat in sullen silence, turning a cold, reptilian stare in my direction at regular intervals. He reminded me of a snake slowly waving his head from side to side, sniffing out idleness, fear or incompetence. He had a spiteful air about him that was underlined by dead eyes, an unsmiling, thin-lipped mouth and dyed black hair, which was swept backwards and set with Brylcreem.

When the shift was officially 'dismissed to its duties', I turned to my new tutor constable, Daniel, who would be my full-time patrol partner for the next ten weeks. It was his job to transfer classroom theory into real-life policing.

'Have I done something wrong? Inspector Cooper kept glaring at me.'

'Well, WPC Foster, you've had the temerity to join the police after the Police Woman's Department was disbanded.'

'That was eight years ago!'

Daniel shrugged. 'What can I say, the man's a dinosaur. He'll ignore you until you do something wrong or,' he winked at me, 'you do something so good he has to acknowledge you!'

I knew I was going to like Daniel. He was only a few years older than me, broad, solid, dependable looking, with dark hair clipped to a half-inch length over his round head. He had an open face with hazelnut eyes that held a continual gleam of mischief and, unlike Coops, his lips loved to turn upwards.

Having been assigned city-centre foot patrol, we set out up St Aldates towards the centre of Oxford. Catching my reflection in a shop window I recall a mental jolt – this was it, I was a proper copper heading out to see what the night would throw in my direction. I kept glancing in shop windows, seeing the uniform and feeling confused, alien, but excited. As we approached one of the several kebab vans scattered around the city centre, an oversized traffic cop was waiting for his meal to be wrapped. The pound note he offered in payment was waved away by the man serving him.

'Alright, Daniel?' he bit into his kebab.

'Not bad, Rodge. This is Chris Foster, she's just joined the shift – first night.' Daniel winked again.

'Well, WPC Foster, let me tell you something,' said Rodge, chewing on both his kebab and the advice he was about to impart. 'Never get off the pavement for anyone and if a black lad looks you in the eye get ready to fight or run.'

I looked at Daniel to see what he made of this advice, but he just smiled and gave another small shrug.

Thud, thud: I could feel the beat of my heart as I stepped out into the rain-soaked road. Raising my right arm to shoulder-height, I held out my shaking palm towards the oncoming, speeding headlight – headlight singular. A light rain ran off my Gore-Tex overcoat, but the slim radio clipped to its lapel crackled comfortingly, reassuring me that I now belonged to the biggest gang; the one with real power. My mouth was desert-dry and the adrenalin coursing through my body continued to make my gloved hand shake as I signalled the approaching car to stop.

Daniel had told me to pull the vehicle over and issue a HORT/1 (a form requiring the driver to produce all vehicle-related documents at a police station within seven days). I was to then instruct them to get their headlight fixed. That was the plan: the simple, straightforward, get-your-toes-wet plan.

As the car slowed, pulled into the kerb and came to a reluctant halt, reggae music blasted from the blacked-out windows and the driver's door was flung open with righteous indignation. The driver leapt out and my heart sank: he was black and the defiantly opened door showed three more black lads inside. Two to four I thought, as I touched my radio for reassurance and luck.

The driver was bopping up and down at my side, gesticulating wildly and demanding to know why I was picking on him. Every stereotype I'd ever heard during basic training slammed into place like a cell door locking. I looked around for Daniel, but he'd stepped back into the shadows of a shop doorway and with folded arms was assessing my progress – or lack of it.

As I slowly made my way through a form that had seemed so simple in a warm dry classroom, the driver became more and more agitated.

'Harassment, man! That's what this is. Harassment, pure and simple!'

He kept sucking in air through clenched teeth and calling me 'Babylon', while his anger was echoed like some Greek chorus of doom by the car's passengers. My 'sirs' became terse, returned through my own tightening jaw as I struggled to control my breathing, my shaking hand and a cheap biro that wouldn't work in the fine rain. I felt vulnerable and scared while struggling to sound officious.

At last my tutor stepped from the doorway. His sudden appearance brought the youth to a standstill, silencing his umpteenth chant of, 'You only pulled me cos I black'. Daniel spoke quietly into the lad's ear and whatever he said turned the youth's eyes hard. His only movement now was the slow clenching and unclenching of his right fist.

'WPC Foster, please issue this delightful young man with a ticket for the defective light.'

As I filled out the form I wasn't sure which was more frightening, the lad's earlier dance of protest or this more chilling, sullen stillness. The chorus had also picked up on the change in dynamic and had fallen silent; the lad in the front passenger seat turned off the music and unclipped his seatbelt. With fear coursing through my body, I forced my hand to grip the pen as I quickly finished off and handed the pad to the driver for a signature. It was delivered with such stabbing force that it dug a hole in the soggy paper. As the car sped off I turned to my tutor with relief.

'What did you say to him?' My question was full of quiet excitement – this was it, this was how real police work got done.

'I simply reassured him that he'd been stopped because his vehicle had a defective headlight.' Daniel smirked before adding, 'but she's booking you *"cause you black"*.' He thought it hilarious and just desserts for giving his probie such a hard time.

I felt obliged to join in Daniel's laughter but inside I was crushed and angry. With only half an hour on the job I felt afraid for the consequences of what had just happened. The race riots of the early Eighties were once more bubbling to the surface in cities all over Britain, and encounters like this just turned up the heat under the pot.

But Daniel was to prove something of a paradox. Later that same night we were dispatched to a disturbance at a local convenience store, where a young white teenager was hurling racial abuse at an Asian shopkeeper who had refused to sell him alcohol.

'You fucking Paki – get back to your own fucking country if you're not going to do your fucking job here!'

The lad was in his late teens and had a skinhead haircut that was only slightly more severe than Daniel's. He also sported a dotted-line tattooed around his neck with the words 'Cut here'.

Grabbing the tattoo, Daniel declared, 'Right you racist piece of shit, you're under arrest!'

He didn't bother cautioning his prisoner as he pushed his face against the brick wall of the shop and proceeded to handcuff the lad – tightening up the cuffs until I saw the white wrists turn bright pink.

The lad was unrepentant. 'Get off me you fucking fascist bastard!'

Back at the station Daniel pushed Sergeant Jarrett for the lad to be charged with a public order offence rather than be merely cautioned for a breach of the peace.

'I can't stand racists!' He declared.

'Fucking uniform-carrier!' Shaz, another tutor constable, stormed out of the parade room slamming the door behind her.

I was entering from the night kitchen with two mugs of tea. 'What's up with her?' I asked Daniel.

'Cherry's tutorship is being extended.'

'So?'

'So, it's hardly fair, is it? If you were as pathetic as Cherry you'd be out on your little white ass.'

'Why thank you, Daniel.'

'For what?'

'A: confirming I'm not pathetic, and B – more importantly – I've got a *little* ass.'

My tutor ignored my fake girliness. 'While you were at Ryton, how many black and Asian probies failed the weekly exam?'

'One or two.'

'As a matter of interest, how many were actually there?'

I did a quick memory sweep, 'Four or five.'

'And what happened to those who failed?'

'Nothing – they did re-sits.'

'And how many times were they allowed to do that?'

'More than the three times I'd have had.' I realised where

Daniel was heading.

'Did any white officer fail three exams?'

'One. An ex-sailor from Portsmouth.'

'And what happened to him?'

'He got the boot.'

Daniel had made his point.

'Scarman thinks it's necessary to...'

'Don't give me that political bullshit, Chris! It's positive discrimination plain and simple – just another fucking example of the government playing fast and loose with what's right and what's fair.'

I'd read up on the Scarman Report for my interview. Following the race riots of 1981, Scarman, a leading judge, headed an inquiry into the reasons behind the unrest. He'd come up with several recommendations on how to tackle the longstanding racial tensions between the black community and the police. The main one involved positive discrimination in the future recruitment of police officers from ethnic minority backgrounds, to make police forces more representative of the communities they policed.

'And what really pisses me off,' continued Daniel, 'is that the good ethnics, like Raj and Chalky, get labelled uniform-carriers, too.'

'Hadn't thought of that.'

'Neither did Scarman! Take Raj – his family disowned him the day he joined our lot. Not one family member came to his passing-out parade.'

'Why?'

'Because he's from a high-caste family that expected him to become a high-caste surgeon, not a low-caste copper. And what about Chalky? We get called *Babylon*, the oppressor, but Chalky's called *coconut* – brown on the outside but white on the inside. He's viewed as a traitor by many in his own community who don't flinch from calling him that to his face.'

I'd never really thought about Chalky in this light before. To me he was just a really funny guy who did Lenny Henry impressions and, like the comedian, told racist jokes.

Daniel was on a roll. 'And on top of all the name-calling crap, they have to put up with the Cherrys of this world who are too scared, too lazy, or generally too useless to do this bloody job. Their only function is to make up ethnic numbers for the sodding politicians.'

'That's a little harsh.'

'Harsh! You might think she's harmless, but her presence screws over all the good ethnics who have to fight every day. Fight their family, their former friends, their communities and even some of us, for recognition as good coppers in their own right and not one of Scarman's freebies.'

'So, what'll happen to Cherry?' As a fellow probationer I had divided loyalties.

'Shaz will have to put right the damage Scarman's caused.'

'How?'

'Wait and see.'

I was about to push Daniel for an answer when a ten-nine shout came over the radio. 'Ten-nine' meant an officer was in physical danger and required immediate assistance. Every other officer responds, even CID turn out from the warmth of the nick; and everyone keeps responding until the shout is cancelled. This was my first ten-nine and we joined everyone else piling into the back yard and any available vehicle. Blues and twos were already ignited and the engines revving hard as the last officers flung themselves through open doors, scrambling for any empty seat.

'Where are we going?' I shouted to Daniel as we rolled

around the caged area of a riot van.

'Cowley. Apparently the acting inspector has sent his turban-wearing Sikh to sort out a Hindu domestic – it's like pouring petrol on a fire!'

Fortunately, the fire was contained by Cowley officers before the Oxford ones arrived, and we were stood down at Magdalen Bridge.

CHAPTER 4

The Importance of
Being Spoofed

Spoof. Such a soft word for what I knew in my heart was a form of bullying. Every new recruit had to undergo this rite of passage. It was not something you looked forward to but I accepted the party line – spoofs were a necessary evil. Spoofing was also a black and white issue; a stress-inducing activity that would prove your reliability, or lack of it, to the rest of the shift.

In the Eighties, officers were issued with only a wooden truncheon, and this lone weapon was made short to the point of uselessness for WPCs, as it had to fit in their standard-issue handbags – no trousers meant no truncheon pocket. Acting on Daniel's advice, I'd already dumped my black leather handbag in the bottom of my locker and, like the rest of the shift, invested in a heavy-duty four-battery metal Maglite to replace the cheap and fairly useless standard-issue rubber torch. Not only was a Maglite more effective at illumination, its length and weight made it a far more formidable weapon than a wooden truncheon. That and 'bottle' was all we could rely on. The sort of bottle that meant you always ran towards trouble, never away from it; the sort of bottle that meant everyone on your shift was happy to place their life in your hands and, when they did, they knew they could rely on you when nothing else existed. Like all probationers I knew that my bottle, my reliability under pressure, would be tested.

Brendan was the first of the new probationers to be tested. During that first set of nights, he and his tutor Richard were sent to 'intruders on the railway line'. As they set off to investigate, Brendan later told me he was convinced this was his spoof; but the knowledge afforded him no comfort. He and Richard climbed out of their panda and started to walk along the top of the steep embankment. They quickly spotted torchlight and two dark figures crouched by the chain-link fence alongside the track. On seeing the officer's capped silhouettes against the station's lights, the figures made a run for it – but in different directions. Richard shouted at Brendan to chase the one heading east while he set off west.

Despite the word *spoof* pounding through his brain, Brendan was determined to prove himself to the shift. The runaway had a good start, but Brendan belonged to Dave's seven-minute pack. By the time he rugby-tackled his man to the ground he was over half-a-mile from the panda and in total darkness. His Maglite was tucked safely in the pocket of the panda's passenger door while his handcuffs had dropped out of his belt during the chase. As he lay on his prisoner, panting and wondering what to do next, the body beneath him began to struggle. It was a huge body.

I was with Daniel when we heard Brendan's call for assistance, but our own radios echoed silence; nothing, not even background crackle.

It was then Brendan saw a second figure walking purposefully towards him and his still-struggling prisoner. The man was dressed in black, including a full-faced balaclava, and he was brandishing a machete that glistened in the moonlight. All thoughts of spoofs forgotten, Brendan was panicking; if this silent figure was the other intruder, come to rescue his friend, what the fuck had happened to his tutor? Was Richard lying disembowelled somewhere or was this a completely separate nutter, from whom he'd have to protect both himself and his reluctant prisoner? In desperation, Brendan upgraded to a ten-nine shout.

Control responded immediately, 'Officer calling ten-nine – ID and location?'

'2497. Railway line mile past Oxford station. One in custody! Second offender with machete!'

'What's his name?'

'He's got a machete for Christ's sake!' Brendan's adrenalin was too high to register that his prisoner had stopped struggling when the second figure appeared, and was now shaking with laughter as he lay quietly beneath him. The penny dropped. 'What do you mean his name?'

'Ask him if his name's Richard. If it's not, we'll send back-up.'

With laughter spilling from his radio, Brendan looked up at the man with the machete, 'Are you a Dick?'

'Never call a man with a weapon a dick,' advised Richard, as he pulled off his balaclava and grinned with pride at his probationer.

''Scuse me,' said a muffled voice from Brendan's armpit. Brendan sat up and let go of Rodger from traffic. He'd stood his ground and passed his spoof with flying colours.

Cherry had been well-named; she was small, round, dark and sweet, but she was not a brave soul. It was the last night of what had been a long but exciting first week, and Daniel and I were in the night kitchen enjoying a late meal break when we heard Cherry being sent to 'intruders on the mound'. It was 4am. Richard and Daniel looked at each other and smiled.

The mound is a small hill in the middle of Oxford. It contains a tiny cell in which, historically, prisoners from the adjacent jail were held overnight before being hanged on top of the mound at dawn. During the day, girls used to climb to the top of the hill to hurl words of comfort and lust at their interned partners, and at night it was a popular meeting place for glue-sniffers.

Cherry immediately asked where Shaz was, but was told her tutor was delayed at the station and that she'd have to go on her own. Denied the immediate back-up everyone knew she'd request, the patrol sergeant watched the beam from her torch as it wound its cautious way around the hillside, eventually finishing at the top. Finding no intruders on the mound itself, Control insisted that Cherry check the death-cell. The sergeant watched the even slower descent of Cherry's light and its disappearance through the heavy iron gate into the small stone cell.

The shift held its collective breath. We were not disappointed.

'Control, there's a body, a dead body, oh my God – it's dead – hanging from a beam… oh my God I need back-up!'

Richard and Daniel burst into laughter as Cherry's panic streamed from their radios.

When she was forced to return to the cell some five minutes later with the sergeant, the body was missing. Paul, the shift member who specialised in playing dead, was nowhere to be seen and Cherry spent the rest of the night filing a report, before being dressed down by Coops – who relished even this faked opportunity to tell a WPC how useless she was. It was only as Cherry was putting away her equipment at the end of the shift, that I felt obliged to confirm to my fellow probationer that the whole thing had indeed been a spoof.

The Importance of Being Spoofed

I tried not to feel too sorry for her. According to Daniel she'd had six spoofs played on her during the preceding six months, and I told myself that by now she really ought to be able to recognise and handle one. But this spoof was the straw that broke poor Cherry's back. On her return to duty after two days off, she handed in a letter of resignation to a smug-faced Coops.

Cherry became a traffic warden in her home town of Slough, where the wardens always hunted in pairs. I avoided speaking to her about her resignation; I wanted to be free to assume that my fellow WPC would be happier as a traffic warden.

When I told Brian about the spoof over breakfast, he didn't understand,

'That's a bit racist isn't it?'

'It's got nothing to do with her colour!' I was spending too much time defending my colleagues to my husband. 'It's about her lack of bottle. If, at the end of our probation, we'd been crewed together, I'd feel vulnerable, I'd *be* vulnerable. If Cherry's default reaction is to scream and run I'd be left up shit-creek without a fucking paddle!'

Brian got up from the table in silence and packed his self-made sandwiches and flask of tea into a grey canvas satchel. He was working as a maintenance man for the ambulance service and had an eight o'clock start, which meant we had about an hour together when I got in from nights. But this planned together-time was actually driving us further apart. I knew Brian was feeling more and more isolated, but that was all part of the plan. I was deliberately freezing him out of my life. I only those shared parts of my work that might annoy or worry him; like how many tickets I'd issued or how many fights I'd been involved in.

'Do you know, Chris, since starting on shift you've not once asked how my day has been.' He closed the front door quietly and I climbed the stairs to bed.

It was a drawn-out way to end a marriage but I didn't feel able to find a different one. Brian was my first serious relationship. I had been flattered by his maturity and the panache with which he wore a cravat. He owned a lovely mare called Playgirl and kept her in livery at stables just outside Oxford, where I was working as a riding instructor. When he had asked me out I said yes and when, six months later, he asked me to marry him I again said yes. On reflection I'd actually said yes to the engagement party, the wedding planning and the dress; not the marriage, to which I'd given no real thought. I still have a photograph of us signing the register and it's accompanied by a clear memory of me thinking *this will never last* as I heard the click of the camera.

It had lasted seven years and the itch was becoming a serious rash.

But, just as I had been too much of a coward to back out of the actual wedding, now I was too much of a coward to ask Brian for a divorce outright. He was too nice a person and he'd always been a good husband to me, so I had no grounds for such a request. I also knew how much his first divorce had upset him and I didn't want to feel responsible for inflicting the same sort of pain. I wanted my job to do the dirty work for me; for it to do all the heavy lifting, to be the perfectly acceptable cause of our break-up.

It was two in the morning and Daniel was munching his way through a large kebab purchased from an extremely dubious-looking van in St Giles. We were sitting in a panda at the deserted Peartree Park and Ride, and the smell of the grease-filled pita bread was making me heave. Despite it being the middle of November, I wound down the passenger window.

'Hotel Alpha two-one.'

It had been a quiet night and the radio made us both jump, causing Daniel to spill chilli sauce on his trousers.

'Shit!' He scrubbed frantically at the sauce, spreading both the stain and the smell.

I laughed and picked up the car's handset. 'Hotel Alpha two-one, go ahead.'

'Are you available for a single vehicle RTA?'

Road traffic accidents were a staple of police work, but I wasn't looking forward to my first. I was concerned that if the injuries were severe, my first-aid wouldn't hold up and my stomach contents wouldn't stay down. But I was learning to hide any fear.

'What's the location?'

'Wolvercote Common – the fire service are in attendance and requesting the presence of a WPC.'

A small but intense knot of fear formed in my already churning innards. Replacing the handset, I stared at Daniel, who had chucked the kebab wrapper onto the back seat and was turning the ignition key with his right hand, while his left flipped the switch for the blues (no siren necessary).

'This is it – this is my spoof isn't it?' My voice, like my innards, was unsteady.

Daniel laughed, 'No, you're alright.'

'But why ask for a WPC at an RTA and on Wolvercote Common? That's a bloody odd place for an accident.'

'Let's go find out shall we?' We sped from the deserted car park, the blue light flashing silently.

'Come on Daniel – admit it – it's my spoof! What's going to

happen?' Fear simmered in my belly, while its heat escaped through the palms of my gloved hands. 'I'll buy your kebabs for the rest of the month – Daniel, tell me!'

Daniel glanced at his probationer's panic-stricken face and turned serious. 'Look, genuinely, it's not a spoof – tutors are always in on them, they have to be, and nobody's said anything to me. We're all lying low 'til the fallout from Cherry's resignation dies down. Trust me.'

I took a deep breath and relaxed back into the panda's grey seat. I did trust my tutor.

'Wolvercote Common,' I slowly recovered some composure, 'is a single track lane. The driver must be really pissed.' I opened the glove-box and rummaged through miscellaneous forms and booklets to retrieve the breathalyser kit and an unopened mouthpiece. I had yet to make my first arrest.

'Atta girl!' Daniel loved his probie's enthusiasm.

The flashing blue lights of the fire engine guided us along the inky-black lane to a small lay-by. As we pulled up, the panda's headlights picked out a bright red MGB GT hard-top, properly parked. The low-slung sports car looked in showroom condition and I wondered if Daniel had lied after all. The sub-officer in charge sauntered over with a smirk and the knot in my stomach tightened. His expression seemed incongruous against the muffled female screams coming from the MG.

'Morning, Daniel. You're going to love this one.'

'Morning Stu...'

'Is someone injured?' I'd already leapt out of the panda and my tone was indignant as I interrupted this leisurely greeting. The sub-o glanced at me but continued talking to Daniel, who had deigned to get out of the panda and face the cold.

'We've got a man and woman doing what men and women

tend to do at two in the morning on Wolvercote Common – only she's had some sort of internal seizure and clamped him inside her. In the struggle to free himself, Romeo here has pushed his foot through one of the spokes of the steering wheel and now they're both... well... they're both well and truly fucked.' The sub-o grinned. 'We thought about trying to remove the steering wheel but we can't access it. We can't amputate his leg so we'll just have to cut the roof off.'

We'd reached the MG at this point and as the sub-o finished, the woman's screams became hysterical.

'Don't worry love, we've got you a WPC – and anyway we've seen it all before.' The sub-o's observation was made with what he thought was confidence-giving cheeriness. 'It won't hurt a bit,' he continued, 'it'll just be very noisy with the grinder and the breaking glass.' As he turned away, he winked at Daniel and added, 'but from the looks of it, you're up for a good grind.'

I thought the sub-o a macho idiot but, on seeing the two bodies entwined and entombed in their shiny red coffin, I had at last relaxed – it was obvious why they needed a whoopsie. It was not my spoof.

I tried to reassure the woman, who was sitting in the driver's seat with her male companion straddling her fully reclined, semi-nude body; his right foot and lower calf were trapped in the vice-like grip of the small wooden steering wheel. I helped feed a fire blanket through from the driver's side. There was only an inch or two to spare between the man's buttocks and the roof of the car and, as a fireman pulled the blanket through from the empty passenger side, I shouted to the woman above the noise of the air-compressor.

'Don't worry, love. It won't take them long. The blanket's just to keep you warm, and protect your modesty and your man's bum from the sparks and flying glass.'

Again, the woman's screams became frantic but were muffled underneath a muscular male torso and now a thick blanket.

Making two cuts through the posts either side of the windscreen, the firemen quickly peeled back the roof of the MG. It reminded me of opening a can of sardines, but done in half the time it would take me to perform that task. With his bum no longer restricted, Romeo hunched up under the rough grey blanket and pulled his own leg free. Rolling off the still hysterical woman, he scrambled back onto the passenger seat, pulled up his trousers and with admirable agility (you could see why he was in this situation to begin with), he leapt out of the car and over a nearby five-bar gate, disappearing into the dark anonymity of the common. The woman was sobbing as I continued to hold the blanket over her while she shuffled beneath it, adjusting her clothes.

'Don't worry, love, he'll be back as soon as the shock's worn off and we've all gone.'

The woman poked her dishevelled head from underneath the blanket. 'I don't give a flying fuck about him!' she shouted. 'What the fucking hell am I supposed to tell my husband when he asks what I've done to his pissing prized car?'

Lost for words, I was relieved when Daniel and I were dispatched to a fight that had broken out at his kebab van.

It was several days later that I heard on the inter-service grapevine that once we'd left the scene, the extremely helpful firemen found a way to save this lady's marriage – a task, it has to be said, not covered by the Fire Service's Act. They apparently managed to connect the MG with a convenient tree, and with the front grill now more of a match with the roof, the poor unsuspecting husband was just relieved to find his wife, unlike his car, intact.

Risk assessment had not been invented in the 1980s – especially risk assessing the likelihood of being sued. So there was still room for the emergency services to take a more creative and even expansive view in how they solved the public's many and varied problems.

While awaiting my own spoof, I was the victim of several practical jokes. I was called into the station to see Sergeant Jarrett in the custody block. 'Ah, WPC Foster,' he said, handing me a sealed brown envelope, 'take this prisoner prescription to Boots, wait for it to be filled and then bring it back here ASAP.'

I duly handed the envelope to a counter assistant at the busy city-centre branch with the words, 'This is fairly urgent.' The assistant opened the envelope and burst out laughing. She then handed it to another assistant who followed suit and this continued until the paper had circulated all the way to the pharmacist. This kindly old gent read the paper, smiled and came to see me.

'You've no idea what's written on this have you, officer?'

'No.' I sighed. 'I was told it was a prescription for a prisoner, but I gather it's not.'

'No... it's not.' He handed me the piece of paper, which read: 'I'm very shy, could you please let me have some extra-large ribbed condoms and anything you've got in a strawberry flavour. Thank you.'

Three or four of the shift, including Daniel, appeared from various corners of the store, smiling broadly.

Brian and I had moved from our cramped rented flat to a large police house on the huge Blackbird Leys council estate.

The house was the one upside to being married and I'd been pleasantly surprised by the grandeur of the four-bed detached residence being offered to a mere probationer. On viewing it, the jungle of a back garden and the mountain of junk mail indicated that it had not been lived in for a while, and I also noticed a large spotlight directed at the house from a nearby lamp-post. Mr Davis, the estate manager, looked sheepish.

'This house is really meant for inspectors and above. But the last occupant antagonised the locals to the point where some of them laid siege to the house – it's not been used since… it's up to you… but there's nothing wrong with the house.'

He was proved right; there was nothing wrong with the house and I found nothing wrong with the location, either. Despite being the biggest social housing estate in Europe at the time, with an overwhelmingly black population, I was given a soft time by residents of the Leys. Some of the locals may not have returned my smiles, but they also withheld the missiles, the dog shit and the graffiti.

Brian and I were both enjoying the size of the house. For Brian it was all about the prestige of living in a four-bed-roomed detached house; for me, I liked the fact we didn't need to share the same space at any one time for too long.

It was the end of lates, and I'd stayed behind to enjoy a drink with the lads in the police bar. Daniel, Brendan and Chalky had been hilarious company and it was past midnight when I drove along the main road leading to the Leys. I was still in uniform, but without my radio, hat, handcuffs or Maglite. Nearing the turn onto the estate a movement caught my eye; someone was climbing over the ten-foot fence sur-rounding the local DIY superstore and garden centre.

I stopped the car and watched a slim figure drop to the pavement, pick up something bulky and disappear into the bushes. Eyes glued to the rear-view mirror, I watched as the person reappeared with something even bulkier. They crossed the road behind me and vanished down an alley leading into the maze of houses that formed Blackbird Leys.

I jumped out of the car and followed the shadow and its bundle. Running quietly in my soft-soled shoes, as I turned down the same alley I was just in time to see the shadow make a right turn. As I turned right, I saw it take a left and so on. Just as I was realising how completely lost I was, I saw the shadow disappear into a mid-terrace house and I followed. Running up the path, past the requisite fridge and old sofa landscaping the front lawn, I pushed open the battered front door, which had been left ajar. As I entered the narrow hall-way, the shadow emerged from the light of the lounge. We stared at each other in disbelief, but I recovered first.

'You're nicked.'

The young lad went for belligerence. 'What the fuck for?'

It was a good question; I still had no idea what the bulky something was. I decided bluff was my only option,

'Don't mess me around. I saw you coming out of Saunders. Where have you stashed the stuff?'

The lad was in his mid-teens and obviously under the impression that I was on duty. Sighing, he pointed to the room behind him and I followed him back into the lounge, where six black plastic dustbins were stacked to one side of the telly – he'd obviously made more than one trip that night. A dog was barking in the kitchen; it sounded bad tempered or hungry.

'Who else is in the house?' I asked.

'Apart from Tyson?' the youth looked towards the vibrating door, 'no one.'

'Is Tyson going to stay where he is?'

'Unless you want me to let him out. He loves coppers – couldn't manage a whole one, though.' He sank onto a well-worn sofa and lit a fag.

'What's your name?'

'Lee.'

'Lee what?'

'That's right, Watt – have you nicked me before, then?'

'No, but I'm arresting you now on suspicion of theft of these dustbins,' and I gave Lee the benefit of a word-perfect caution. 'Do you actually live here?' Lee nodded and took another drag on his fag. 'What's the address then?' The question was delivered in a 'prove it' tone, which Lee fell for, and he reeled off the full address, including the postcode. 'Are you on the phone here, Lee?'

'Course we are. Why?'

'My radio's dead, so I'll need to phone in for transport.' He hadn't registered my lack of equipment.

'It's in the hall. Leave ten pence.'

wLee seemed resigned to his fate and I closed the lounge door before dialling 999. After explaining the situation in a hushed voice, Control promised to send immediate on-duty assistance and I went back into the lounge to wait. Lee had switched on the telly and when the doorbell rang, he just looked up at me,

'Spect that's for you.'

As I opened the front door, a second youth, holding six black dustbin lids, backed into the hallway.

'Why didn't you leave the door open?' When he got no reply he looked up. 'Shit!'

'Guess what?' I smiled at him.

'I'm nicked?'

'Got it in one! Lee's through there – let's all watch telly until my mates arrive.'

'Fuck it.' Was his only reply to my caution.

My weekend off dragged on, although a visit to Frilford Market on Sunday provided something for me and Brian to talk about. It was though we were back on a first date, with the same sort of 'I don't know you' politeness but none of the sexual tension. Sex had been mechanical for a long time and now we'd stopped even pretending that it was something that either of us actually enjoyed anymore. I was relieved when Monday and a new set of nights came around.

When Coops entered the parade room, he was accompanied by the divisional superintendent, who proceeded to congratulate me on my 'outstanding police work' in relation to the single-handed off-duty arrests of Lee Watt and Justin Ledbetter. The inspector looked like he was sucking lemons.

I thought the praise a bit OTT for six plastic dustbins, but according to the superintendent, Lee and Justin had been regular visitors to Saunders and had amassed a lock-up full of stolen property, which they were selling every Sunday at Frilford Market. While the rest of the shift congratulated their newest whoopsie, I noticed Daniel looking grim, and as soon as we were in the panda he turned on me,

'You're a fucking idiot WPC Foster – you could have been seriously hurt! That bloody tunic you're wearing is not bulletproof – it's not even stab-proof. The rest of them may think you've proved your bottle, but to my mind you've shown an incredible lack of judgment and, if we have *any* luck keeping us safe in this job, you've probably just used up a career's worth!'

I was indignant, but as I opened my mouth to defend myself, I saw in my tutor's brown eyes something more than a tutor's concern, and I closed it again without comment. Brian had the same reaction to my commendation; but where Daniel's concern made me feel special, Brian's was irritating.

Spoofs died a natural death towards the end of the 1980s. Officers were issued with better equipment: reliable radios that worked anywhere, quick-cuffs with fixed-link leverage that meant a small female could floor a large male, side-handled batons followed by extendable ones, pepper-spray and, most recently, Tasers – all of which meant that having 'bottle' became less and less important.

CHAPTER 5

'Yer Doona Wanna Do That'

After nearly two weeks on shift I was beginning to fret. I still hadn't made my first arrest and, like a pregnant woman whose first child was overdue, I felt that people were beginning to look sideways at me. Blu-tacked to the night-kitchen wall was a piece of A3 paper that listed, in fat red marker pen, the names of all the station's probationers. To the right of these names were two columns, 'Reported' and 'Arrests'. Every time a probationer reported someone for a summons or made an arrest for more serious offences, their tutor placed a tick against their name.

Following a morning rush-hour trap set by Daniel to catch cyclists cutting through the no-entry sign in Holywell Street – my Report column now held twenty-two ticks, but the pristine whiteness of the Arrest column was blinding and I felt this was beginning to reflect poorly on the rest of the shift. So at the start of my first late turn, I set out from the station with Daniel in tow, determined to bag my first prisoner before the end of our shift at ten.

Despite my urgency to be out there catching a criminal, Daniel insisted his probationer learn to walk more slowly.

'We've got twelve hours to kill – there's no point in hurrying. You're not a harassed shopper now you know. We're here to see and been seen – giving the public the reassurance of bobbies on the beat.'

Eventually, we reached the fertile hunting ground around Bonn Square. The square is situated in the heart of Oxford, opposite the Westgate shopping centre. It used to provide a small patch of calming green amidst the hustle and bustle of the city. The modest stepped war memorial was surrounded by a small area of grass, which in turn was surrounded by a low stone wall. This wall divided not only the grass from the concrete, but the haves from the have-nots.

Oxford's ten or so regular 'dossers' – homeless alcoholics who spent their days begging from tourists and students – called the square home. Depending on the success of their begging and therefore their level of intoxication, they'd sit on the wall, stand around the steps of the memorial, or lie on the grass, enjoying loud debates, physical fights and singing. All these activities were carried out with equal frequency and gusto.

At night, when the shoppers, tourists, and students had all gone home, the dossers swayed their way down to the only 'wet' night-shelter, behind the Court House in Speedwell Street. This shelter took in alcoholics who were still drinking, and when it was too full or too violent, some of its clients would doss down in shop doorways, stairwells, or under hedges along the canal bank. Daniel told me he'd once found one there, frozen to death on Christmas Day. Dossers, shoplifters, and shoplifting-dossers provided the bread and butter arrests for probationers.

Christine had been drinking steadily all day, and was now dancing along the low wall that bordered the square. She was multi-tasking, singing loudly and out of tune while waving her less than spotless knickers in the air.

'If yer wanna see ma booty, wave your knickers in the air! If yer wanna feel ma boobies, 'ave a lick or 'ave a stare…'

'Christine! Get off the wall and put your knickers back on.'
Daniel's tone was one of stern amusement.

'Hiya, Daniel, how're they hanging?'

'Mine are fine – for God's sake cover yours up!'

'Bollocks!' said Christine, cheerily.

Her total lack of self-respect and lack of respect for Daniel
made something inside me snap. Taking hold of her arm I
pulled her off the wall and onto the pavement.

'That's it – you're nicked!' I declared.

'What for?'

'D&D.'

Once off the wall, Christine was a good six inches
shorter than me. Screwing up her eyes, which could have
once been blue but had been diluted by alcohol to a watery-
grey, she swayed gently as she pulled back her bedraggled
head to inspect the contents of the shiny new uniform
rising before her.

'You're new ain't you? She's new, 'ain't she?' She asked
Daniel

'Yes, Christine,' my tutor confirmed.

'She really going to arrest me?'

'It would appear so.'

'Yer doona wanna do that…no, yer doona wanna do
that… yer doona….' Christine continued to chunter away
while I radioed for transport back to the station.

'You sure 'yer wanna do' this?' mimicked Daniel.

'Yes, I'm sure. What's the problem?'

Daniel just smiled, while Christine continued to sing to the
passing shoppers, 'Yer doona wanna be doing that, nah, yer
doona wanna be doin' that….'

Her singing was drawing a small crowd as she tried to
dance around me in a tight circle. Her knickers were still

being twirled above her head, which meant they rotated directly under my nose at regular intervals.

'Daniel, mate – a bit of help wouldn't go amiss,' I whispered angrily.

'Oh, this one's all yours, WPC Foster – your decision, your arrest.'

I was considering handcuffing Christine, but that would have meant touching her knickers, when Big John arrived with the transit. Big John was a quiet man, cruising towards retirement with the studied calm of experience; he'd seen it all and not been impressed by much. As he started to unlock the back doors he caught sight of Christine and promptly slammed them shut again.

'You're not putting her in here!'

'But I've arrested her!'

'Well bloody well de-arrest her!'

'She's my first prisoner. I can't just de-arrest her and anyway, she's still drunk and disorderly.'

As if to prove my point, Christine turned up the volume on her homemade ditty to full throttle and threw her knickers at John.

Coming up from a duck that was pure reflex, he fixed her with a stare. 'Christine, you do *anything* in the back of my transit and I'll be hosing you down, too – clear?'

'Quite clear thank you, Johnnie!'

Christine knew the names of all the Oxford bobbies. She saw it as her unofficial role to nurture the probies, keeping a watchful eye on their progress and training them up in the pecking orders and realities of life.

I was so busy hanging onto my prisoner that I didn't really register John's threat, but Christine smiled knowingly as she climbed slowly into the back of the transit. The same smile remained fixed on her lips as John locked us in. Through the glass in the rear doors, I saw John shake his head and heard him mutter, 'Probationers'.

Daniel chose to sit in the front of the van with John.

By the time we reached the station, the smell in the rear was toxic. As a meths-drinker, Christine sweated alcohol. The smell of this pungent spirit mixed with that of stale urine to produce an aroma known in custody as 'channel number five'. With corrosive efficiency it soon burnt up the little oxygen available and left a cloying imprint at the back of my nose and throat. As I stumbled through the heavy iron door into the custody office, Christine was swaying at my side like a trawler in a force nine gale, and smelling much the same.

We both heard Sergeant Jarrett sigh. He was a tall, gangly, man with thinning hair and a long face, his drawn-in cheeks intersected by an eagle-beak of a nose. Despite looking stern, Sergeant J was by nature a mild-mannered man who had drifted into supervision by doing nothing wrong or risky and upsetting no one higher up the food chain. It appeared I was about to test his mildness.

'Christ, not Christine... Daniel, what the fuck!'

Daniel just leaned against the door-jamb, shrugged and smiled.

Before I could formally book in my first prisoner, Christine cried out, 'Hiya Sarge! Nice to see you, too – get us a cuppa!' and with this warm greeting she once more flung her knickers into the air with gay abandon. They landed with an ominous slap on the custody records lying on the desk, directly under Sergeant Jarrett's long nose. With a look of disgust he used his biro to flick the offending garment onto the floor, before putting both the biro and unused custody record into the bin.

'Right, Sarge,' I began, 'I've arrested this woman for D&D.'

'Why?'

'D&D – she's drunk and disorderly.'

'Christine is permanently drunk. Disorderly, incapable or just plain drunk – why arrest her?'

'Look, Sarge, she was swaying along the wall in Bonn Square singing songs so lewd they'd make a rugby team blush and waving her knickers at all and sundry. What was I supposed to do? Leave her to fall off and maim a passing shopper?'

'Fair enough – your decision. Well, Christine, looks like you're staying with us for a few hours. You know the routine, empty your pockets.'

Without further warning, Christine emptied more than her pockets. Hitching her dirty green skirt up to her ample waist, she crouched in the middle of the custody room floor and proceeded to pee – long and loudly. Daniel, who knew the lie of the land and the slope of the floor, stood and watched the stream of urine pass a few inches from his boots, but as the ever-increasing puddle flowed towards me, I jumped out of the way.

'Shit, Christine!'

'No, love – just pee... this time.' She grinned up at me from her crouched position.

Standing up, Christine picked her knickers off the floor and gave herself a perfunctory wipe, before she swayed off down the corridor leading to the female cells, humming her satisfaction at a job well done,

'I warned yer, I warned yer, yer doona wanna 'ave dun that....'

When she got to the first empty cell, I heard her kick off her smelly plimsolls and go inside, heaving the metal door shut behind her. I remained open-mouthed, still standing in the custody office.

Sergeant J pointed to a cupboard, 'Mop and bucket in there, WPC Foster – use plenty of disinfectant.'

'I'll put the kettle on,' Daniel was smiling broadly as he left the custody office.

'Ay – good idea,' came a voice from the cells.

Over tea, Daniel explained that Christine had a rather unique method of registering her protest to some types of incarceration.

'If you'd had the decency to arrest her for a proper crime, like shoplifting or assault, she'd have quite happily waited until she'd reached the cell and used the bog there.'

Drunks were a growing problem at this time. It was rumoured that Barlinnie Prison in Scotland gave its inmates one-way coach tickets to Oxford on their release. It was the chosen dumping destination because the tourist and student population could support their begging-for-booze habit, while the council provided both wet and dry shelters. In an attempt to deal with the fallout from the swelling dosser population, the police and courts had instigated an unofficial cautioning system.

This involved the drunk getting four hours in the drunk-tank before receiving a written caution and being released. If they took longer than four hours to sober up sufficiently to sign for their caution, they would usually be charged – as punishment for incurring the expense of a visit from the police surgeon. When a drunk had collected two cautions and was arrested for a third time, he or she was charged and put before the court.

Despite having numerous arrests under my belt within months of starting on shift (I'm ashamed to admit that, with my mind always on that night-kitchen chart, I once arrested the same dosser three times in the space of one fourteen-hour shift), it was nearly three months before I actually found myself in the witness box of the local magistrates' court.

I'd been summoned to the court building on several occasions prior to this but, if my drunks had remembered to turn up at all, they had turned up drunk. This would result in their being arrested by court officers and detained in the court cells for 'contempt of court'. They would be released 'at the rising of the court', usually around 4.30pm. This detaining until the court's rising would have been the likely result of any drunk-dosser case. Alcoholics, who have slipped to the bottom of life's rubbish heap, do not possess any property or cash to which fines can be attached. So the local justice system was being used as a form of refuse collection; keeping them in police and court cells for a few hours meant that the streets of Oxford were temporarily cleared of the undesirable and unsightly.

Billie was a legend among the inhabitants of Bonn Square and he was to be responsible for my first court appearance. Bylaws were local oddities that rarely got repealed and could prove very useful. In Oxford, there was a bylaw that any busking within the city limits was lawful only if a police officer in uniform considered it to be good value for money.

When Billie was sober he was quite effective with an old banjo and rusty harmonica. His Long John Silver-styled wooden leg and a scruffy dog added to his ability to collect compassion cash, and on a good morning he could earn around five pounds. Unfortunately, Billie would then blow the lot on a liquid lunch of Special Brew and cider, and by early afternoon he'd be unable to manage his banjo and would busk using just his harmonica; which would often spend more time up his nose than in his mouth.

After one such lunch, I'd ordered Billie to put his snot-covered harmonica away and move on from Bonn Square.

He complained loudly and bitterly, 'I have every right (hic) to be here! (hic). I am neither drunk (hic) nor disorderly!'

I ducked backwards as he waved his banjo in an expansive gesture towards the passing shoppers, in the hope of getting someone sober to back him up. His statements were delivered with slow, slurred words, deliberately not shortened to indicate both previous education and sobriety. He swayed artistically, his one good eye screwed up in an attempt to stay focused on the source of his impending incarceration.

As I took a step towards him, Billie leant back too far and fell flat on his bum. He lay like an upturned beetle waving his banjo and one good leg and shouting 'fuck' at two-second intervals. When I first saw Father Ted on TV, I became convinced that Billie had been the inspiration for Father Jack.

I arrested Billie and, as this was his third arrest, he was charged.

I became a little nervous when, several weeks later, I attended court regarding this arrest and found Billie had not only turned up on the right day, but was relatively sober; and I didn't know whether to laugh or cry when the usher told me that Billie intended defending himself. Sure enough, when I was called into court two, Billie was not in the dock, but at the desk in front of it, where the defence solicitor usually sat.

Entering the witness box I declined the automatically proffered bible. I was agnostic by nature and had seen too many of my colleagues gabble their way through the oath, reading it from a laminated piece of card while the bible waved around in their loose grip. This gave an impression of nonchalance that made me wonder if magistrates and juries took their subsequent evidence as lightly as the officers appeared to be taking their oath. So I made a point of keeping my eyes on the magistrates' faces as I raised my empty right hand and slowly recited, from memory, the words of the affirmation.

'I do solemnly sincerely and truly declare and affirm, that the evidence I shall give shall be the truth, the whole truth and nothing but the truth. [No mention of God – helping or otherwise,] I am Woman Police Constable Christine Susan Foster, currently stationed at St Aldates Police Station, your worships.'

Because the affirmation was not often used by police officers at this time, whoever was sitting on the bench would invariably look up from their scribbling and scrutinise me. More importantly, they continued to listen as I gave my evidence.

Having delivered my affirmation and identity with what I considered great aplomb, I turned to the prosecuting police inspector. The Crown Prosecution Service (or as it was subsequently known, the Criminal Protection Service) had not yet been invented. The inspector asked me to relate the facts surrounding Billie's arrest and I in turn asked if I could 'refer to my notes'. And so we played through the opening rally of set questions and answers regarding when the notes were made and how clear my memory was of the incident at the time they were made. This format was followed in every court case I was ever involved in, and it was not long before I realised that courts of justice were more like tennis courts when it came to establishing the truth.

Trials became matches that merely facilitated the re-playing of set pieces in a set way: serves, aces, forehands, backhands, lobs and volleys – truth was often bounced around, misdirected, or disallowed on a technicality and there were plenty of dodgy line calls, too. The best players, be they witnesses, offenders or solicitors, would get the umpire's decision; delivered from the raised height of the judicial bench. The result often came down to who was the stronger player on the day and who had the greater stamina, or the professional coach and expensive racket. Nevertheless, I found this very predictability reassuring during my first venture into the arena of theatrical racket slamming which was, is, the British legal system.

On completion of my evidence the magistrate turned to Billie. 'Have you anything you would like to put to this officer?'

Billie stood up and attempted a passing impression of Rumpole. Placing his dirty thumbs under the lapels of his even dirtier jacket, he declared, 'No, milord. I shall be calling my own witness.' He sat down again.

The chairman of the bench tried correcting Billie. 'I am referred to as your worship, not my lord.'

Billie stood and gave a little bob, 'Quite so, milord, quite so,' and he sat down again.

There were no other prosecution witnesses as police officers are considered 'experts' regarding levels of intoxication, and I was released by the court. I was free to go, but wild horses wouldn't have dragged me from that courtroom – not until I'd seen Billie and his witness in action.

The prosecuting inspector stood up. 'That concludes the case for the prosecution, your worships'.

The middle-worship addressed Billie. 'You may call your first witness.'

Billie Jade with authority, 'Certainly, milord, certainly. Call Mr Seamus O'Lynn!' he boomed at the usher, who was waiting expectantly by the door.

Seamus was a giant of a man, an ex-bare-knuckle prize-fighter. What little sense he may have been born with had been knocked out of him in the many and bloody fights to which his broken nose, cauliflower ears and missing teeth stood testament. When sober he was quite a gentle soul (if still five cans short of a six-pack), but he had fists the size of hams and, when fighting drunk, it could take eight of us to get him into the back of the transit and as many to get him out again at the station. I didn't even recall Seamus being there when I'd arrested Billie.

As the big man was led into court, squeezed into the witness box and guided through the oath and his details, I wondered what on earth he was going to say. The magistrate turned to Seamus,

'Well, Mr O'Lynn, can you please tell the court about the events of the 16th November?' Seamus looked blank. 'The incident that took place in Bonn Square, Mr O'Lynn?' Still nothing. The magistrate sighed. 'The officer over there,' he pointed at me seated in the public gallery, 'has told the court that on November 16th last, Billie was drunk and incapable in Bonn Square.'

The light came on and Seamus started to nod vigorously, 'Oh yes sir, yes sir!'

'Well?' the magistrate persisted, 'what is your recollection of the event?'

'Well, your highness,' collective smiles were quickly hidden behind hands and downcast eyes, 'if that officer over there', Seamus waved in my general direction, 'said Billie was drunk sir, and incapable, sir – he was drunk and incapable, sir.'

No sooner were the words out of Seamus's mouth than Billie was limping around the desk, waving his banjo at Seamus's head and shouting. 'Yer feckin' Irish eejit! Wot'd you say that for!' The prosecuting inspector, the usher and myself managed to disarm and restrain Billie and, when the magistrates had stopped laughing, they sent him down for contempt of court. Seamus left court wearing the same bewildered look with which he'd arrived.

CHAPTER 6

Taking the Rough
with the Rough

'I knew it.' Inspector Cooper declared. 'You whoopsies are all the same! They never should have disbanded the policewomen's department. Trouble, that's what you lot are, guaranteed trouble!'

It was the first time the inspector had deigned to speak to me directly. I'd just arrived for another twelve-hour shift, filling in for the men deployed on the miners' strike, and had been summoned to the inspector's office via a worried-looking Sergeant J. During my first weeks on shift, Coops had cut me dead on the two occasions Daniel had tried to introduce me; he had literally turned his back without comment and walked off in the opposite direction.

Daniel tried to reassure me. 'He'll come round when you've proved yourself.'

Despite my off-duty arrests of Lee and Justin, the inspector had not 'come round', and I had no idea why I was standing to attention in front of his overly tidy desk listening to a tirade of abuse, which included threats that if I continued to behave in this manner he would personally see to it that I was removed from his shift, if not the force. It seemed like several minutes before he eventually got to the point.

'I know you're having an affair with Daniel!'

'I am not!' My reaction was instant. Torn between disbelief and indignation, the volume and tone of my denial was not what the inspector was expecting.

'I beg your pardon?' His voice dropped to a threatening rumble, 'Are you calling me a liar?'

That's exactly what I'm calling you, you chauvinistic cretin, I thought, but I bit my tongue – I literally held it between my teeth while I thought of a more acceptable reply.

'What I'm saying, *Sir*, is that I am not having an affair with my tutor constable.'

'That's not what the Gen 22 says.'

'With all due respect, *Sir*, the Gen 22 can only say that we both booked off-duty at ten o'clock last night. It can't tell you that I went home and apparently Daniel didn't. I don't know what Daniel did after he left here last night, *Sir*, but I can assure you he wasn't doing it with me!'

The previous day, Daniel and I had been assigned to football duty, making up the numbers in a Public Support Unit. WPCs didn't usually work in PSUs, which were unofficial riot control vans, but the continuing miners' strike meant physical numbers counted more than actual experience. So, while the rest of the shift had worked from two in the afternoon to two in the morning, Daniel and I had worked a ten-ten day. We'd therefore booked off duty earlier than the rest of the shift. I had gone home to an increasingly sullen husband, while Daniel had obviously not gone home to his wife. When his suspicious spouse rang the station at midnight she was put through to Inspector Cooper who, on checking the register, had put two and two together and made five. He was now glaring at my reddening face.

'Would you like my husband to confirm this fact for you? I could phone him now.' My challenge was offered with a cold fury that made the inspector blink and swallow.

'That won't be necessary.'

I remained standing defiantly to attention, waiting for an apology that I knew would not be forthcoming.

'You may go, WPC Foster.'

I managed to refrain from slamming the door, which Coops would have viewed as hormonal, but I was devastated. I stood holding onto the outer doorknob for support, hot fury pricking at my eyes as I fought against unwanted tears and a deepening flush of frustrated anger. I was determined not to be seen as the clichéd WPC who slept with her tutor and then left the job to have babies. Most importantly, neither Daniel nor I had acted on any sexual tension there may have been between us, so Coops was well out of order. Railing against the unfairness of the accusations and the fact this powerful man thought so badly of me as a police officer, I turned, head down, to walk back along the corridor and bumped straight into Daniel's broad chest. Forewarned by Sergeant J, he'd been eavesdropping.

'Wait in the canteen,' was all he said before he marched into the inspector's office without knocking and closed the door firmly behind him.

I was not hopeful about Daniel sorting things out without making matters worse, but I did as I was told and waited for him in the canteen; trying to hide my burning rage, but the redness of my eyes indicating to the whole world that I'd not managed to stem the tears.

As I drank the depressing putty-coloured water that passed for canteen tea, Bob Adams burst into the canteen, purchased his own cup of dishwater and bounced over to my table. The training sergeant was well named; he didn't walk, he bobbed, bouncing on the balls of his highly polished shoes like an over-enthusiastic puppy – always up for a game. I liked Sergeant Adams; despite years in the job he still chose to see the best in people.

He'd recently been out on patrol with me, to make sure I was up to scratch and ready to be unleashed on the public unsupervised. I was impressed when he selected an early turn to do this. Bounding into the parade room at 5.45am, he'd pointed his clipboard at me. 'Right, WPC Foster, let's see what you're made of.' His small bright face was lit by a huge grin.

He'd trudged behind me as we climbed the stairs in the Westgate car park. The concrete steps smelt of stale urine but the tuneless whistle following me showed that Bob Adams remained unaffected by the early hour and his surroundings.

'So, Chris, what's the plan?'

'Warrant hunt, Sarge.'

He looked at the wad of papers sticking out of my coat pocket, arrest warrants that I would try to match with wanted people out on the street.

'Anyone in particular?'

'Failures to appear, dossers mainly, if you get them early doors they'll be sober enough for court.'

On reaching the next level I found a heap of old clothes asleep in the corner of the small landing. A fresh rivulet of urine trickled towards us from the snoring mound of old over-coats. I rocked the mound gently with my toecap, reluctant to use even a gloved hand, and a head of matted hair appeared from one end, watery eyes blinking. I'd not seen those eyes before.

'What's your name, mate?'

'Eric.'

'Eric what?'

'Smith.'

'Yeah, right.'

'Believe me, if I could change it I would – but someone's got to actually own it.' Eric's voice was booze-gravelly but well educated.

'What's in the bag, Eric?' As he struggled to sit up, a plastic bag had fallen from the folds of his layered coats. Bending down, I picked up one of several packets of Marks & Spencer's biscuits. While dossers couldn't afford to shop there, they did sometimes shoplift from the food-hall; its rear exit made this easy, almost an invitation, and the biscuits were right by the exit. I handed the packet back to Eric. I had no proof they were stolen and at least he would have some quality food along with the booze that day.

'Why aren't you in the night shelter?' I asked.

'It's full of nutters.'

As I continued to climb the stairs, Bob rejoined me. Like Daniel on my first shift, he'd stepped into the shadows to watch and assess.

'Good job!' was his verdict, as we continued to climb. 'You'll make CID, checking the expiry dates on those biscuits. Good solid police work that.'

Sergeant Adams had obviously assumed the biscuits had come from the skip rather than the shelves and I didn't want to disappoint him with the truth; about me or Eric.

'What's up?' he now asked, as he pulled out the plastic canteen chair opposite me.

'Inspector Cooper's just accused me of having an affair with Daniel and is threatening to get me thrown out – or at least off his shift.'

'Are you?'

'No, I'm not!' I slammed my chipped cup into its saucer.

'Didn't think so – he's having it off with someone from headquarters isn't he?'

Taking the Rough with the Rough

'I don't know and I don't care,' I hissed. 'What I do care about is that Inspector Cooper *thinks* I am and that because of that he'll move me and because of the move no one will take me seriously! I'll become one of those *four-year whoopsies* everyone talks about – women who only join to find a well-paid husband.'

'And you've already got one of those.' Bob's grin was met by a glare. 'It could be worse you know,' he tried moving from irony to reassurance, 'you could be considered frigid … or a dyke! Look I'll speak to Cooper – don't worry, I'll sort it.'

Between them, Bob and Daniel could not achieve an actual apology from Inspector Cooper, but they managed a return to the status quo – the inspector once more ignoring the presence of a WPC on his shift.

'Now, I need you to do something for me in return.' Daniel was sitting in the parade room with a fistful of blank interview sheets. 'I've told Charlotte I had a football prisoner and was doing overtime at Cowley last night. I'm going to write out a mock interview and I need you to pretend to be the prisoner and initial all the answers and sign each page.'

Daniel had saved my career and I was happy to help save his marriage.

The woman was old, as frail as a dry twig. I lifted her bony shoulders into a sitting position in order to remove her hand-knitted cardigan and, as the air trapped in her lungs was forced out, she groaned. Considering the size of her frame and the fact she was dead, the groan seemed disproportionately loud. I screamed and jumped back and the woman fell off the slab, landing on the mortuary floor with a sickening thud. She was my first corpse and I was supposed to be booking her into the out-of-hours mortuary attached to the nick.

Any sudden deaths, occurring after four in the afternoon and not in hospital, were brought to St Aldates.

On entering the mortuary, Daniel had directed my thinking.

'Right, Chris, treat this lady like you'd want your own relative to be treated – she's probably someone's gran.'

This advice helped. Many probies were told to view corpses as empty vessels, lumps of meat even, but throughout my career I continued to be touched by the humanity of a dead body and this helped me deal with any physical unpleasantness of death. I was lucky with my first body; she was a clean corpse. Many deaths result in more than life leaving the body. However, while imparting this philosophical outlook, Daniel had neglected to tell me of the dangers, and resulting horrors, of air trapped in a body.

As the old lady hit the floor, Daniel yelled. 'For fuck's sake, Chris!'

I was mortified. Apart from thinking how I'd feel if someone chucked a dead relative of mine onto the floor, a body that had died peacefully in its sleep was now sporting a head wound and what looked suspiciously like a broken neck.

Daniel's face was as white as the wall tiles. 'Get a grip!' he demanded and I realised I was still screaming. 'It's not as though you've actually killed her.' The tightness of his voice contradicted his words and tears replaced my screams. 'Help me lift her back up, then go get Sergeant J.'

Sergeant Jarrett saved the day. After bollocking Daniel. 'You dickhead, Daniel, fancy not telling her about trapped gas,' he turned to me and his tone softened. 'Crack on and undress the old biddy and book her in. I'll call the undertakers.'

I undressed the woman and put her safely to rest in the

fridge, before making the proverbial pot of tea.

Sergeant J completed his phone calls, 'Right you two, your luck's in. There's no post-mortem, her GP's already signed the death certificate and the undertakers have assured me they'll mask any visible injury – not that an open casket viewing has been requested.'

Done and dusted; another first out of the way. I did however slip back to the mortuary in my meal break, and resting my hand on the fridge door I made a silent apology to someone's gran.

My first solo foot-beat resulted in my first ten-nine shout, and I blame this embarrassing fact entirely on Maggie Thatcher. It was a direct result of her Care in the Community policy, the government-sponsored abandonment of the mentally ill so that mental hospitals, situated in large grounds on the outskirts of expensive cities, could be sold off for the development of lucrative luxury apartments.

Fergus was a schizophrenic who, to all intents and purposes, had been made homeless by this policy. He'd been placed in an unsupervised halfway house where he'd been left to his own devices; which did not include taking his medication on a regular basis. Thus, I was dispatched to sort out a disturbance in an alleyway called Fryers Entry that runs down the side of Debenhams.

On my arrival, Fergus was ranting obscenities at passing shoppers and at first I mistook him for a new dosser – he certainly looked and smelt like one – but he did not play by the same rules. When I took hold of his arm to place him under arrest, he spun to face me and with a wild roar grabbed my throat in a vice-like grip. His thin, filthy fingers were topped with yellow talons and I'd felt this same manic-strength once before.

I had a flashback of a skinny white arm reaching across my shoulder to grab a slice of quiche at a barbeque in a friend's back garden. My reflex reaction then had been to grab the arm, but that thin white arm, with a wrist that looked like one good twist could snap it, managed to knock my well-fed body onto its well-fed arse. The lad had then bounded from the garden, eating as he ran. He, too, had been a resident of Littlemore, the local mental institution that was in the process of being closed down.

Fergus threw me to the ground and, with his grip still choking me, tried to bite my face. I can still feel the shock of his spit hitting my eyeballs as we struggled on the urine-stained paving slabs of the dark alleyway. Two workmen in hard hats tried to haul him off, but Fergus's strength was almost superhuman. All they could do was hold him clear of my throat and face. Freeing an arm, I managed to yell 'ten-nine Debenhams' into my radio, before Fergus knocked it from my hand with such force that the grey plastic block smashed and died.

By now he was actually frothing at the mouth and, leaping to his feet, he knocked the two burly workmen backwards. Freeing himself of their feeble restraint, Fergus raised his bearded face to an invisible moon and howled at the after-noon sky. I crawled away from the distracted animal and while the workmen stood bravely blocking his escape from the alley in one direction, I and my pathetically small wooden truncheon, blocked his escape in the other. None of us wanted to take hold of him again.

Fergus then collapsed to his knees as though he had been shot and, whimpering, started to bang his forehead on the pavement as though trying to shatter his own pain.

Taking the Rough with the Rough

I sighed with relief as a multitude of sirens closed in on the four of us, trapped so unexpectedly in this spectacle of broken humanity. Daniel was the first to reach Fergus, and his touch made Fergus roar again. It was as though human contact burned him, electrifying him into violence. It took six of us to carry him to the van and six of us to sit on his still-struggling frame as we made the short journey to the station. As we manhandled Fergus into the custody office, each of us tried desperately to avoid his snapping, rabid mouth as he was pushed face down onto the recently polished floor. We all sat on his writhing body with Daniel holding his hair, ensuring his head was turned to one side so that he could breathe, but keeping it in constant contact with the floor to avoid his spitting.

It was a wonder that we didn't suffocate him. Safe prisoner restraint was not something that had been considered at this time — it was every man or woman for themselves.

Fortunately, the police surgeon was already in custody for another prisoner, and diving into his case he quickly produced a syringe with a clear liquid that rendered Fergus compliant within seconds. I booked him in under Section One of the Mental Health Act as being a danger to both himself and the public.

When I came back from my meal break an hour later, Fergus had been released back into the community. To be more specific, he had been released into the care of his mental-health nurse – the one who had not seen him for the previous two weeks. I didn't hold out much hope for either Fergus or the community.

Littlemore hospital was up-cycled. It once more provides a gated-community, but this one is made up of houses and apartments costing upwards of a quarter of a million pounds apiece.

CHAPTER 7

Black Man's Wheels

It was my first set of nights since successfully completing my tutorship. I'd been given my regular city-centre foot patrol, but I knew the rest of the team, especially Daniel, would be keeping an ear to their radios, keen to support me in this, my first solo night flight.

As I practised a slow plod around the still-busy streets, I felt proprietorial. This was my city now and when everyone else eventually went to bed, the streets and alleyways would become truly mine. I was especially looking forward to my first sunrise alone, and planned to watch it from Christchurch Meadows. But right now the business of policing was at the forefront of my excited mind. Meandering down The High, I saw another duff headlight travelling towards me. Swallowing hard I stepped out into the road and signalled for the car to stop.

Once more my heart sank, the driver was black and I could feel prejudice and intolerance about to pollute the crisp night air like a smelly fog, blinding people to anything other than a person's skin colour, or the uniform. This time the driver got out with tired resignation.

'Ah man, black man's wheels, again?'

I glanced at the BMW, a car favoured by many young black men. It was a rather upmarket example with highly polished chrome trim, a clutter-free dashboard and no crap hanging from the rear-view mirror.

'Seriously – it's the third time this week you lot have pulled me. I'm spending more time at the nick than I am at home!'

The man's eyes held mine, but they were too beautiful to be threatening. I took in the oval head, which he kept shaved as if to show off its attractiveness, his finely chiselled lips and perfectly square white teeth. *'You're one handsome dude,'* I found myself thinking.

During basic training we'd been taught that, when faced with authority, Asians did not like to meet your eye because it was considered impolite on their part. We were also told that black youths would not meet your eye either; although the reason for this was never specified, natural evasiveness was implied. However, if their eye contact moved from the pavement to you it could be taken as an early warning of impending violence, and staring a black lad in the eye might invite confrontation – which was fine if that's what you wanted.

It wasn't what I wanted, but I wasn't going to let the colour of someone's skin dictate how I talked to them, and this man seemed to invite eye contact.

'Well now, Sir – how long has your headlight been out?' He gave a small shrug, 'If you don't get it fixed *us lot* will just keep *pulling you.*' I smiled at him. The smile hiding the fact that duff lights were also a good excuse to try for a breathalyser. 'When did you last have a drink, Sir?'

Daniel had taught me always ask *when* not *if.* I couldn't smell anything on his breath but then, because of the defective light, I didn't need to. The breathalyser, or a refusal to be breathalysed, could produce another arrest, another red tick.

'Man, why do you lot always assume I be drinking? Well I 'ain't been drinking, I don't drink, I respect my body, and don't tell me I been pulled for a light, man. I'm a black man driving a smart car and you lot just assume it's nicked.'

Walking in front of the smart BMW I beckoned my black Adonis to come and stand in the road next to me. 'See this car coming towards us – the one with two working headlights – tell me what colour the driver is?'

'How the fuck do I know – the light's blinding me, man.'

'So what am I, fucking psychic?' I felt safe enough to echo the man's use of the f-word. I'd never sworn much before joining the police, but it was everyday currency in the parade and locker rooms; a way to be seen as one of the lads.

'Fair 'nough,' the man smiled appreciation of my point.

'So, what's your name?'

'Marlon, Marlon James.'

I was about to ask him for ID, but he was already pulling a small wad of papers from his tight-fitting, well-cut black wool coat.

'There you go – my documents – save your ink and my time.'

Daniel pulled up in a panda. Parking it in front of the BMW, he wound down the window. 'Everything alright?'

'Everything's fine, Daniel.' I smiled at Marlon and I handed him back his documents, 'On your way then Mr James – and get that light fixed.'

I strolled up to Daniel's window. 'You going to shadow me all night?'

'No!' the exclamation mark indicated a yes. 'You know who that is?'

'Obviously,' I waved my notebook.

'No, I mean Marlon James has got previous for assaulting police as well as theft. He's a professional shoplifter.'

'That seems an odd combination?' I felt somehow disappointed in the man I'd only just met. 'He told me he works as a bouncer at McDonald's.'

'Yes, at night. During the day he shoplifts to order. I'm telling you he can take an Austin Reed suit, put it in an attaché
case and deliver it to his own customer without so much as a
crease.'

'Do I detect a note of admiration?'

'Probably, if he wasn't into bobby-bashing, too.' Daniel
looking concerned. 'Seriously, watch him!'

Over the following nights I spent a lot of time watching
Marlon James. He would end up saving my life.

Oxford, like any busy city, could be a rough place after dark
and every night-trading premises employed bouncers. The
large and privileged student population and lager-drinking
yuppies rubbed uneasy shoulders with the even larger population of unemployed youth; while non-English-speaking tourists sometimes added to this explosive mix of high ambition
and low expectation.

The first time Marlon saw my uniform approach
McDonald's, he turned his back on me and sucked in air
through clenched teeth. I wasn't sure if I should take this personally as I was quite a way off when the back was turned: my
white hat, like my white shirt, could be seen from quite a distance. So, when I walked past I made a point of looking
directly at his muscular back.

'Evening, Mr James.'

He turned and looked at me. I saw recognition in his eyes,
but he turned to the other bouncer with a closed, sullen face.
The other man was already quizzing him.

'How she know your name, Marlon?'

'She's Babylon – 'cause she know my name.'

I felt a sense of deflation and disappointment that was out

of all proportion to the situation. What did I expect? Marlon James was black CRO and I was white police – what did I think was going to happen?

Nevertheless I decided I would keep on trying as a matter of pure principle, to break through this stereotypical, mutual hatred. So, every time I passed Marlon (which was roughly once an hour), I'd glance at him and smile. He continued to turn and hunch his back, but now he made excuses for the action: to check what was happening inside the restaurant, to say something to his fellow bouncer, to light a fag, once he even bent his beautiful head to blow warmth onto gloved hands. The fact that he was bothering to justify his reasons for ignoring me gave me hope.

Hope of what? I asked myself; hope of a friendly relationship, I told myself. Anything else was a non-starter on so many fronts. Not least of which was Brian.

My husband had been so supportive of my new career, especially since moving into the police house, and he'd made a point of not complaining once about my shifts and overtime, so my guilt was beginning to build. I'd decided early on that my career had to come first; before Brian, before Daniel, especially before the likes of Marlon James. Nevertheless, Marlon was floating my sexual boat in a way I'd never experienced before – and the fact that he was an active criminal and I was a copper just added to the whole forbidden-fruit fizz.

I was drawn out of this reverie by the sound of breaking glass. As I ran back past Marlon I could feel him staring at my retreating figure. Turning into The High from Cornmarket, I saw a small woman struggling to remove a drum-kit from the smashed window of the music shop. She was shouting and sobbing as she pulled at the smaller snare drum and cymbal, while a crowd of onlookers stood in a semi-circle, shouting encouragement. I pushed through the crowd and grabbed the woman's arm,

'Right, you're under arrest – theft and criminal damage.'

The woman was too drunk for me to bother cautioning and, when she registered my uniform, she gave up and crumpled to the pavement; her tiny frame wracked by sobs. I radioed for transport and asked Control to notify the shop's keyholder. Daniel arrived within seconds,

'Nice one!'

'Bit of a gift.' I smiled a thank you for Daniel's quick response. 'But I'll have to wait for the transit – I'll need to get the drum kit back, too.'

By three, the woman was sober enough to interview; it would be my first solo interview.

'Want someone in there with you?' Sergeant J asked.

'No, Sarge, I'm good – expecting a cough and a caution.'

Sergeant J nodded as he handed me the cell keys.

The interview lasted 20 minutes. The woman admitted the offences straight away and was full of remorse and embarrassment.

'So why, Jane? Why try and steal a drum kit?'

'It was for my son... a Christmas present.'

'How old's your son?'

Tears began to flow once more, but now she was sober they were silent. 'Nearly sixteen... but he's dead now... he died... in a car crash, last week... he'd always wanted a drum kit.'

And I thought I had problems.

By the time Jane had been cautioned and I was back out on patrol, the city centre was deserted. McDonald's, like all the pubs, clubs and restaurants, was closed; the streets were finally mine but I felt sad and a little lonely.

CHAPTER 8

Domestic Bliss

I loved being crewed with my ex-tutor, it meant being in a car and therefore available for more exciting and demanding jobs. Sergeant J had just summoned us back to the station for an urgent task, but Daniel just made a beeline for the night-kitchen and the kettle, telling me to seek out Sergeant J and see what he wanted. I found him in the parade room, holding a screaming tot at arm's length.

'Someone's just handed in this at the front counter.' Sergeant J immediately tried to pass the toddler to me. 'Here, I think it needs changing.'

Keeping my hands glued to my sides I replied, 'I've never changed a baby in my life, Sarge.'

'Well, now's your chance.'

'But Sarge, you're a father, surely you can do it.' The smell floating between us was alarming.

'WPC Foster, I'm ordering you to take this baby!'

'Can you at least show me what to do?' I asked, now holding the crying toddler at arm's length.

'No.'

'Ah come on Sarge...'

'I can't show you because I don't know how. It's what wives do – not husbands.'

Daniel entered the parade room holding two mugs of steaming tea.

'What the fuck's going on? Poor kid!' Putting down the teas he swept up the toddler and folded it into his arms while Sergeant J and I looked on in disbelief as Daniel started to cluck at the screaming baby and stroke its angry wet cheek with his stubby, nicotine-stained index finger.

'Didn't know you had kids, Daniel,' I was impressed.

'I don't, but my sister's got three – love kids, me.'

'Great!' I backed away from the smell and the screaming, 'You deal with that and I'll go find a shoplifter or something.'

An hour later social services had collected the baby and Daniel and I were back out on patrol.

It had quickly become clear that the three Ds made up a probationer's life – drunks, drivers and domestics accounted for the majority of early arrests, when quantity not quality was the measure of success. We didn't have long to wait for the first of that afternoon's Ds.

'Alpha two-one, can you take a domestic at 325 Summertown.'

'On our way!' My response was immediate and enthusiastic, but Daniel just sighed and didn't turn on the blues and twos. 'Get a move on, Daniel – someone could be dying!'

He smiled at the continued over-eagerness of his probationer. 'These two are regulars – driving slowly will give them time to get over their hissy fit and, with any luck, they'll have kissed and made up by the time we arrive.'

'But, what if he's beating the hell out of her and she's bleeding to death while you continue driving this panda like a hearse?'

Daniel laughed. 'There is no *she*.' He allowed the panda to creep slowly towards a green light.

'Who's having the domestic, then?'

'Claude and Jason – two poofters who have jealous natures and hot tempers.'

Despite our delayed arrival, Claude and Jason were still going strong. We could hear them clearly from the street, even with the panda windows wound shut against their shouted obscenities.

'Fuck. This sounds like a hands-on one.' Daniel's face folded into a grimace. 'Look, you know a domestic can quickly turn nasty, but the problem with gays is they combine female hysteria with a bloke's strength, so be careful!'

Daniel climbed reluctantly out of the panda and pulled down the strap on his reinforced helmet. I leapt out and followed Daniel's lead, pushing down at my soft-topped hat. With our respective protection in place we headed towards the communal stairwell of the two-storey flats. As we reached the door the sound of breaking glass crashed from above and turning around we were in time to see a large telly cartwheeling merrily through the air as it plunged towards the bonnet of the panda.

'Right, those bastards are coming in for that!' Daniel took the stairs two at a time, with me following hot on his heels. Barging through the flimsy lock on the front door we rushed down a well-trodden path into a purple lounge. The two men were standing by the broken window surveying the murdered panda below. Daniel broke their stunned silence.

'Which of you buggers threw that telly?'

Claude offered up his wrists, while Jason flung a protective arm around his boyfriend's shoulders.

As we drove back to the nick with a tearful Claude, I thought I'd love to have a proper screaming match with Brian, but he wouldn't allow it. Every time I found myself building up to a blazing row where, under the cover of battle-fire I could tell him how I really felt, Brian just turned and walked away. Even the cut-glass ashtray thrown at his retreating back had not made him stand and fight.

It was gone eleven when I got home. It had become something of a habit to always stay for a post-shift drink after a late turn: team-building and husband avoidance – two birds with one stone. Pulling into the drive I was surprised to see no lights. Brian was usually in bed and asleep by this time, but he always left the hall light on. *Pig* I thought, but I also felt a little uneasy. Opening the front door the house felt cold and empty.

As I felt the cool radiator I realised the feeling of emptiness was physical, down to a lack of clutter in the hallway. Only my coats were on the pegs and only my shoes were by the phone table, which wasn't displaying Brian's car keys. Running upstairs I opened the bedroom door. The bed was pristine in its flatness. I flung open the wardrobe doors and grinned at the gently swinging empty wire hangers.

'Yes! Yes! Thank you God!'

Going back downstairs and into the kitchen, I found that it, too, was beautifully bare. No flask, no sandwich box, no canvas satchel. But there was a note, propped up against the limescale-stained plastic kettle.

Sorry – but I'm not doing this again. B

I screwed it up and lobbed it into the open bin. When it hit its target I did a fist pump and flicked on the kettle.

'He's left you?' Daniel's tone was tinged with expectation.

'He sure has! Fancy breakfast at mine after work?'

Daniel's hazel eyes sparkled. 'I feel some overtime coming on,' he grinned and leant in for a kiss, but he pulled away with a knowing smile when we heard feet climbing the concrete stairs to the locker room.

Brian's leaving had not only given me an unjustified sense of the moral high-ground, the empty house now gave me and Daniel an away-from-work opportunity to do something about the chemistry that had been simmering between us.

I was given city-centre foot patrol again, but I didn't mind. It was Friday night and the cherry on my cake had been delivered without too much pain (on my part at least), and later Daniel and I would have a few hours together before he returned home to sleep. We took our meal break with other shift members in the police bar. Although the bar closed at eleven, the pool table was still in operation, along with several packs of cards. But Daniel and I chose to sit by ourselves; which caused one or two raised eyebrows but no comment.

'You're going to have to put a report into Coops and they'll take the house off you pronto.' Daniel took a swig from his can of full-fat Coke.

'What's my marital status got to do with Coops?'

'Technically nothing, but you can't send stuff straight to headquarters.'

I nodded, and then changed the subject. 'Who did Marlon James assault?'

'Someone in Metpol – decked him during a stop and search, broke the bloke's nose.'

'Has he ever had a go at one of us?'

'Nope – but Marlon doesn't shit on his own doorstep. He does all his business in the smoke and, in fairness, Metpol officers ask for it the way they use their sus-law, continually stopping young black lads "on suspicion" of offending, when their main offence is usually the colour of their skin.'

'You don't like the Metpol do you?'

'Neither do you from what you said about basic training.'

The shift finished without incident and Daniel phoned his

wife before following me home. We were in the shower when the front door opened and Brian shouted up the stairs,

'I've come to give you my new address and return the keys.' His voice sounded flat.

'I'll be right down!' I shouted, as I shrugged my wet and still-tingling body into an oversized dressing gown.

Planting a kiss on Daniel's panic-stricken face, I went downstairs and into the kitchen. Brian was standing by the kettle looking lost; his house keys lay splayed on the otherwise empty kitchen table, a forlorn centrepiece.

'So where are you living?' I purposely avoided asking him how he was – I didn't want to know, didn't want to be made to feel guilty; but in an effort to appear reasonable I raised the kettle and shook it at him, 'Got time for a brew?'

Brian looked at his watch, nodded and sat down at the table, 'I've got a bedsit in Rose Hill.' It was a simple statement of fact delivered without bitterness or self-pity.

We sat in silence, waiting for the kettle to boil; I didn't know what to say and I wondered why I'd invited him to stay for a tea – natural perverseness my mother would say but I did feel sorry for Brian and I wanted us to try and stay on friendly terms. I think I needed his continued amiability to salve my conscience. Brian felt obliged to fill in the growing silence.

'Sorry I left how I did. I just wanted to make it easy... on both of us.'

'No problem.' The kettle flicked itself off and I poured the boiling water onto two tea-bags.

'Will we be getting a divorce?' Brian was staring at the floor.

'I think so... that way we can both get on with our lives.' I thought it best to kill any hope he might be harbouring in the recesses of his large heart.

Brian was a kind man whom I liked but never truly loved. I felt the same way about Daniel, waiting patiently upstairs; but neither man would rock my world and I could just as easily live without either one in it. I had never held expectations of meeting a soulmate; I was sure they probably existed but I was happy enough with my own company and had no intention of making the compromise of marrying again.

'Who's going to divorce who?' he asked.

'You petition me – you'll get legal aid, I won't.'

'On what grounds?' His voice remained level. I think he was aiming for a tone of neutral resignation but the continued flatness was the sound of utter defeat.

'Unreasonable behaviour should do it. Refusing to cook, refusing sex, that sort of thing.'

Brian nodded once. Then, standing up, he walked over and planted a soft kiss on my forehead before he walked out of the house that had always been a temporary refuge for him; somewhere he was never going to belong.

I waited to hear the click of the front door before I raced back upstairs. Daniel was getting dressed.

'What the fuck!'

'Where are you going?' I was bemused by his anger.

'Where do you think? Home – to my wife! There's only so much overtime she'll turn a blind eye to and if you want to waste it with your ex that's your lookout!' Thundering down the stairs, Daniel slammed the front door shut behind him.

Walking slowly up the neatly raked gravel path, the sun glanced off the tips of my once-shiny toecaps, a residue from basic training not yet dulled by real life. I was about to deliver my first death message.

Many officers find this the hardest part of the job. They

would rather be at the scene of a fatal road accident, dealing with paperwork and body parts, than go and inform a living person that the loved one they saw at breakfast will not be home for tea. I grew to feel the opposite: your actions can't affect the dead but they can help those still living and left behind.

With four months in, I'd been enjoying a meandering foot patrol around the ancient honey-coloured buildings of Oxford's colleges, stopping to give directions to tourists and have my photograph taken with them. When my radio crackled, Control cast a shadow on my sunny shift and I was summoned back to the station. There I was given details of a macabre industrial accident.

A man called Francis had been cut in half by an industrial saw on a trading estate in Banbury, and I was being dispatched to inform his wife of forty years.

Daniel dropped me off at their home in the Oxford suburbs.

'Do you *need* me to come with you?' he asked, knowing his emphasis on the word 'need' would make me say no.

Daniel was one of those who coped better with the physical rather than the emotional side of death. Luckily, we shared the same outlook on sex, enjoying the physical side of things but neither of us looking for emotional commitment. After releasing the sexual tension that had been built up between us, we'd just gradually drifted apart with no hard feelings.

I saw a woman twitch open the bright white net curtain as I continued up the path to the house, and was therefore expecting the door to be opened before my actual arrival at the newly painted doorstep.

I had already learnt that the approach of a police uniform to someone's front door produced one of two distinct reactions. Regular customers would be dashing out of the back door as their mothers or partners delayed us at the front with protestations of their loved one's innocence and rants against the continued persecution of their significant other. The other reaction – the one I was expecting – was fear. We were, after all, never the harbingers of good news.

Despite this, the door remained stubbornly shut and my palm felt sweaty against the coolness of the dolphin-shaped brass knocker. I banged it once, in what I hoped was a businesslike but friendly manner. A smartly dressed lady in her late fifties answered the door with a smile and a disturbing lack of trepidation in her pale green eyes.

'Hello, are you Kathleen, Francis's wife?' I hoped the question would trigger alarm bells and make my job a little easier, but Kathleen merely nodded and continued to smile at me, apparently totally unconcerned by my presence on her doorstep. 'May I come in?'

'Certainly.' She opened the door wide, holding out her well-manicured right hand before showing me into her neat lounge. The furniture was old-fashioned and there was a strong smell of lavender wood polish. 'Would you like a cup of tea?' Kathleen's tone remained disconcertingly even.

'No thanks – please, have a seat, Kathleen. I'm afraid I have some very bad news.'

Still no reaction. Kathleen's face remained set with a fixed smile that was impassive, implacable; she reminded me of a 1970s shop-window dummy. She sat with a ramrod straight back on the edge of a chintz-covered armchair, but I got the impression this was to preserve the plumpness of the arranged cushions rather than a sign of mental stress. Fetching a dining chair from the nearby table, I placed it at the recommended forty-five-degree angle – comforting rather than confrontational.

Scanning her face for signs of comprehension, I noticed a fading but large bruise on her left temple, underneath expertly applied make-up.

'Can I confirm that you're Kathleen Smith and you're married to Francis Smith, who worked at Burns and Co in Banbury?' She didn't pick up on my use of the past tense.

'That's right, dear,' she replied, 'he's there now.' Still there was no tension or distress in her voice and I began to wonder if perhaps Kathleen was a little... slow.

'Well, as I said, I'm afraid I've got bad news...' This, in theory, is where the person leaps up and tells you someone must be dead or injured – but nothing. I pushed on. 'I'm afraid Francis was the victim of an industrial accident at work this afternoon.'

'Is he badly injured?' The question was asked in a 'milk and sugar?' tone.

I bit the bullet. 'I'm afraid Francis has died, Kathleen.' I fumbled for the clean hankie I had ready in my tunic pocket.

'He's dead? Not just injured?' Kathleen's tone held an edge of expectancy.

'No, I'm afraid he died at the scene.' Silence; I could sense the information being processed behind the still-closed face.

'Right. So he's definitely dead?' I nodded. 'And it's definitely Francis?'

'Yes Kathleen, his colleagues identified him to police at the scene.'

'He won't be coming back then?'

'No. He won't be coming back.'

As this devastating information finally filtered through her rigid frame, a slow smile spread slowly across Kathleen's face, lighting up her dry eyes.

'Do you know,' she said, 'it's the best thing that bastard has ever done!'

I was speechless. Kathleen looked at my shocked face and took pity on me. Still smiling, she leaned forward and patted my knee.

'I expect you could do with that cuppa now.' And, jumping up, she walked purposefully into the kitchen, humming.

I closed my mouth. I should be making the tea and she should be sobbing, not singing; she's in total denial I thought, I must get through to her. I followed Kathleen into the kitchen where the hum had grown into a full-blown rendition of 'Born Free', and Kathleen was waltzing around a small table, teacups in hand.

'Kathleen, you do understand what I've just told you?'

'Oh yes, dear, I do. Francis is dead, and he's not coming back – simply wonderful! Oh sod the tea! I'm opening the champers, well the Asti, can't afford the real stuff. Will you join me?'

'No thanks... on duty... but I could do with that tea.'

'I'll do both.' Kathleen continued to waltz and hum around the tiny space as she opened and closed various cupboards and dropped a teabag into a fine china mug painted with poppies.

She stopped suddenly and faced me with a slightly defiant look in her eye. 'I expect you think I'm mad?'

The thought had crossed my mind. 'Well, it's not the reaction I was expecting from someone who's been married forty years and is so suddenly made a widow.'

'And such a *merry* one?' Kathleen raised an eyebrow. 'Well,' she paused and a dark shadow crossed her face, closing down her smile and eyes, 'if your husband had come home drunk every payday for the last four decades and beaten seven bells of shit out of you, you'd not be sorry to see him go, would you?'

'True.' I said, light dawning over the faded bruise. But it was her use of the word 'shit' that hit me; it was as though a real person had broken through the Stepford Wife exterior. Seeing me glance at her temple again, she touched her bruise self-consciously.

'That was last week – he got careless. Normally he took care to punch and kick where bruises don't show.'

I felt a twinge of guilt. We, that is the police, were crap at domestic abuse. But I wasn't about to burst Kathleen's bubble with further questions now. Within the last few minutes she had turned into a living breathing human being; her husband's death seemed to have pumped her full of life. The cloud vanished and Kathleen skipped, literally skipped, back into the lounge, where her excited voice now came from the depths of the sideboard.

'Blast!' Her exclamation drew me back to the lounge, 'the bastard's been at the Asti, too.' Kathleen emerged waving the half-empty bottle, grinning wildly.

Her joy was infectious and I smiled back, before returning to the kitchen to collect my tea. When I re-entered the lounge, Kathleen had kicked off her shoes and was laid back into the full plumpness of her chintz; her feet resting on the polished coffee table.

'I've just thought of something else that's brilliant!' She declared

'What's that?'

'I'll get his pension, won't I? He won't be able to piss it away down the pub.'

'Yes.' I confirmed, before dropping a metaphorical strawberry into her bottle of Asti, 'I expect there'll be some compensation from the company, too.'

Kathleen's eyes widened as she laughed out loud at the thought. 'I told you it was the best thing he's ever done!' And she waved her now nearly empty bottle above her immaculately permed hair.

'Cheers!' she sang.

'Cheers.' I replied, as I clinked my teacup against her bottle.

Kathleen's story was, unfortunately, all too common. In the 1980s the police still had a very poor and, it has to be said, deserved reputation regarding their ability to ignore domestic abuse; or at least for treating it too lightly. Considering well over seventy per cent of murders were a direct result of domestic abuse and, as with shoplifters, few culprits are unlucky enough to be caught first time; common sense alone should have directed officers to a far more proactive approach.

But wife-beating had an historical legacy. For much of our history, women moved from being the legal property of their fathers to the legal property of their husbands, and men could treat their property however they saw fit. Male-dominated police forces still clung to these echoes of chauvinism, allowing them to state that domestic violence was not really 'police business' and the crimes committed 'didn't count'.

Throughout my career I found myself fighting tooth and nail to give the victims of domestic abuse the confidence to make statements against their abusers, but the courts would rarely acknowledge the courage this took and would often release their attacker on bail. Within twenty-four hours the majority of these women would withdraw their complaints. But even when we got a conviction and had a husband or boyfriend imprisoned for the hospitalisation of the partner they professed to love, that woman would often be found with a similar partner within a matter of months, if not weeks.

I used to rage against this weak stupidity, even declaring to one or two, 'You made your bed – now lie in it.' But I was to learn from the women who started to set up and run shelters for battered wives, that domestic abuse caused chronic damage that wasn't just physical. The mental abuse that accompanied the violence and sexual abuse made women believe they belonged at the bottom of the shit-heap that was their life. And some found a strange sort of comfort there; it was far easier to remain a punch-bag than struggle to become an independent thinker with self-respect. Such women felt that if they stayed in 'their place' no one would expect more of them than they felt capable of giving.

During a regular sermon on self-respect, I was once interrupted by one of my more articulate victims. 'Do you know how hard it is to aim at something you've never felt?' she asked.

The one time that some of these women became the worm that turned, was the first time that assaults were extended to their children. Sometimes this would bring out the fighter in them; they might deserve a beating but their children didn't.

It was to take me, and society in general, another 20 years to learn that men could also be the victim of such abuse.

I was fortunate enough to have accumulated a full six months' experience before being asked to deal with my first sudden-death scene. But where Kathleen's reaction to her husband's death had been a revelation, Irene's was heartbreaking.

I sat on the edge of the armchair, my notebook and pen providing a surprisingly effective barrier to this woman's frantic grief. As she paced the lounge, a Kleenex was turning to mush in her constantly wringing hands. Her answers to my invasive questions were interrupted by gulps of air, as she tried to control the sobs that rose from deep within her. Alfie, the family Alsatian, was lying flat to the floor, his eyes following her every move.

Irene confirmed that Phil, her husband for over two decades, was a 40-year-old self-employed builder. She was a nurse and had been in the shower getting ready for work, when Phil had returned home mid-morning. He'd shouted to her that he was feeling unwell and was going back to bed and, as she stepped out of the shower, she'd heard a loud thump. Running into their bedroom, Irene had found Phil lying dead on the floor. He had suffered a massive heart attack and, despite her best professional efforts, nothing could alter the outcome of this devastating event.

Imagine your life partner has just died: totally unexpectedly, no warnings, just literally dropped dead, like a stone hitting the ground; one last swift movement before total eternal inertia. A complete stranger then arrives and insists on completing an extraordinarily long form, full of seemingly inane and irrelevant minutiae such as what the deceased had for breakfast. This same stranger also asks you to decide what firm of undertakers you'd like to employ but, most incongruously of all, she needs you to formally identify your partner's body.

The ambulance crew had arrived shortly before the lady's own GP, who confirmed what they all knew – her husband was dead. I had arrived as the empty ambulance was leaving. Having confirmed Phil had no medical history to speak of, the doctor was now in the kitchen making tea, while Irene and I climbed the stairs to her bedroom. As we climbed, my feet felt like lead and my chest was tight. In a much lesser way

I was feeling as overwhelmed as Irene.

After formal confirmation that the man lying dead on her bedroom floor was her husband, Irene asked if she could spend some time alone with him, to say goodbye. The answer should have been no. If foul play was involved she could be doing all sorts of things to any evidence. But as I closed the bedroom door, tears streamed down my own face as I caught her first words.

'What will I do without you, Phil?'

Scrubbing a uniform sleeve across my eyes, I returned downstairs to find the doctor in the hallway, about to leave.

'I've left half a dozen Valium on the coffee table in the lounge. Tell Irene to take one now and another in four hours if she feels she needs it. There will obviously have to be a post-mortem to establish exact cause of death.'

Great, on top of everything else I'll have to tell this poor woman that her husband's body is now the property of the Crown. Walking back into the lounge en-route to the kitchen, I noticed Alfie licking the top of the glass coffee table. He'd come to sniff me on my arrival but, as with many dogs, he could sense the sorrow surrounding him and been very subdued.

As the licked-clean table-top clicked into my consciousness, the six Valium tablets he'd just swallowed had an immediate and, in canine terms, opposite effect. Within seconds, Alfie was performing wall-of-death circuits around the lounge, interspersed with pit-stops for manic chewing of the carpet. Finding myself trapped in the middle of an Alsatian whirl-wind and having no idea what to do about it, I radioed Control.

'Is there a dog handler in the area?' I asked.

'Why? Haven't you found the body yet?' The riposte was

irritating.

'Stow it.' I replied, and quickly explained the situation.

'We'll get a vet out to you ASAP,' was the more useful reply.

'If we've a dog handler in the area I'd appreciate their help.' I tried to keep the squeak of rising panic from my voice. Alfie was now on his back, with his eyes rolling in opposite directions above an open mouth that was chewing air.

'Afraid not – our only dog has just finished nights.'

Fortunately, there was a small animal surgery at the end of a nearby road and within a few minutes a shiny new vet was standing next to the shiny new copper, as we both watched Alfie resume his wall of death around a now decimated lounge.

'Valium, you say?'

'Six tablets.'

'Right, we'll have to inject amphetamine.'

'We?'

'Two-man job. I'll grab the sharp end, you hold the rest of him down. Let me get the syringe filled first.'

I eyed the blown-out hurricane of fur that was once more slowing to a drunken walk and when the vet gave me the nod I threw myself over Alfie's torso to prevent any relaunch. It was at this point that Irene entered her war-zone of a lounge, and was met by the spectacle of two strangers wrestling her household pet to the floor and injecting him with an unknown substance.

Returning to the house a few days later for a welfare check and coroner's update, I saw the lounge had been put to rights and the signs of Alfie's drug-induced rampage cleared away. But there was an emptiness to the room, as though Phil's existence had been cleared away with the broken china and torn cushions. New cushions sat straight but sad and the curtains remained half-drawn against the sun. This echo of loss had fallen over the whole house and the light had gone from two sets of eyes. Alfie was left lost in the moment, knowing his master was not there, but still hopeful of his return. Irene on the other hand could see an empty future stretching before them and she clung to Alfie for the warmth she would no longer receive from her obviously much-loved husband.

CHAPTER 9

Life's A Riot

All this time I had continued to smile and nod at Marlon whenever I walked past him outside McDonald's. He'd stopped turning away and, although he didn't return my smiles, he did smile when his fellow bouncer teased him with 'Man, she got the hots for you, bro!' and 'Here comes your girlfriend' whenever I hoved into view.

Then, in the early hours of one Sunday morning, it happened – Marlon James nodded back. He didn't say anything, but I felt thrilled. I felt the nod acknowledged me as an individual; for the first time he hadn't just dismissed me as my uniform. I still had no idea where any relationship could possibly head, but I'd woken up from more than one erotic dream involving this particular man.

For the next six months I'd stop and chat with Marlon and some of his mates. I was even being invited to share a coffee with them at the back of McDonald's. Cultivating new 'tea-stops' was a mark of growing experience in a probie, and I was especially proud of this one. It was during one of these regular coffees that Marlon asked me out.

'So, how about it?'

'How about what, Marlon?'

'You and me... you know... getting it together.'

My coffee spurted everywhere as I choked on the idea dreamt about so vividly but never voiced. My reaction amused his friends no end. They stood in a semi-circle, grinning and their excited back-slapping and hand-clasping gave me the distinct impression that money had been at stake on my answer.

'I'll take that as a 'no' then, shall I?' Marlon's tone remained neutral.

'Yes.'

'Yes, yes, or yes, no?'

'Yes, no.'

'I suppose it's *cos I'm black*?' The observation was delivered with a wide grin.

'No, Marlon. It's cos *you're CRO* [Criminal Records Office], and active at that!'

'Fair 'nough — had to ask though.' He replenished my wasted coffee while his mates exchanged money and told-you-so looks.

I was flattered rather than seriously tempted, despite my saucy dreams. No man would be allowed to get in the way of my career again, and his criminal record constituted a serious, insurmountable obstacle.

Meandering down George Street in the small hours of the following morning, I was beckoned over by two bouncers from Downtown Manhattan, a below-street-level nightclub.

'Think you'd better get your pals, love. We've just been steamed by a dozen Rastas and we think they've stabbed Stan.'

'Steaming' was a tactic used by groups of black youths to push through crowded areas, stealing as they went.

'Where is he?'

'Think he's in the bogs downstairs.'

My lack of experience, bolstered by a much-remarked upon level of over-confidence, was about to reveal itself.

Rather than radio Control and await back-up, I nonchalantly walked past the worried-looking bouncers and descended the dark stairwell into the bowels of a monster belching noise and smoke. Stopping at the foot of the stairs I looked around the club, letting my eyes adjust to the darkness and strobe-lighting. The only other white face in that packed basement belonged to a barmaid, who stared at me open-mouthed. But no alarm bells rang.

Pushing my way across the sticky floor towards the gents, the strong smell of stale beer was matched by the aroma of weed mingling with thick tobacco smoke. People stopped talking and stared at me with either indignation or disbelief. Still the alarm bells did not ring. Finding the door to the gents locked, I banged loudly and shouted 'Police!', but got no response – at least not from the toilet side of the door.

As I turned back into the club, a huge hand grabbed my throat and shoved me up against the locked door. My feet were lifted from the floor and I found myself looking into the very angry eyes of a very large Rastafarian, who spat into my quickly reddening face,

'What the fuck you doin' here, Babylon?'

Alarm bells now sounded so loudly that they was ringing in my ears. I tried to use my radio but there was no signal underground – oh the irony of being in a radio 'black spot'! My breathing became ever more difficult and my lungs began to burn as they struggled for oxygen. As my sight was beginning to blur, Marlon appeared; the surly crowd parting silently as they recognised him. He tapped the Rasta on his shoulder.

'Put her down, man.'

'Who the fuck are you?' The Rasta ignored Marlon and continued staring into my slowly closing eyes.

'My name's Marlon,' said Marlon. 'Put her down.'

'She's Babylon.'

'She's ok, for Babylon.'

'She's on our turf – uninvited.'

'You're on *my* turf – uninvited.'

My captor looked at Marlon for the first time, before glancing back at me and then looking at Marlon again, who was now surrounded by a large group of his friends, some of whom I recognised from McDonald's. The Rasta's mates stood behind him facing the local crew, but they were outnumbered at least five to one.

After sucking his teeth once, the Rasta released his fist and I fell onto the filthy carpet like a piece of dropped litter. I wasn't sure if the purple swirls were part of the carpet-design or the result of oxygen-deprivation. Breathing heavily, I picked myself up and leant against the locked door for support. Maintaining eye contact with the Rasta, Marlon flicked his head towards the stairs.

'Get the fuck out,' he advised.

So I did. Walking back across the dance floor towards the stairs and freedom, it was not a sense of bravado that dictated my slow pace, but the lack of coordination in my legs. It was then I caught sight of Bob Keylock.

Bob was a fairly new probationer and he was standing alone at the foot of the stairs. As he waited for me to reach him he took off his glasses, folded them and placed them in his tunic pocket. Bob was not a big bloke but this action was done with such a studied air of menace that several people standing by him took a step back. On reaching the stairs I grabbed him and hissed, 'Let's go!'

We could hear a large-scale fight breaking out behind us in the club as we hurried back up to stairs to the fresh air of George Street. Still very concerned for the bouncer in the locked loo, I also had a hunch that Bob and I might be followed into the street by those black lads not under Marlon's influence. I was right, and I put up my second ten-nine shout.

In the seconds it took other officers to start arriving, all hell had broken loose and within minutes Bob and I were in the centre of a full-blown riot.

Race riots had reignited in St Paul's, Handsworth and Brixton that autumn and in a year's time PC Keith Blakelock would be stabbed to death on Broadwater Farm. Scarman's philosophy had not worked. It was never going to work against the dark halo effect created by the Metropolitan Police's institutionally racist use of their 'sus-law'. Because of what was happening in London, black youth in all cities saw the police as their enemy, and as witnessed on my very first shift, behaviour breeds behaviour.

Tonight it was Oxford's turn. My ten-nine resulted in Police Support Units responding from as far away as Abingdon, Banbury, High Wycombe and Reading. I was still trying to let supervisors know that we had a seriously injured man trapped in the toilets of Downtown Manhattan as shop windows went in and the looting started. When I finally managed to speak to a dog section sergeant about the stabbed bouncer, I went back down into club with him and another handler.

I learnt many valuable lessons that night. One was not to lead dog handlers into a crowded space. Although the club was clearing quickly as its customers ran up into George Street to join in the 'protest', the police dogs were hyper, barking wildly and the sergeant's particularly large shaggy specimen jumped up at me, grabbing the thick sleeve of my uniform coat and nearly shaking me off my feet.

'Leave! Leave!'

'Christ, doesn't he know I'm on his side?' I yelled.

'The only side this dog's on is mine,' he yelled back, 'and we train them to attack wearing old uniforms, so you need to keep your fucking distance!'

I didn't need to be told twice, and the advice served me well at a football match many years later.

Support group officers managed to break down the loo door and rushing inside they leapt on two black lads who were backed up against the far wall with their hands in the air and utter terror on their faces. 'Not the dogs, man! No dogs! We dun nuffin!' Within seconds they were face down and hand-cuffed on the filthy wet floor. I ran to the bouncer who was slumped over a basin holding his bleeding side.

'It wasn't them,' he gasped, 'it was the Rastas. . . locked myself in... thought they'd come in and finish the job.'

The two males were de-cuffed without apology and they sidled warily past the barking dogs. I helped the bouncer to a waiting ambulance where his wound was examined and found to be the sort that would need stitching but was not life-threatening.

I don't recall many other details of the riot itself, other than helping a Support Group officer called Mark. Support Group specialised in public order offences such as assault and affray. They were stereotypically made up of adrenalin-fuelled alpha-males, who continued to wear their black leather gloves in summer and had a reputation for hitting first and asking questions later. But when you found yourself in the menacing situation of 'my dad's bigger than yours', Support Group was our dad.

Mark was fighting in a shop doorway with a tall, well-dressed, black male. The glass door was set back from the street, with large windows either side of it, which meant the two men were fighting in a U-shape made of glass. I could see

Mark was suffering from red mist, where adrenalin replaces thinking with hitting, and rather than making an arrest he was just punching out at the man, who was punching back. In a weird sort of slow motion I also noticed that several other black youths had clocked this fight and were making their way down the road to offer assistance.

Pulling at Mark's right arm I shouted at him for what seemed several minutes, rather than the seconds it probably took, before I got his attention through the adrenalin-fuelled mist.

'Mark, leave it! Leave it!'

Mark tried to shake me off in the same frenzied way the dog had. Fortunately, unlike the dog, he recognised the uniform and therefore which side I was on. As the red mist began to clear, he also recognised the danger he was in, from both the glass and the approaching group. The black lad's mist was lifting too and he smiled as he saw the approaching youths.

'You're going down, man,' he sneered, but he made the mistake of relaxing his stance and lowering his raised fist.

'It's not me going down.' In a move that would have put Bruce Lee to shame, Mark swept the lad's legs from underneath him until he was face down in the doorway, a groan replacing the sneer.

I sat on his wildly kicking legs as Mark secured the handcuffs and as we pulled the struggling man to his feet, his would-be rescuers reached the doorway.

'Let him go, Babylon!'

'He's under arrest and if you don't fuck off, you'll get nicked, too.' Mark was still panting from the fight.

'You and whose army, Babylon?'

'This army, mate.' I pointed to the riot van that had drawn up silently behind the group. The sound of its approach had been masked by the scream of other sirens, breaking glass and shouting from further up the street. Six officers I didn't recognise leapt out of the sliding side-door; their visors were down and their batons raised.

'Shit!' The four lads legged it back up the road, while Mark and I manhandled his prisoner into the back of the van.

The man subsequently made the mistake of using a London barrister to defend his public order charge in Oxford's magistrates' court. Magistrates did not like being lectured by local barristers, never mind ones travelling in from the capital. Although his London barrister got him off prison, the magistrates made his fine earnings-related; and this particular rioter was a stockbroker.

Around four that morning, Bob and I found ourselves in the canteen, drinking tea and 'making up' in our pocket notebooks, (this is a procedural rather than literal description of what we were doing).

Bob was a gentle soul whose career (following a ride on the roof of a Cortina), subsequently took him into CID and then Special Branch.

I looked up from our interminable scribbling. 'So, what was all that macho stuff with your glasses?'

His grin was rueful. 'Well, when the bouncers said you'd gone down into the club alone, I became worried.'

'But you didn't think to call for back-up first?'

'Like you, you mean?' I smiled acknowledgement of a mistake duplicated.

'Well, you know what it's like with us new probies – you can't be shouting for back-up every five minutes. Of course, once inside, when I saw you being throttled by that humongous Rasta, I didn't know whether to rush to your rescue or rush back upstairs for help. Then I saw that other black guy do the rescuing, so I stayed put.'

'Cheers, I appreciate it.'

'Well, to be perfectly honest, Chris, I was so shit-scared that keeping upright was as much as I could do.'

'And taking your specs off?'

'Same thing – didn't like what I was seeing. I've only had them a week and they were bloody expensive. If I was going to get the shit kicked out of me I could at least try and protect my specs... even if I couldn't protect you.'

We were interrupted by the duty superintendent, called from his warm bed by the rioting.

'WPC Foster?'

'Sir.'

'I understand you put up the first ten-nine.'

'Yes, Sir.'

'You certainly got things started. Are you ok?' He was staring at the extensive purple bruising around my neck, made more spectacular by the white of the shirt collar.

'Yes, Sir, mainly thanks to Marlon James. He probably saved my life.'

'So I understand. I'm thinking of putting him up for a chief constable's commendation.' He seemed pleased with this idea.

'That's great, Sir. I could deliver it when I serve his next warrant for non-payment of fines.'

The superintendent looked confused, but I knew Marlon wouldn't want official police thanks; it would ruin his street-cred. What he'd done for me was despite my uniform, not because of it.

When I eventually got home that morning and saw the bruising in the bathroom mirror, I'd have given anything to feel Brian's arms around me. But it was a fleeting moment of self-pity and it was Marlon's arms I dreamt of when I fell into an exhausted sleep.

The next time I saw Marlon, we were both at work. Despite this I walked straight up to him, stood on tip-toe and planted a kiss on his cheek.

'Cheers.' Was all I said.

He just smiled and nodded.

I maintained a good 'working' relationship with Marlon for the two years I pounded the beat in Oxford and, when I went to his home address to serve a summons, he invited me in and introduced me to his mum.

CHAPTER 10

Angel Dust Andy

I had replaced my husband with a new horse. Now that I was working shifts, I could easily fit in riding and time at the stables around my job. Evicted speedily from the police house, I had managed to buy a new-build studio flat in Abingdon with the help of a 110 percent mortgage. Rynghmor, my ex-racehorse, was stabled not too far away near Didcot.

'Make everything legal!' the professor declared, as our horses ambled over the downs, enjoying the still air of a sunny afternoon. I was hacking out with a fellow livery owner who was also a fellow of Oxford University, working for the Home Office on the cost to society of drug abuse. He had a radical and brilliant idea for dealing with drug-related crime.

'Heroin, in fact all class A drugs, can be produced safely for pence,' he said. 'If you *give* addicts what they want in a controlled environment, a health centre say, they won't have to commit crime to fund their habit. They could probably hold down jobs, too.'

'You're joking. How can a junkie hold down a job?'

'Have you any idea how many coke-heads manage large hedge funds in the City? The only difference between them and a street addict is that they can afford their drugs. They don't have to waste time worrying about where their next fix is coming from.'

'But wouldn't you create a whole new generation of junkies?' I leant forward to pull a large piece of pinched cow parsley from my gelding's mouth.

'It's a risk, but I believe it's a small one. If you take the mystery, the cult, the taboo, out of drug-taking, it becomes a bad habit for losers, with no street-cred amongst the young. Who wants to be seen standing in line outside a health centre? It'd be as cool as grannies spiking their hair with gel and putting a safety-pin through their nose.'

I smiled at this lovely image and used the retrieved cow parsley to swat the flies buzzing around my face.

'I reckon you could reduce all theft-related crime by eighty per cent within a few years and deprive organised crime of millions. But the government just doesn't have the balls for it.'

This conversation threw up a memory of Angel Dust Andy being dragged into the custody office during my recent six-week stint as jailer. It was a grunt of a job, involving searching prisoners, doing half-hourly checks on juveniles and drunks, and hourly checks on the rest. I also made tea, handed out meals and loo paper, mopped up vomit and urine and recorded everything I did on the handwritten custody records.

Andy was a local addict whose own collection of custody records started shortly after his twelfth birthday. A teacher had caught him smoking behind the bike sheds, not normally an offence requiring police intervention, but Andy's fag was a spliff. Continuing steadily along his chosen career path, by the time he was eighteen Andy had graduated to a very expensive heroin habit. He'd been arrested three times in the previous month for burglary or theft from vehicles. Like many addicts he was painfully thin and weedy, with a weasel face and flaky, ash-coloured skin; but Andy was not usually violent.

As Support Group walked him in, he seemed distracted.

His eyes constantly darted around the custody office and he kept licking his cracked lips. Every now and then he'd jump sideways in an attempt to spot an imaginary person creeping up behind him. By the time Sergeant J had booked him in and he'd been carefully searched for needles, his actions had grown from tension tics to a full-blown frantic dance.

When Sergeant J told Support Group to take him to the cells, Andy exploded. Breaking free he tried to merge into the back wall of the office. It took both arresting officers to pull him away from the wall and down the cell corridor. When we got to the cell, Andy braced his legs against the door frame; he was screaming incoherently. The officers picked him up and walked his kicking and writhing body into the cell, before placing him face-down on the floor. While one of them leant on Andy's shoulders and undid the handcuffs, the other managed to fold his kicking legs over each other and lean on them, too. This was supposed to have the effect of deadening the prisoner's legs for a few seconds, which meant he wouldn't be able to get to his feet quickly. It was supposed to give the officers enough time to leave the cell safely.

Both men gave one final push on Andy's upper body and folded legs, before they jumped up and ran for the door. I just managed to slam it shut before Andy launched himself at it with such force that the solid metal shuddered under my hands. He immediately started to pound at the closed inspection hatch with his bare fists, all the time screaming like a banshee. He wasn't shouting the usual obscenities. His screams were a non-human sound that made the hairs on the back of my neck stand up. Even Support Group looked apprehensive.

There was no let-up in this screaming and banging and, as I returned to the cellblock to check on another prisoner, I was amazed to see that Andy's continual hammering on the metal hatch had actually started to bend it outwards. Approaching his cell with caution I could hear Andy kicking at something. Peering through the scratched glass of the door's tiny viewing window, I saw him kung-fu kicking the porcelain toilet – which he'd managed to crack. I watched, transfixed by the power this weedy body and stocking feet were producing, as the toilet smashed. Andy picked up one of the bigger pieces, using it to rain down fatal blows on what was left of the offending utility. Water gushed like blood and ran towards me, quickly seeping out from under the door.

I raced back to get Sergeant J and in the short time it took us to return Andy had taken off a sock, stuffed it with bits of broken porcelain and was now swinging it above his head like a medieval mace. Again, he was doing this with such force that he had cracked several of the oblong cream tiles that covered the Victorian cell walls and he'd even managed to crack one of the six-inch glass bricks that provided the cell with daylight. His screaming was continuous and contained such a raw rage and sense of undiluted hatred that I felt genuinely scared. Sergeant J looked as worried as I felt.

'Chris, get onto Control. I want Support Group back here and any PSU-trained shift members to custody – immediately! Check if there's a dog handler in the area, too.' Glancing through the porthole he added, 'Better get onto ambulance control – if he doesn't need medical treatment we might.'

Calls complete, I returned to the cellblock where Sergeant J was in the process of evacuating the other four prisoners from that corridor; escorting them one at a time to the female block. By now Andy had succeeded in bending the thinner metal of the inspection hatch out so far that he was able to chuck smaller pieces of the toilet down the corridor. The missiles themselves could not be thrown at an angle needed to hit you, but they were causing an amazing amount of dust, which was billowing along the corridor. As I helped Sergeant J drag a semi-conscious Billie from the drunk-tank, Andy's screaming continued undiminished.

It didn't take long for the troops to mass in the custody office. Sergeant J told everyone to don full riot gear and form into three shield parties. Andy's screaming was so unnerving that no one considered this overkill. When the dog handler arrived, Sergeant J instructed him to stand at the entrance to the cellblock, just in case Andy got past all three shield parties, and again no one saw this as ridiculous.

Andy's screaming caused retaliatory barking in the police dog. Their combined howls echoed and reverberated, bouncing off the tiled walls. This high-pitched density of noise was one of the most incredible sounds I've ever heard, and Andy won. The dog's pricked ears now lay flat against its lowered head, the strain had gone from its leash and its hyper-barking became a whine before it fell silent. Meanwhile, Andy's wailing continued undefeated and unchallenged.

Once the ambulance arrived, I led the first shield party down the cell corridor, which was now swimming in a good inch of water. It made a sticky paste with the debris intermittently thrown by Andy. There was still nothing intermittent about his screams.

Shield parties were made up of two officers with interlocking 6ft plastic shields. They were held in a side-by-side position by a third officer, standing behind his colleagues and holding firmly onto their belts. This third officer was also responsible for talking to the 'subject' and guiding the shield officers; whose aim was to back said subject into a corner, or at least against a wall, and hold them there. The second shield party would then enter to restrain and handcuff the person, while they were still pinned against the wall by the first set of shields. Having witnessed the damage that Andy had already inflicted on the structure of his cell; no one was confident that one shield party would be able to hold him, which is why Sergeant J had the third on standby. I, too, was dressed in riot gear. It was my job to check where Andy was in the cell, quietly unlock the door and then signal to the shield party when I was about to pull it open. All cell doors open outwards for just these situations.

The only good thing about Andy's current state was that while he was so busy on 'planet Andy' he was taking no notice of the outside world. The small porthole was now cracked and covered in spit, so I tried looking under the gap in the bent hatch. But it was too bent to move either up or down and my visor was preventing me from getting an angle from which I could see into the cell – so I took my helmet off. I was fairly confident, from the direction of Andy's wailing, he was now at the back of the cell.

My hunch was right and, better still, I could indicate to the shield party that he was actually sitting in the far right-hand corner, cradling his knees and rocking himself in time to his wails.

As I swung open the door the first two shield parties rushed into the cell, while the third formed a protective see-through temporary door. The first three leapt onto Andy, pinning his body to the ground, but it still took the other three several minutes to control Andy's limbs enough to get the special public order cuffs on. These thick plastic loops hooked over a person's wrists and ankles, before being pulled tight with a quick jerk – no need for time-wasting keys. Once tight they could not be loosened and would have to be cut off to be removed.

It took four officers to carry Andy, face down and trussed like a chicken, out of his decimated cell and into a fresh one, where the ambulance crew examined him. Bit by bit, the Support Group officers held the relevant body parts still for medical examination. The only injury the ambulance men could find was the smallest of cuts to a little finger. There appeared to be no broken bones. Andy was left lying on his stomach with his wrists and ankles bound for nearly an hour – it took him that long to stop screaming. When the police surgeon eventually arrived, he was reluctant to administer any sedative in case it reacted with whatever he'd taken.

At last Andy went quiet. He had fallen into a deep exhausted sleep, and once we were sure he wasn't pretending, the cuffs were cut from his hands and feet. I placed him in the recovery position and covered him with a grey blanket, which matched the colour of his skin. The next morning when he woke, early-turn reported that he was groggy but otherwise fine. Several impressive bruises had developed on his hands and feet, but Andy could recall nothing of the previous night – apart from trying Angel Dust for the first time.

He was imprisoned for both the initial theft and the criminal damage to his cell, but the sentence was not long enough to get him clean, and on his release Andy would once more steal in order to feed his habit. He would cause extensive criminal damage to several cars on a daily basis in order to get at stereos, which he'd steal, together with anything else of value. He also broke into people's homes, stealing the sentimental as well as the valuable, including an irreplaceable fifty-year-old wedding photo in its insured silver frame. As with all burglaries, the salt of fear was often added to the open wound of material loss.

Angel Dust Andy

Patsy was my dressage trainer. She was a typical horsey woman, strong-minded, no nonsense, practical. Yet the day-time burglary of her family's home left her feeling so vulnerable she slept fully clothed for the next few weeks. The thought of a stranger rummaging through her underwear was as upsetting as the loss of the television and stereo. Some burgled parents were even forced to sell up and move, as nothing they said or did could make their children feel safe again.

Stolen property would be 'fenced' at around twenty percent of its market value; which is why multiple offences would need to be committed each day by each addict. And I couldn't help but think that the professor's proposal might eliminate both the financial and emotional cost to all these victims. Thirty years on and nothing much has changed – legalisation of all drugs is still being talked about.

CHAPTER 11

Driving, Drinking and Discretion

'Stop him, Chris! Stop him!'

It had just gone midnight and I was standing in a shop doorway in Cornmarket. I'd heard a car approaching at speed and stepping out to investigate I saw a blue Ford Cortina speed past me, heading towards St Giles. Bob Keylock was on its roof. He was banging his Maglite on the car's windscreen with his left hand and yelling at me.

As I put up a ten-nine shout for Bob, a Support Group car parked in Turl Street had also seen him and was already giving chase. The chase ended on a roundabout near Kidlington, some three miles away, when two traffic cars and Support Group managed to box the driver in and bring him to a halt with Bob still on the roof.

He'd stopped the car in St Aldates, and the driver had been friendly enough until Bob had requested a breath specimen. Half out of the car at the time, the driver had panicked and leapt back into the driver's seat, slamming the door shut and trapping Bob's right thumb in the rubber seal of the door. He'd stupidly been resting his hand on the roof as he spoke to the driver.

'Never touch a vehicle that still contains a driver,' was a lesson I passed on to probationers in future years.

As the man started the engine, Bob had shouted at him to stop, but the driver was in a total panic and he drove forward, leaving Bob no option but to leap onto the roof or be dragged along the road. When the car was eventually stopped and the door reopened, Bob had a small cut to his thumb that didn't even need stitching. He did, however, require a change of underwear. The driver was treated for a broken arm.

It was morning rush-hour and traffic was building steadily along Oxford's High Street. Crawling towards me was a red VW Beetle, his snail-like speed was creating a tailback towards Magdalen Bridge. I recognised the driver as Christopher.

Christopher's was a tragic story. Shortly after leaving school, a building site accident had left him with a serious head injury, and a large metal plate now replaced the smashed part of his skull. He'd not been the brightest button in the box to begin with but, when sober, he was a pleasant, chatty bloke. Because of his disabilities Christopher's provisional driving licence had been withdrawn. Unfortunately, withdrawing a piece of paper had not removed his passion (and it had to be said, some skill) for driving. Christopher viewed any vehicle with keys left in the ignition as a direct invitation. He once took an open-top tour bus from the depot on the Cowley Road and drove it to his home in the small terraced streets of Jericho – leaving it neatly parallel-parked outside his front door.

Christopher now seemed blissfully unaware of the honking queue of traffic behind him. His sedate pace was due to his severely restricted line of sight, which was forcing him to lean forward over the steering wheel with his face a tongue-out picture of concentration. When he saw me signal him to stop, recognition replaced concentration and he smiled and waved. Indicating left, Christopher pulled into the kerb and applied the handbrake. At my mimed signal he also turned off the engine.

The tailback sped past us with rude gestures and one last indignant honk from the line of angry commuters. Christopher remained oblivious to them all as he leant across and opened the front passenger door for me. I crouched on the pavement, Bob's roof-ride still fresh in my mind.

'Morning, Christopher.'

'Morning, WPC Foster. How do you like my new car?'

'It's lovely, but it's not really yours is it?'

'It is too.' We both knew his affronted tone was put on.

'Christopher, you've just *borrowed* this from that new garage on the Iffley Road haven't you?'

He looked sheepish. 'Might have... how do you know?'

'These.' I said, standing up to peel off the four large red stickers plastered over the windscreen, which read £599.

Where Christopher was a naturally talented driver, I was not. If I wanted to take the wheel of a police vehicle, however, I needed to pass their driving course. Probationers posted to city centres could often wait three years to take the course, as officers on rural beats took priority – very few of their jobs being within walking distance. But just under two years in I was being honoured with a basic driving course. I had recently passed my tutor constable's training and, as a tutor, I would need access to pandas and riot-vans. Rumours abounded about how intense the course was and how hard the instructors were. Like running, I'd always hated driving, although it involved far less physical effort in getting from A to B. I was fortunate, however, to have as my instructor Rob Nurden, who combined the unusual qualities of being an excellent driver and compassionate teacher – not that I knew any of this on the first day.

Driving, Drinking and Discretion

Day one started with the allocation of three officers to each instructor and a specific car. The morning was spent in the classroom revising the Highway Code and being instructed on the need for good hygiene. The course would, we were assured, produce a lot of sweating. After lunch, Rob showed his three new students what advanced driving was all about. His demonstration was a thrilling fairground ride accompanied by a running commentary on what he was doing and why. It included observations like, 'small child walking large dog on left, dog may break free,' and 'Newcastle number plate in front – may not know area and so may brake suddenly.'

Overwhelmed by such smooth expertise, we then took turns in the driver's seat while the maestro assessed us. He wanted us to drive 'normally' so that he could see how many bad habits we'd picked up since passing our tests. I'd never been behind the wheel of such a new car; it was less than a year old. The driving school was based in Banbury and on the narrow country lanes surrounding the town I kept well away from the hedgerows in case I scratched the gleaming bodywork. I was so nervous that I fluffed a simple gear change in magnificent style and Rob turned to the two lads sat in the back.

'Looks like we have ourselves a Scandinavian driver, gentlemen.'

'Scandinavian, Rob?' I could detect a level of male smugness.

'Oh yes, that was a classic Swedish gear-change if ever I heard one.'

'Swedish, Rob?' The back seat drivers sounded positively gleeful.

'Well,' he sighed, 'one more *grind* like that and we'll all be fucked!'

Glancing in the rear-view mirror I could see my so-called colleagues sniggering, but when I looked at Rob his face showed no emotion as he stared ahead serenely. Instead, his right hand came up to the gear stick, palm up with fingers flicking backwards, indicating he wanted more speed.

Over the following three weeks it became a matter of honour within our car that we each completed our forty-minute stint in the driving seat without Rob feeling the need to flick his fingers. And, to our instructor's credit, the lack of facial expression he displayed on day one stayed with him throughout the course. Not once did I see the fear in my eyes reflected in his.

The next day, Rob took us to a deserted airstrip where we practiced double de-clutching and killing road cones by attempting to slalom and then reverse between them. At one point, having flattened my third cone, I stopped the car, banged the steering wheel and demanded some 'team work' from my errant vehicle. Much to Rob's amusement this technique worked and it was not me who had to fork out for drinks that night; a penalty for murdering the most cones.

Lots were drawn each Monday morning of the three-week course to see which set of students would be lumbered with the Mondeo for that week. As the Mondeo straw was drawn on the second Monday by another group, it looked as though our turn for the shit-brown car which handled like a tractor would come in the final week and therefore for the final exam. So our car really cheered when we passed the Mondeo nose down in a large ditch, while its former occupants surveyed their handiwork from the safety of the verge.

An over-enthusiastic corner by one of the drivers had resulted in the temporary demise of this hated vehicle. This was a cause for much celebration amongst both pupils and instructors; although the sergeant in overall charge was a little hacked off that no one had thought to remove the sticker running along the back windscreen proclaiming 'Thames Valley Police Driving School' when they'd abandoned the vehicle.

We were trained in unmarked cars to enhance our driving abilities. Too many panda drivers have a misplaced trust in their blues and twos. They think that a flashing blue light and two-tone siren provides them, and everyone else, with some sort of celestial air-bag. Later on in my career when, as a sergeant, I conducted the one-hour driving assessment of new probationers that had replaced the three-week courses, I would make the following observation:

'We do not have the death penalty in this country, not even for the rape and murder of children. When you decide to activate the 'blues and twos', run red lights and break speed limits, make damn sure that what you're racing to is worth the risks you take. The risks not only to yourself, but to the other officers in the car and innocent members of the public who will not always see the lights or hear the sirens.'

However, my own experience as a police driver was not without blemish. After nearly four years of driving on blues and twos without incident, I had a spate of three (minor) 'Polacs' (police accidents) in as many weeks. My shift started to call me Chi Chi – she who fucks pandas – and the sergeant felt obliged to send me on a week's remedial driving course. But some drivers would never learn their lesson... .

It was early turn, and I was standing in the doorway of McDonald's debating whether to treat myself to an egg and bacon McMuffin for breakfast, when a dark blue BMW made a slow right turn against a no-entry sign into Cornmarket. The car crept to a halt in front of me, half on the pavement and half in the road, abandoned rather than parked, at a very rakish angle. With the engine still running, I watched with growing incredulity as the driver's door opened and a yuppie, complete with red braces and yellow socks, fell softly out of the driver's seat and onto his hands and knees.

With considerable concentration he started to crawl towards McDonald's and me. As he reached the doorway his hand touched my shoe and his eyes travelled slowly up my freshly pressed skirt, white shirt, black tie and epaulettes, to my unsmiling face, which stared down into his rather haggard, unshaven one.

'Shit,' he said. Giving up the unequal struggle to get breakfast, he turned over and sat with his back against the wall. After fighting with his jacket pocket, which refused to give up his own cigarettes, he tried unsuccessfully to suck life into an unlit fag-end he picked up from the pavement. The smell of booze floated upwards in gentle waves, and bending down I whispered those immortal words, 'You're nicked.'

While Adrian finished his pretend fag, I re-parked his car, turned off the engine and placed a 'Police Aware' sticker in the windscreen before radioing for transport. It was only a matter of 800 yards back to the station, but Adrian was not going to make even that distance under his own steam.

When Paul arrived in a panda, it took both of us to pour Adrian into the rear seat and throughout the short journey back he kept repeating, 'My mother's going to kill me.'

'You're lucky to be alive so she can kill you,' I retorted. 'More to the point, you're bloody lucky you haven't killed anyone else, driving in that state. Where have you come from?'

'London,' was his astounding reply.

We decanted Adrian into the custody office, where he

managed to confirm his details, including the fact that he worked as a stockbroker. He explained he'd had a spur of the moment whim to visit his girlfriend in one of the colleges, but what had seemed like a good idea at five in the morning was looking decidedly dodgy now. Once the booking-in procedure was complete, I followed Adrian and Sergeant J into the intoximeter room. My breakfast could wait; I needed to see what reading he would produce – I was betting on treble figures.

Sergeant J started working his way through the paperwork and when he got to the part that asked, 'Have you taken anything that might affect the reading of this machine?'Adrian replied, 'Bottle of Bolly and some vodka,' before he fell off his chair, laughing at his own witticism.

Sergeant J was not amused. Adrian was so drunk it took him several attempts to summon up the necessary concentration and lung-power to provide a successful specimen. The legal limit was thirty-five – Adrian's reading was a hundred and twenty-six. Technically he should have been dead from alcoholic poisoning. It took the rest of the shift for him to become sober enough for me to complete his antecedence form, which tells the court about a person's education, employment record and current financial situation.

'So, Adrian, what do you do for a living – when you're not drinking?'

'I'm a stockbroker.'

'And how much do you earn?'

'Around ninety.'

'Ninety?' I struggled to process the figure against my own annual income.

'Yeah, around ninety... plus bonuses.'

'Does that make you a good stockbroker?'

'No such thing as a bad one. You're either successful or you're not a stockbroker – for long.'

'Have you been in trouble with the police before?'

He nodded. 'I seem to get myself into this particular scrape fairly regularly. This is my third drink-driving – am I going to lose my licence again?'

'You're going to lose more than your licence, mate. With such a high reading there's every chance you'll go down.'

'Go down?'

'Adrian, you're likely to go to prison.'

When I charged him with the offence of driving with excess alcohol (which in the circumstances seemed a woeful under-statement) his reply was, 'My mother's really going to kill me this time.'

I was at court swearing out a warrant the day of Adrian's trial. His solicitor had confirmed my opinion that he would serve time and Adrian had come prepared. There was no sign of his mother, who I imagined sitting alone in an elegant London drawing room, pale with shame. Adrian cut a forlorn figure as he sat with a small brown suitcase and a teddy bear, tucked under the arm of his Savile Row suit.

'Brideshead Revisited', which had been filmed in and around Oxford, was on the TV and Aloysius teddy bears had become something of a fashion accessory amongst many of the male students. The bear was a good-luck mascot from his girlfriend, who appeared from the Ladies and flung both arms around the dejected Adrian. I approached the couple to offer some advice.

'Adrian, mate, leave the bear with…?' I looked at the girlfriend.

'Lucy,' she offered, looking affronted by my intrusion.

'Good looking isn't he, your bloke?' She nodded and

caressed his expensively encased free arm.

'Well, there are men in prison who will feel the same as you and his possession of this bear will act like a neon arrow – come and get it here!' Adrian looked alarmed but Lucy just looked bemused, so I clarified things, 'Lucy, if Adrian goes into prison holding that, the chances are he won't come out the same man that he went in.'

As the usher called Adrian back into court he shoved the bear at a tearful Lucy. He got six months custodial and a five-year ban from driving. Good job he could afford a chauffeur.

Because of the pressure of that probationer chart in the night-kitchen, I believed I could not use 'discretion'. I kept having to prove my worth to both myself and people like Coops; and the only measurement used was numerical. My natural competitive streak ensured I was top of that chart most months, and I was therefore expecting a pat on the back at my first annual review with the divisional superintendent.

'Well, WPC Foster, you're setting the bar very high aren't you?'

I smiled at the words but felt confused by the tone with which they were delivered.

'You're married, are you not?'

'Separated, Sir.'

'So you're not planning to start a family in the foreseeable future?'

'No Sir, I don't want children.'

'Hmm.' He didn't sound convinced, but returned to my career prospects. 'The problem with getting ticks in all the top boxes is that the only way for you now is down.'

'Well, Sir, I can only do my best.' What was to become a

regular sense of indignation in these types of interview, where my personal life featured more heavily than my professional, flared for the first time and I added, 'I'm afraid I was not brought up to aim at failure.'

It was shortly after this appraisal that I was to receive an important lesson in life's shades of grey. Ironically it came from a Support Group officer. This particular member of Support Group had passed his sergeant's exam and was doing a stint of acting sergeant with the shift. His name was Paul 'Smokey' Brightwell, a nickname gained from his time on the tactical firearms team. Smokey was well over 6ft and whippet-thin. His face was gaunt, built for scowling, but he was always willing to smile at life.

The previous evening Smokey had been acting as the custody sergeant when I'd brought in another excess alcohol arrest. The driver was an extremely nice man who'd been on his way home from an anniversary dinner with his wife. I felt I'd gone through the breathalyser procedure with professional but friendly warmth.

'Your defective headlight means you're actually committing a moving traffic offence.' I looked apologetic. 'Because of this I now require you to provide me with a specimen of your breath. Failure to do, refusal to do so, or a positive test will result in your arrest and possible prosecution. Do you understand?' I smiled encouragement.

The driver's own smile faded and he looked old-paper-yellow in the orange glow of the street lamp, but he remained polite and helpful. When he blew into the little black box, the light went to amber quite quickly, meaning the device was registering alcohol, but it took much longer to go to the amber and red-light verbal warning combination. Watching the continual flicking of the second hand on my watch I knew it was nearer fifty seconds, rather than the recommended forty, before I got the solo red light that indicated a failed breath test. Another arrest, another tick.

Back at the station, omitting the ten-second extension, I related the legal minutiae to Smokey. He booked the man in and got on with obtaining the evidential reading from the intoximeter. On a roll, I resumed my patrol; on the hunt for further work. During my meal break I bounced back into custody to check that my prisoner had been charged. Smokey's confirmation came with a disapproving, sideways look.

The next night he organised patrols so that we were crewed together. I was still half expecting a 'well done' for the previous night's arrest but it was not forthcoming and, in the small hours of the morning, Smokey parked-up in Turl Street and turned to face me.

'You realise what'll happen to that bloke you arrested last night?'

I bristled. 'He'll go to court, plead or get found guilty and be banned from driving.'

'He's a taxi driver.' Smokey's tone was accusatory.

'He should have known better then.'

'So he'll lose his livelihood as well as his licence.'

'That's not my fault!'

'You could have... helped it.'

'Look,' I said, indignation burning through every pore, 'the man broke the law. It's my job to enforce the law – are you saying I should have ignored the red light?'

'No. The red light's pretty final, although he only just scraped a positive reading with me.' Smokey tapped the steering wheel while he considered his next move.

On reflection, he was being extremely brave. Most acting supervisors wouldn't have dared broach the subject, much less persist in the face of such dogged opposition.

'What made you stop him in the first place? Was he driving erratically?'

'No. He had a duff light.'

'So, what made you think he'd been drinking? Could you smell it on him?'

'No, he told me he'd had a glass of champagne when I asked.'

'What made you ask?'

'Standard procedure, good practice. Jesus!'

'What made you decide to breathalyse him?'

'Because the law says I can.'

Smokey sighed. 'But it doesn't say you *have to* ...'

'What do you mean by that?'

'I mean discretion. I mean if you had used some, this very nice man might still have a job to support his wife and their new baby.'

I was furious, 'I'm a probationer, I don't have any bloody discretion!'

Smokey sighed again and started the car. We finished the shift in silence.

Everything was very black and white to me then and I didn't give that poor taxi driver another thought. At the time I felt vindicated, I just did what was necessary to play the game and fight for my place in a world where the odds were still stacked against me; but that was no excuse. Thirty years on I feel bad. Those extra ten seconds made a crucial difference. It was to take me a while before I could use discretion with confidence.

It was several years after that argument, on Wednesday 19th August 1987, that Smokey found himself part of the TVP response to the Hungerford Massacre. Michael Ryan had shot dead sixteen people in that bustling market town: his own mother and a police officer, Roger Brereton, were among the dead. Ryan had also wounded fifteen others, including medics who had been dispatched to help the wounded, and firemen who were trying to tackle the house fires he'd started.

At the end of an unimaginably stressful, traumatic and incomprehensible day, where terror and panic had been at the core of individual fights for survival, Smokey found himself leading the tactical firearms team maintaining an armed cordon around the perimeter of the John O'Gaunt Secondary School. Ryan had been seen entering the school around lunchtime. Fortunately, the school (like me) was on its summer break. It was Smokey who saw Ryan standing at the third-floor window of the empty school. This confirmed sighting allowed the other emergency services to finally aid the injured and dying, unhindered by fear for their own safety. It was Smokey who persuaded Ryan to throw his assault weapon out of the window and it was Smokey who had Ryan's unprotected forehead in the sights of his rifle, but he refrained from shooting him dead.

Several months later I was enjoying a quiet drink in the police bar, when Smokey plonked himself down next to me.

'How's it going?' he asked.

'Good – you?'

He nodded, and took a sip of Coke.

I turned to face him, 'Can I ask you something?'

'Let me guess – why didn't I shoot Ryan when I had the chance?'

'I'd have pulled the trigger, no problem.'

Smokey smiled knowingly at the still gung-ho girl sitting next to him, and I was instantly taken back to the last time we'd been sitting side by side. His sigh this time was one of indulgence.

'I didn't shoot because I could see both his hands and they were empty. When he picked up the gun it was to throw out of the window. At no time I had him in my sights did Michael pose a threat.'

I was startled by his use of Ryan's first name. 'But you could have killed him? Procedurally – legally?'

'Probably, yes,' Smokey took another sip of Coke, 'but I decided not to.'

Smokey had walked the walk. He had used his discretion in the most challenging of circumstances. No one would have criticised him for shooting Ryan; he might well have become a hero instead of a Googled-footnote to history. Instead, Paul Brightwell had spent the next ninety minutes trying to persuade Michael Ryan to give himself up. During their intermittent, shouted, conversation, Ryan had yelled at him.

'It's funny, I killed all those people but I haven't got the guts to blow my own brains out.'

Despite Paul's best efforts, at six-twenty-five he heard a single shot. Ryan had found the guts.

CHAPTER 12

On Death and Dying

It was another wasted day at court and I was doing battle with a coffee machine in the corridor, when a sergeant I didn't recognise called me back to the confines of the police room. It was a small, windowless oasis, where officers could find sanctuary from those they had arrested and their supporters. The sergeant was from headquarters.

'Either of you know a Kevin Thornly?'

'I do, Sarge.' The only other officer in the room was a bobby from Cowley. 'He's a right nutter.'

'The usher from court one has requested police assistance. Thornly's about to have his bail withdrawn and the magistrates are expecting a violent reaction to this good news. I've contacted St Aldates for back-up.'

'Do we need it? There's three of us here.' I was keen to be viewed as a reliable asset.

'We'll need it.' The Cowley bobby's voice was doom-laden.

There's a criminal cliché that divides offenders into one of three categories: sad, mad, and bad. Thornly's category was apparently bad with a serious streak of drug-related madness. I rang the court cells to tell the three officers there to 'get ready for incoming', and was relieved when it was Pete who had picked up the phone. Pete was a bodybuilder, the current holder of the Mr South West title who would go on to become

Mr Great Britain and was even runner-up in something like Mr World, Universe or Cosmos. Like me, Pete was still in his probation. Unlike me, he was having his whole uniform made to measure – starting with twenty-two inch collars.

The Cowley bobby had been called to give evidence in court two, but Thornly must have guessed something was up when the sergeant and I followed him into court one. His suspicions were confirmed when two more officers entered via the dock. Len had come up with Pete. Where Pete was young, strong, black, and bald by choice, Len was nearing retirement, white and with a receding hairline that he resented. They stood at the back of the dock, one in each corner, like mismatched bookends.

Despite assuming the look of a hunted animal, Thornly followed the nod of his solicitor's head and he walked warily into the dock; his eyes darting over the four police officers he could see and his head cocked as though listening for more. The sergeant and I stood by the door and I flicked my lowered hand at the usher hiding behind us, indicating he needed to move. If Thornly did a runner the usher could get hurt if he stood between a nutter and his freedom.

The three magistrates filed in. They remained standing as the chairman of the bench declared, 'Mr Thornly, we are setting a trial date for three weeks from today and we are withdrawing your bail and remanding you into custody.'

All three filed out again as quickly as was seemly, but only just quick enough.

Thornly's reaction was instantaneous. Leaping over the top of the open dock he screamed, 'You fucking bastards!' and ran towards the raised bench, reaching it just as the last magistrate pushed her colleagues through the door to their chamber and slammed it shut. As Thornly tried to scale the empty bench, the sergeant and I grabbed him in a pincer movement with Len, while Pete stood still. Thornly clung to the carved crest decorating the front of the bench like a manic limpet, while Pete continued to watch the three of us struggle to pull him off and place him on the ground.

Finding himself face down on the brown nylon carpet of the courtroom floor, Thornly tucked both his arms tightly into his body so we couldn't get handcuffs on. He was used to being restrained by the police. He continued to struggle wildly, kicking and snapping and, even with the sergeant straddling his back and me desperately trying to control his bucking legs, Len couldn't get a good enough grip on one of his arms to pull it out. In fact, every time Len went anywhere near Thornly's head, Kevin tried to bite him.

It appeared my initial confidence in Pete had been misplaced. He may have been big, he may have been brave, but he was vain and avoided all physical situations, claiming he didn't want injuries and bruises to spoil his oh so perfect torso.

'For God's sake, Pete!' I yelled. 'Get your big arse over here and help us.'

'It's not big – it's in perfect proportion to the rest of me.' Pete strode over to the struggling mass of humanity rolling around in front of him. Kneeling down he took hold of Thornly's right elbow and gently squeezed it. A howl of pain was added to Thornly's free-flowing abuse and a bony arm shot into view. Len grabbed it and held onto the twig-like wrist with all his might; he was nearly sixty and had presumed this sort of work was behind him.

It was at this point that we realised none of us had handcuffs.

'Shit. I think there's some in the police room,' I said. 'Wait here.'

'Where the fuck could we go?' Pete observed.

As I jumped off the thrashing Thornly, the sergeant moved back to sit on his legs, while Pete reluctantly took the sergeant's place. Leaning the mass of his upper body away from the fury beneath him, Pete's massive biceps held Thornly's spindle of an arm at a pre-break angle across his back.

Fighting my way through the crowd of spectators at the door, I saw Bob Keylock running up the stairs.

'Get your cuffs!' I yelled.

The sergeant from headquarters was looking knackered and I wondered how long it had been since he had seen active service. Bob clipped a bracelet onto Thornly's right wrist, and Len swapped places with Pete so the latter could work his magic and retrieve Thornly's left wrist. He managed this one as easily as the first; like a squeezed boil it erupted into view above Thornly's head and, without thinking, I reached for it.

I had intended to pull his arm out, down and back so I could attach the second bracelet, but Thornly's jaws snapped. He sunk his teeth into my own left wrist and he had no intention of letting go. It was like being savaged by a pit-bull, complete with snarls. The pain was made bearable by the adrenalin that rushes to join any fight, but I felt violated. A human bite is primeval and it aroused a primordial reaction in me.

I could not fly, so I fought. Clenching my right fist I hit Thornly on the left of his face. It wasn't a punch, the angles were wrong, it was a hammer blow − like someone banging on a locked door. The signet ring on my little finger gave a cutting edge to each of the three blows. Pete pushed his head down on the floor and held it there, while I punched out my fear into the side of Thornly's bloodied face. When he still refused to let go, Pete started to push his considerable weight down onto Thornly's head and, as his skull appeared to flex,

Thornly finally went limp and let go of me.

Sitting back on my heels, I clutched my wrist as Pete secured the cuffs. I glanced over at Thornly's solicitor, standing by the door with the usher and miscellaneous spectators. For a second I wondered if he'd say anything, but he just smiled apologetically at me before disappearing through the crowd. I took the smile as acknowledgement of reasonable force – in the circumstances. Pain was beginning to make itself felt through the ebbing waves of adrenalin, but we still had to get Thornly down the narrow stairs to the court cells.

Once bitten, forever shy. Avoiding the sharp end, I grabbed one of his legs, which occasionally gave an involuntary kick accompanied by a snarl. Len took the other leg and Pete, using the handcuffs as a handle, picked up Thornly's body while Bob grabbed his hair and held his bleeding head; ready to pull his neck back if he tried to bite again. The sergeant had remained a sweating heap on the courtroom floor, but he recovered enough to manage the door. We made our way slowly down the narrow stairs and were met at the bottom by two prison officers who had just dropped off another inmate.

'As I live and breathe, Mr Kevin Thornly,' one of them said. 'He can be a right handful.'

'Tell me about it.' I replied. 'The bastard's just bitten me.'

The prison officer's face fell. 'You know he's HIV?'

'He's what!' I dropped Thornly's leg and jumped backwards.

The word HIV brought out the same reflex from the rest of the lads and Thornly landed with a thud, face down on the concrete floor. Leaving him lying there I quickly pushed up the sleeves of both my tunic and shirt and we all gazed at my wrist. The bite had been hard enough to penetrate the thick serge of my tunic and the cotton of my long-sleeved shirt; a dentist would have been proud to create such a clear impression. The individual dents made by each tooth were already starting to bruise, the aggressive shade of puce giving clarity and depth to the injury.

It was then I took in Thornly's dried blood smeared over my right hand. Realising the import of this I held it aloft like Lady Macbeth and shouted 'Jesus F Christ!' The lads backed away from me, Bob checking his own hands for Thornly's blood.

'Are you sure about this AIDS thing?' I asked the prison officers.

'Fairly. I'll phone the admissions office and get them to check his records.'

Len was the first to recover. 'Look, let's get that that blood washed off and then we'll get you to hospital for a check- up. Are you free to take her Bob?'

Though Bob nodded, neither man moved towards me. It was clear I was on my own until the blood had been dealt with. I let the water in the sink run so hot I was in danger of scalding myself and as I left the cells, with Bob still walking several paces behind me, I saw Len reach for a bottle of bleach. None of us had a clue about HIV and AIDS; we didn't even know they were two different things. We didn't have the facts – just the fear. As I climbed back up the stairs, with Bob trailing behind me, Pete shouted after us.

'Still, it could have been worse.'

'How's that?' I shouted back.

'He could have bitten me – I've got a big competition this weekend.'

At the hospital I was reassured that even if Thornly was HIV positive, the saliva was unlikely to have penetrated the serge and cotton and the bite mark itself was only a contusion with no actual puncture wounds. Although I had punched him with an ungloved hand, my own skin had remained unbroken, and so his blood could not have contaminated me either. Still, they took a blood test and gave me a tetanus jab for good measure.

Over the next few weeks, I was to find myself waking regularly in the small hours of the morning with an undefined sense of panic and loneliness, until the negative result finally allowed my brain to sleep peacefully once more.

Thornly died a year later, while once again in police custody. He had a habit of banging his head repeatedly against cell doors and one evening he suffered a massive brain haemorrhage in his sleep. There was no one at his funeral – a touch of sad to complete the mad and the bad.

It was a week of late turns and, as it turned out, my week for bodies. During briefing, observations had been requested for one Andrew Little. Andrew was not well named. He was six-foot-five, extremely thin and had bright copper-red hair. He had last been seen wearing a multicoloured striped jumper and two pairs of jeans – not likely to blend into a crowd then, I thought. Andrew was not a shoplifter; he was one of the last patients at the soon-to-be-closed Littlemore mental hospital. He'd been missing since just after breakfast and since being told about Littlemore's closure – his home for the last decade – he'd made several attempts at suicide.

It was a freezing day at the start of December, and I was once more on foot patrol in the city centre. I didn't mind. With Christmas approaching, the shops were crowded and I was virtually guaranteed a shoplifter within an hour, which would enable me to return to the station and spend some time in a nice warm custody suite.

My radio crackled. 'Hotel Alpha one-two – are you free for a body on the line?'

'Where's BTP?' My reply was instant reflex. British Transport Police were responsible for everything that happened in and around railway lines and stations.

'They're en route from Reading, but Sergeant Jarrett has asked that you attend in the first instance.'

'Okay, exact location?'

I had yet to deal with a suicide, and I couldn't complain as it was Sergeant J who had signed my probationer's book to say that I had attended a post-mortem, when I hadn't. Like me he didn't see the point of this gruesome exercise; the sights, smells and sounds of a post-mortem would never be replicated on the street. In the fresh air of a road accident we would not be expected to stand and watch the slow dismemberment of a body that was already putrefying. We would have a job of work to get on with and a constructive reason for our presence, rather than merely enduring the academic exercise of proving you could keep your breakfast or lunch down. Like spoofs, the obligatory attendance at a post-mortem was an initiation rite that was dying a natural death.

As I approached the body, I immediately recognised it as Andrew Little. As the body had no head, this impressed the railwaymen no end. I had been bracing myself for bits of flesh scattered everywhere, but what I found was surreal, clinical, Damien Hirst-like. Andrew may have been suicidal, but there was no sense of chaos in the way he'd organised his death.

He'd gathered together a pile of undergrowth and used this to cover his body, which he'd laid at right angles to the railway line. Andrew had then rested his neck on the cold metal and waited patiently for death. His camouflage worked. By the time the driver of the train spotted his bright red hair, the job was done. When the train decapitated poor Andrew, it was travelling at such speed that the wheels appeared to have cauterised his neck, leaving very little blood and gore. I knew it was Andrew by the multi-coloured wool of his jumper showing through his blanket of under-growth and the two pairs of jeans sitting loosely across his extremely narrow hips. He looked like someone who had fallen asleep under the cosiest of duvets.

Andrew's head had been scooped up by the engine's undercarriage. It was subsequently brought back from Goring, to sit on a separate shelf above his body. The mortu-ary register held the rather bizarre entry of, 'Shelves 5 & 6 John Doe, (believed to be Andrew Little Born 4.9.62)'. But formal identification would not be made until a pathologist confirmed that the head belonged to the body and the dental records of the head were those of Andrew.

The following day was my last late turn, but I was not fin-ished with body parts. I'd only been out on patrol a few hours when I was again called to the railway line, this time for an attempted, rather than actual, suicide. Bloody BTP, I thought, never there when you needed them.

The incident had taken place a short way down the track from Oxford station and I arrived on scene at the same time as two medics. A young woman in her mid-thirties had changed her mind at the last minute and decided not to jump in front of a passing train, but as she pulled back, the train had caught her arm and removed most of it from just below the elbow. She was now kneeling at the side of the track, screaming hysterically and holding her right elbow with her left hand. Unlike Andrew, there was blood everywhere.

Thank God for the medics; my first-aid abilities would have been stretched to say the least. They whipped on a tourniquet, injected her with sedatives and morphine and dressed the stump within seconds – brilliant. The woman's screams reduced to body-heaving sobs as one of the medics climbed back up the steep bank to fetch a carry-chair from the ambulance. The woman kept moaning, 'my hand, my hand,' and the remaining paramedic tried to comfort her with his business-like tone.

'Can't worry 'bout that love, it's probably in Reading by now.'

'It's not.' I said and pointed to a glint of gold near the medic's knee. He leapt up. Buried in the thick grass, sticky with blood, was the woman's hand, ring and all. I took over comforting the woman, while the paramedic packed the hand into a plastic bag. He wasn't hopeful of it being re-attached as the lower arm was too fragmented, but they had nothing to lose.

In all, that job showed up on the police log as lasting a total of eighteen minutes from arrival to departure. The medics were fantastic and certainly saved her life, if not her hand. I was therefore outraged when, a week later, I found myself being formally interviewed under caution by a superintendent from Complaints and Discipline about the theft of a gold ring. The woman had made formal complaints about everyone involved: the medics, me and numerous hospital staff. She wanted the 'thief' prosecuted. The ring was subsequently discovered a few weeks later in the hospital's property store. The person booking it in had just misspelt her surname.

CHAPTER 13

Big Thief, Little Thief

The Blacks' family business was run on numbers rather than intellect. On one memorable occasion we managed to get nine of them, spanning three generations, either into care, on remand, or actually serving time simultaneously. The local crime rate fell by twenty-five percent for that glorious three-month period.

The first member of the Black family I ever met was Joey, a 13-year-old specialising in theft from cars. It was the small hours of a weekday morning, and I was crewed with Big John. Unlike many nearing their retirement, John didn't 'swing the lantern' with tales of how things were in the good old days. In fact, he would barely speak for the whole eight-hour shift, and the only time I recall him showing any emotion, was when I had randomly used the word *hate*. John was a Jehovah's Witness.

'You shouldn't hate anyone.' His rebuke was softly spoken but adamant.

'What about those Irish bastards that bombed the horses in Hyde Park. I hate them with every fibre of my being,' I declared. 'Put those bastards' necks in a noose and I'll sing as they swing.'

I had just brought a chalk-drawn charity print of a cavalry horse's head, which had running through its mane the words *In memory of an outrage to the honour and beauty of men and horses. Hyde*

Park, July 1982' and my own outrage had been reignited.

John looked at me with horror, concern for my soul shining from his light blue eyes, 'You don't mean that.'

'Try me,' I replied.

He shook his head and I felt his silence was now full of prayer for the damned.

As I drove slowly past a garage forecourt, John's huge frame was so still in the front passenger seat and his breathing so deep that I'd assumed he was having a nap.

'Stop the car.' His voice held an urgency that was at odds with his relaxed body. I pulled into the kerb and was about to turn off the engine when he added, 'Keep it running – if you see him do a runner, give chase.'

'Who?' I was totally bewildered.

John nodded towards the back of the forecourt, 'Eyes open,' he ordered, as he exited the car with surprising speed. He walked quickly through the rows of cars before suddenly ducking out of sight. When he stood up again a few seconds later, one of his hands clutched a wriggling shadow dressed head to toe in black and the other held a car stereo. I turned off the engine and joined him.

'Are you psychic or what?' I was impressed.

'Meet Joey Black,' John replied. 'He's the family's car thief – steals from them, not the cars themselves – yet.'

Joey grinned at me, 'Nice to meet you.' He turned to John, 'My dad's going to kill me.'

'For stealing?' I asked

The boy smiled at my naivety. 'For getting caught.'

I turned to John, 'How did you know he was there? I didn't see a thing.'

John handed me the stereo and just tapped his nose, unwilling to divulge trade secrets in front of the enemy.

Later, with little Joey safely deposited in the detention room, Big John educated me on his powers of observation.

'Didn't you see the interior light in the car?' he asked.

'God, no.'

He winced at my profanity. 'Well, he obviously heard our engine and assumed it would be coppers at that hour, driving that slowly, so he hid under the car. Unfortunately for him, he hadn't closed the door properly so the light was still on. Like a little neon arrow it was.' John smiled with quiet satisfaction.

Theft supports both naturally talented loners and those who are raised into a family business from a very young age and, as criminal liability doesn't exist on a day-to-day basis for those under ten, the younger the better. More than one nine-year-old, or those who could get away with claiming they were still nine, have been stopped leaving supermarkets with a trolley full of goodies. Like some supermarket sweep, the adults would fill the trolley before sending little Johnny running through the door with it. If he was stopped, nothing much could happen. 'It's his idea of a joke officer, what can you do?' And if he wasn't, the family got a free week's shopping.

My first juvenile prisoner had been a loner and a dead ringer for the Milkybar Kid, even down to his round rimless spectacles. He was eleven years old and had been caught shoplifting a word processor cable from Tandy's. On my arrival at the manager's office, he sat calmly as the store detective told me what she'd seen. His nonchalant attitude grated and I decided to make his arrest as formal as possible, including a full caution. It had about as much impact as a fart in a gale; the boy remained unmoved, surrounded by a bubble of self-contained stillness that clashed with his years.

'So, what's your name and address?' I asked.

His answer was an expressionless stare.

'He had this on him, too.' The store detective handed me a carrier bag containing a new shoebox.

The box felt too heavy for shoes and looking inside I found the seven paperbacks that made up the Chronicles of Narnia. They were all brand new and carried price tags from several different shops. I was not going to give the kid the satisfaction of ignoring me again so I radioed for transport – making a special request for the riot van, with its iron grilles fixed to the windows and roof.

As usual, the van was being driven by Big John, and when he walked into the office the Milkybar Kid stood up and held out his arms, the glint of excitement in his eye indicating he was actually looking forward to being handcuffed. As much as I would have liked to oblige the little tyke, we weren't allowed to handcuff children and women unless they were very violent or had actually made an effort to escape; and even then you were expected to hang on to kids without cuffs.

The riot van did not have the desired effect either. It could just as easily have been a chauffeur-driven limo for all the Milkybar Kid seemed to care. As he sat quietly by my side, his general calm and apparent lack of fear was unnerving and the theme music from The Omen started to run through my brain. If I'd been arrested at his age I'm sure I would have been in floods of tears and wailing for my mum, but pure indifference continued to radiate from his slight frame.

When I marched him into the custody office, Sergeant Jarrett bent over the charge desk and peered down his hooked nose at my prize catch.

'Right, WPC Foster, what have we got here?'

'Shoplifter, Sarge. He's nicked a word processor cable from Tandy's, and these.' I showed him the boxed books.

'Well young man, what have you got say for yourself?' Sergeant J used his best headmaster's voice.

'Nothing.' The reply was as short as the person it came from.

Sergeant J ignored the rebuff. 'Let's start with your name and address shall we?'

'Let's not.'

Sergeant J leaned over his desk and once more peered down at the Milkybar Kid. 'Let's get one thing straight, me laddo, while you're in my police station you'll do as you're told. And when I ask you a question, I expect an answer – got it?'

'No.'

Sergeant J's usually relaxed posture grew taut. Leaning over the charge desk he slowly reached out and took hold of the lad by the lapels of his blazer. The Milkybar Kid did not flinch. The sergeant slowly lifted him off the ground until they were eye to eye and, as Sergeant J was well over six foot, this meant the kid's highly polished black lace-ups now dangled a good few feet off the floor. Still he did not blink, continuing to meet the sergeant's glare with a Buddha-like expression of utter tranquillity.

'What's your game lad?' Sergeant J growled.

'I'm not playing games. She,' he pointed at me, while continuing to hold the sergeant's eyes, 'told me I *do not have to say anything and anything I do say may be used in evidence,* so I'm not going to say anything.'

Sergeant J lowered the Milkybar Kid to the ground, letting him drop the last few inches. Letting out a long sigh, he turned to me. 'After you've searched him, take this little bugger straight to the detention room.'

I wanted to shove him into the cell next to the drunk-tank,

where the noise and the smell might have seeped through his hardened exterior, but I knew the sarge would not agree and I didn't want to lose another battle in front of this horror-film escapee. The search drew a complete blank. He had no money and no ID and I wondered if I put him in front of a mirror if he'd even have a reflection. As I marched my mini-mastermind into the detention room, I pointed something out to him.

'If you don't give us your name and address you'll just sit in here until your parents decide to report you missing. I suppose they will *miss* you?'

'Why do they need to be involved?' I felt just the tiniest ripple in his armour of indifference.

'Because you're an eleven-year-old who's been caught stealing. You'll have to be interviewed and we can't interview you without one of your parents being present – end of story.'

'If I tell you where I live can I have my books to read while I'm waiting?'

'They're not *your* books – they're evidence of your criminal activity, but give me your name and address and I'll find you a comic, deal?'

'Okay, but I'd prefer a magazine.'

'I bet you would.' I slammed the detention room door shut.

His father arrived within the hour and apart from the difference in height and age, the kid could have been his clone rather than his son; even down to the matching blazer and black lace-ups. The Milkybar Kid's calmness was obviously genetic and the father initially dismissed his son's arrest with the same indifference his son had displayed.

'I'm sure it was just the result of some stupid dare by friends,' he asserted.

I explained that his son, Joseph, had acted alone and when

I showed him the seven books, he admitted that he would not have had the money to purchase them. Having already checked records for any previous arrests and drawn a blank, I advised the father that if his son told the truth about both the cable and the books, he would receive an instant police caution and the matter could be dealt with that afternoon. After speaking to a solicitor to confirm what I'd said, he entered the detention room to discuss the matter with his errant heir.

During Joseph's interview the full extent of his criminal intellect was revealed – to the obvious delight of his father, who couldn't help smiling at some of his offspring's answers.

'So, Joe -'

'- Joseph,' corrected the Milkybar Kid.

'Joseph, where did you get the box from?'

He looked at me as though I was a complete moron and indicated the name of the shoe shop plastered over both the bag and the box. 'You will note that the box matches the bag. This would help convince *most* people that the box contained shoes.'

'How did you get the box and bag without the shoes?'

Joseph sighed. 'I just asked the assistant for an empty box for a project and then asked for the bag, too.'

'What did you do next?'

'My plan was to visit seven bookshops and take a title from each shop or book department.'

'Lucky you were in Oxford then – not many other cities have so many booksellers.'

'Luck had nothing to do with it.'

'So why go to all this trouble? Why not just take all seven titles from the same premises?'

He looked at me as though I was being purposely obtuse, before explaining in a tone of exaggerated patience that taking one title from each shop took one seventh of the time and therefore, statistically, reduced his chances of being caught by the same amount. He added. 'Two had sold out of the right title, so I had to go back to two of the shops.'

'Well at least you remained flexible.' His father's remark was full of paternal pride.

'So you had actually visited all seven shops before today, to 'case' them for the relevant title?' I was stunned.

'Of course I did. As Father says, if something's worth doing, it's worth doing well.' Father had the decency to blush.

Shoplifters varied in their abilities. Known faces like Christine from Bonn Square were rarely successful, as their motivation was booze. When they reeled into a department store looking for something they could re-sell quickly or swap for more alcohol, they might as well have been wearing a cowbell around their neck. Uniformed security staff and plain-clothed store detectives would be on to them before they could summon up the concentration needed to successfully mount the escalator, never mind commit an actual theft.

Wally Jackman held the record for the most shoplifters ever arrested at one time. It was several weeks after joining the shift that I realised Wally's real name was actually Peter. He'd recently been given a bollocking by Inspector Cooper for the downward turn in his arrest rate, and I couldn't help wondering if the bollocking was also a result of a female now heading the league table of arrests. But, whatever the reason, Wally was determined to rectify the situation.

He didn't have to wait long. The following Saturday he was called to W.H. Smith to deal with a juvenile shoplifter caught stealing some felt-tip pens. The only trouble was she was French and part of a large group of students on a day's sightseeing trip. With the aid of her marked map and shouted sign language, Wally established the location of the coach taking the students back to London and there they both waited for her fellow students and teachers to return.

When everyone was back on the coach, and with the numbers game in mind, Wally made an announcement via a teacher,

'Attention! If anyone has any property on them that they haven't paid for and can't prove they've paid for with a receipt, they will be arrested. Because you're foreign nationals, you'll all be kept in custody until you appear in court.' The teachers, like their pupils, had turned pale. 'However,' he smiled encouragingly, 'if you co-operate and return any stolen items now, you will all be dealt with by way of a caution – a telling-off.'

Wally watched relief flood back into the mass of faces in front of him. The teacher, who had been doing the translating of this doomsday (and totally illegal) scenario, smiled encouragement to her teenage charges. Of the forty-eight students on the bus, forty-two held something up for Wally's inspection; ranging from postcards and an expensive-looking scarf, to a single pencil with a funny rubber creature stuck on the end. He arrested all forty-two on suspicion of theft before getting the coach driver to convey them to the rear yard of St Aldates Police Station.

Sergeant J's face was a picture, and so was Coops's. The whole shift was called back in to set up a processing conveyer belt for the juvenile prisoners. They were taken off the coach one at a time and put before Sergeant J, who booked them in and read them their rights, with one teacher acting as translator. Supervised by another teacher, they were passed to either a female or male officer who physically searched the appropriate gender and put any stolen property into a plastic bag. On completion of a caution form, they were shown into the closed police bar where they waited for the last of their friends to be processed.

Once all forty-two prisoners had been processed, Coops strode into the bar and stood on a table. With one of the teachers translating each sentence, he administered a formal police caution, like some form of mass baptism. As he left the bar he barked at the smiling Wally,

'Jackman, my office - now!'

A decade later, that afternoon was to provide me with a template for organising the mass arrests from the Newbury Bypass demonstration.

Towards the end of my probation, I made it onto the Christmas shoplifting squad. Every year from mid-November to mid-January, several officers were selected from each shift to form this prestigious plain-clothes squad. The year I was on it, the team made nearly two hundred arrests and recovered over £350,000's worth of stolen property. Stuart Hudson was to account for £30,000's worth. Where the Black family had been middle management, the Hudson family were CEOs in the world of shoplifting.

We worked in pairs and I was partnered with Carl, a lad from B shift. His pale freckles matched the washed-out brown of his floppy Hugh Grant hair, while his pigeon-chested torso was built for running rather than fighting. We'd only been on duty ten minutes when Control sent us to see Doreen, the store detective from Boots. Doreen was not her usual cheerful self.

'What's up?' I asked.

Shaking her head, she switched on a CCTV tape made

twenty minutes earlier. 'See what you think, but he looks like an off-duty copper to me.'

The black and white picture showed a short middle-aged man who was beginning to go bald. He was wearing a dark bomber jacket over an open-necked white shirt, dark trousers and black shoes. Several pens were sticking out of the breast pocket of his shirt.

'Well, if he's police, he's not Thames Valley.' Carl said.

'He could be an inspector or above.'

'Could he be Prison Service?' Doreen asked.

As we watched the tape it became evident he was working with a 'blocker'. An attractive blonde in her late teens was shielding his actions as he placed several bottles of designer perfume into a bag.

Carl and I decided to split up. We had seen enough to know we were dealing with professionals, probably stealing to order. Perfume seemed to be on that day's shopping list, so we concentrated on covering the relevant counters in all the big stores. But we had no joy and after an hour we were returning to the station when Carl spotted the man walking down George Street with the same blonde. Stopping our unmarked car, we leapt out and confronted the pair, shoving our warrant cards into their calm faces.

'What's in the bag?' I asked the heavily made-up girl.

She opened it without comment and I found several packets of expensive bedlinen from a number of different shops.

'Receipts?' I asked.

She just looked at me. We both knew the score.

Carl and I arrested them both on suspicion of theft, splitting our arrests along gender lines to keep things simple. By searching the person we arrested, our statements and the exhibiting of any evidence found remained straightforward.

Neither of them had the four bottles of perfume from Boots and neither had any form of identification. No credit cards, driving licences, bills or letters; absolutely nothing, and as we drove back to St Aldates they didn't look at each other or speak.

Once in custody they did give their names and date of births, as they knew they would not be released without doing so. Stuart Hudson may have looked like an off-duty copper, but he gave his occupation as unemployed; the girl was his nineteen-year-old daughter, Linda. They refused to give their address until they had spoken to their solicitor, and the fact they could independently recite their solicitor's number spoke volumes. After speaking to the latter, they waited a further twenty minutes before revealing an address in Aylesbury that could be verified for bail.

The DS in charge of the squad wanted the address check combined with a search. It took us an hour to obtain the relevant paperwork and another to travel to Aylesbury. Carl and I were not overly surprised to find the address was in the middle of a fairly run-down council estate, but there was nothing run-down about the Hudsons' home. It had obviously been purchased under Maggie Thatcher's right-to-buy scheme and then extended to almost double its size. Apart from all the new double-glazing, two other things made this house stand out from its neighbours. One was the gold coloured Rolls-Royce parked in the driveway and the other was the CCTV cameras, which formed part of an extensive security system.

Another part of this system were the Rottweilers, who jumped up at the shadows we cast as I rang the bell of the partly glazed front door. A female voice silenced the dogs with a single command; I wondered what the 'attack' word was.

The same voice asked us to hold our warrant cards up to the small camera situated inside the porch. I could see the outline of a slim woman checking these on a monitor in the hallway and once satisfied as to who we were, she put the dogs into the back garden.

Like an extra from Dynasty, Stuart's wife was immaculately turned out, with big shoulder pads and bigger hair. She was obviously expecting us and we found nothing that could not be accounted for. The family were clearly familiar with warrants, as the lady of the house asked us to, 'Please leave the rooms as tidy as you find them,' before also asking, 'Would you like a cup of tea? I imagine you'll have time.'

I asked Mrs Hudson how her husband and daughter had got to Oxford from Aylesbury (Stuart had no keys in his possession, either house or car), and she confirmed her family's story of travelling by train. I didn't believe them and I didn't believe her. This was not the sort of family to rely on public transport, especially with so much heavy shopping to carry.

Returning to Oxford, Carl and I charged Stuart and Linda with the seventy pounds worth of stolen bedlinen, but we could do nothing about the perfume. Having been presented with the evidence of the CCTV tape in interview, they independently claimed to have left it elsewhere in the store when they realised they had been caught on camera; quick, professional thinking.

However, we'd done some quick thinking of our own, and two other squad members were now waiting outside the front of the police station for the pair to be bailed and released. Convinced they had a car in Oxford, these two officers followed Stuart and Linda, but it became obvious that they were 'tail-conscious', as father and daughter spent over two hours going in and out of various bars around the city centre. So the

DS called in a favour from his drug-squad mates, who picked up the surveillance of our two suspects.

It was past midnight when the Hudsons eventually made their way to the deserted Westgate multi-storey car park. Because it was so empty, drug squad dare not follow them inside. Instead they hid in the bushes at the side of the only vehicle exit in order to identify the Hudsons' car as it left. They were driving a battered old Escort and drug squad radioed its registration to the traffic car on standby in the one-way system. The Hudsons were stopped within half a mile of the car park and the perfume was found in the boot, together with booze worth over three hundred pounds.

Stuart and Linda were re-arrested and after no-comment interviews they were charged with these additional thefts; together with a traffic offence relating to the Escort's false licence plates. The keys to this deliberately cheap car had been left on the inside of a wheel rim, making the vehicle easy to abandon if necessary.

Because shoplifting was obviously a full-time family business and because their house and second car indicated just how successful that business was, the DS liaised with Aylesbury CID and arranged for Stuart to be followed over the next few days. He must be storing his stock somewhere and we knew it wasn't at his house.

Sure enough, after lying low for twenty-four hours, Hudson was followed to a lock-up on the estate, from which he recovered a boot full of items. He was followed home and several callers visited the house during the afternoon, each leaving with one or two items. It appeared that the Hudson family were running their own branch of Argos. The mother would take orders during the first part of the week and Stuart and Linda would then fill them over the second half. But they had also built up a back-stock of goodies, which the continued following of Stuart revealed were stored in two more lock-ups. When Aylesbury CID eventually raided the Hudsons and all three of their lock-ups, over twenty-nine thousand pounds worth of stolen property was recovered.

Mr and Mrs Hudson and their daughter were to spend that Christmas, and several others, at Her Majesty's pleasure.

CHAPTER 14

All in a Day's Work

I was on patrol one Saturday afternoon with a young female special constable called Helen. She was petite but tenacious. On reaching Bonn Square, we started to clear the dossers so that families could shop without being badgered by sometimes aggressive begging. I always gave the assembled down-and-outs five minutes to drag their collective butts elsewhere, but if any of them were still in the square on my return they knew they could look forward to four hours in the drunk-tank.

A dark-haired male whom I'd never seen before was sitting amongst the regulars. He was relatively young and had a huge frame that took up two spaces on the wooden bench, with a semi-conscious Seamus taking up the rest of the space. When I'd told everyone to move on, the stranger muttered,

'Why don't you move on and fuck off.' His accent was foreign, Dutch I thought, but couldn't be sure.

I'd resisted calling for the transit immediately as I wanted to give my regulars the chance to find a more secluded spot. I also knew that Sergeant J would not be best pleased if I filled his cells with drunks when they'd shortly be full of shoplifters and, as it was a home match for Oxford City, the overflow of football supporters from Cowley. But I felt confident that when Helen and I returned from our preamble, this particular customer would still be waiting.

He was. With the exception of Billie and Seamus, the other

regulars had made their weary way to more sheltered surroundings, probably down to the bushes by the canal. As I radioed Control for the transit, Billie was trying to pull Seamus's bulk off the bench, but the ex-prize fighter was too far gone.

'Nice try, Billie,' I said, 'but it looks like Seamus is for a lie-down and if you don't want to keep him company, you'd best be on your way before the van arrives.'

'Right yer are, WPC Foster. Just need a sit-down 'til it comes though, yon man's fair knackered me. Useless great lump of Irish lard!' Billie sank down onto the empty second bench.

'Two minutes,' I agreed.

I turned my attention to the stranger, who was still swigging from a party-sized cider bottle. 'You'd best be on your way too, if you don't want to spend the rest of this lovely afternoon in the cells.'

He took a last swig from the glass bottle and looked me straight in the eye, 'I'd like to see you try and get me anywhere near a fucking cell.'

I shrugged and waited for the transit. As I saw it winding its way slowly towards us through the afternoon shoppers in Queen Street, I told Billie to get going and arrested Seamus for being drunk and incapable. The arrest was for the benefit of the shoppers. Under the old Judges' Rules, police didn't have to formally arrest and caution anyone who was not sober enough to understand, or who was too violent. But Daniel had told me to still do it in order to ease the collective mind of passers-by; people don't like seeing others being bundled into the back of a police transit for no specific reason. Not that anyone would really wonder why Seamus might be taking a trip to the nick. His reply to the caution was a belch.

'You're not arresting him and you're not arresting me.' The Dutch voice was heavy with threat.

Helen and I looked up from hauling on Seamus's arms and saw the stranger looming over us. The cider bottle was now being held upside down by its neck, transforming it into an effective weapon.

'Grab his other arm!' I yelled at Helen as I lunged at the one with the bottle.

Helen grappled with his free arm and as we both clung on to our respective limbs we quickly realised just how tall and strong he was. While I was forced to stand on tip-toe, Helen's feet were lifted completely off the pavement and we found ourselves dangling like a pair of gibbons from the branches of an enormous and now slowly revolving tree. I shouted to Helen not to let go, while I hung on determinedly to the arm with the bottle. If he managed to shake either of us off, that bottle could inflict some serious damage.

As the stranger paced about Bonn Square with two WPCs hanging off his huge biceps, a small crowd of shoppers gathered in a semi-circle to witness this impromptu piece of street theatre. Billie joined in this display of freestyle mayhem by slowly climbing onto the bench and launching himself at the passing back of the stranger, shouting:

'Leave them alone, ye feckin eejit! Yeh're feckin under feckin arrest. Seamus! Seamus yer useless lump, give us a hand!'

Seamus, momentarily roused into action by Billie's shouting, tried to get up off the bench but failed miserably. Falling flat on his face he gave up gracefully, closed his eyes and went to sleep, curled around the leg of the bench as a child would curl around its favourite teddy.

The transit van drew to a soft halt and Sergeant Wilson

slowly squeezed his portly frame from behind the steering wheel. Everything about Sergeant Wilson was round. He had a round head on top of a round body, with circular patches of red on his cheeks and a matching circle of baldness on the back of his head. If he'd been wearing a trilby instead of a police flat cap, he would have passed for Farmer Giles and, as he sauntered up to us, hands deep in his trouser pockets, all he was missing was a piece of straw to chew on.

'Now then, girls, stop messing around and get this idiot cuffed.'

'We're trying, Sarge,' Helen puffed, as we completed another 360-degree slow-motion spin, which came to a stop facing Sergeant Wilson.

The sergeant's hands moved to his ample hips as he stood shaking his head at our pathetic attempts to subdue our prisoner. The drunk had stopped directly in front of Sergeant Wilson, who in turn had stopped directly in front of a huge pebble-dashed concrete rubbish bin. The Dutchman head-butted Sergeant Wilson – hard, and the force of the blow pushed the sergeant backwards and the top edge of the bin caught the back of his buttocks. Holding his now-bleeding nose, Wilson fell backwards into the bin and his considerable weight forced the rubbish inside to collapse. Like some cartoon character, he folded in two and disappeared from sight, leaving just his feet and one arm sticking out.

Helen and I were still hanging on for grim death, unrealistically hopeful that we were wearing our opponent down. Billie had slid off the vast expanse of back on the second or third rotation and was now collapsed back on the bench looking seasick. Having been sufficiently entertained, and seeing our male colleague out of play, several men now stepped forward from the semi-circle of spectators and gallantly helped

Helen and me to push our drunk on to the ground by kicking his legs out from underneath him. We then struggled to attach the handcuffs.

We each managed to attach one bracelet of our handcuffs to one of his thick wrists, before pulling at the free bracelet of each set until they eventually met in the small of his back where we finally snapped them together. Meanwhile, two more men were heaving poor Sergeant Wilson out of the bin.

Being seen as the weaker sex could occasionally bring out the best in people, and there was one occasion when my gender was responsible for something really cool. King Juan Carlos and Queen Sophia of Spain were visiting Oxford, where the king was to receive an honorary doctorate from the university. Our own Queen had lent her European counterparts her Rolls-Royce for the occasion – the one with the particularly large bulletproof windows designed for safe-visibility for any watching subjects. I was part of the number-one uniform police presence, there to control the throng of flag-waving and flower-carrying schoolchildren.

As the royal couple went walkabout around the Sheldonian Theatre, they were followed by bodyguards wearing sunglasses and ladies-in-waiting wearing hats. About three paces behind them was the chief constable, while the Rolls-Royce crawled behind them all; a mobile haven of security. Queen Sophia was overwhelmed by both the warmth of the greeting and the quantity of flowers she was given. When her hands became full, she passed bunches of blooms to her ladies-in-waiting. When their hands became full, they passed the flowers to the chief constable – who looked nonplussed and immediately scanned the line of uniform bobbies for an appropriate flower-collector. As I was the only skirt and white-topped hat in the line, he signalled me over and handed me an enormous collection of daffodils, irises and cellophane-wrapped, garage-bought tulips.

'What shall I do with them, Sir?'

He indicated the creeping Rolls-Royce with a nod of his head and turned back to the royal couple, his gloved hands now clasped firmly behind his rigid back.

Seeing my predicament, the chauffeur stopped the car and got out. Standing to attention with a smile on his face, he held open the back door and saluted me as I stepped into the rear of the royal vehicle and walked to the back seat over a thick cream carpet. I'm not exaggerating; it literally took me two steps to reach the upholstered back seats, which reeked of leather and power. I had to kneel on them in order to place the flowers on the wide ledge behind and I remember thinking, 'How cool is this – my knee is where the Queen's bum has been.' When I'd sworn allegiance to Her Majesty the previous spring, I'd never dreamt of such close, physical proximity. I couldn't wait to tell Mum.

This process was repeated twice more, with me walking a pace behind my leader, ready to step forward and accept the flowers from the ladies-in-waiting while he kept his own eyes raised – focused on matters regal rather than floral.

When the royal couple entered the Sheldonian for the ceremony, the chauffeur knew he now had precisely forty-one minutes to wait before he'd be needed again. As I placed the last bunch of flowers on the rear shelf and turned to exit the Rolls-Royce, he produced a small instamatic camera from his jacket pocket.

'Have a seat, love,' he said, indicating the camera and his intention to take a picture of me inside the Queen's Rolls-Royce. I stood stock still, stooped by the door with a large cheesy grin on my face. 'No, no,' he said, 'do it proper, have a seat.' I glanced over to where my chief constable was standing, a mere six feet away. 'Don't worry about him, clear case of royal fever.' I took a deep breath and lowered my bottom to where royalty had placed theirs. 'Now give us a wave,' coaxed the driver. So I did, and as my white-gloved hand gave a regal twirl, the camera clicked. I finally exited the Rolls with a smile as huge as the backseat.

The driver put the camera back in his jacket pocket and took out a scrap of paper and a stub of pencil. 'Right, give us your name, number and the address of your station.' He'd obviously done this before. I was not overly hopeful of ever seeing the photograph, but the experience had been great fun.

I should not have doubted Her Majesty's chauffeur. A week later, an intrigued-looking Sergeant Jarrett walked towards me with a small brown envelope.

'We don't encourage personally addressed mail,' he said, flexing the envelope as he handed it over. 'It feels like a photo.'

Ripping the envelope open, I was greeted by my own image, smiling through the open door of the Queen's Rolls-Royce. I turned the same smiling face to Sergeant J.

'Bloody hell!' was all he said.

My royalist mum displayed the snapshot on her mantel-piece with great pride.

Daniel was on leave and I was once more out in the transit van with Big John. It was a midweek night-turn and things had been fairly quiet. Around three, Control sent us to Cowley's patch to pick up a stolen moped and convey it back to Cowley nick.

As we headed east, Control dispatched Cowley officers to an activated burglar alarm at Garsington Sports and Social Club. Having picked up the moped and booked it into the property office at Cowley, John started up the transit, intending to return to Oxford. But radio traffic confirmed that there had been a break-in at the club and the three fruit machines had been broken into. Someone was walking around with a hell of a lot of pound coins.

My ears had pricked at the mention of Garsington, it was where Rynghmor was stabled, I suggested to John that we join the area search. We had nothing better to do and from off-duty hacking around that area, I had a detailed knowledge of this particular group of villages. John agreed and we started to make our way slowly out into the blackness of the unlit countryside. There was no point rushing, the crime scene was covered. It would be our job to scan the wider area for any signs of unusual activity.

Driving in the general direction of Garsington, I saw a beam of headlights travelling along the top of a line of small hills which lay in front of us. The lights were on our left, travelling at right angles towards the road we were on and we would meet them at the next junction. As they were coming from the general direction of Garsington and belonged to the only vehicle we'd seen moving, I asked John to switch on the blues and pull the car as it made a left turn out of the junction in front of us.

John remained in the van, while I got out to speak to the two males sitting in the fairly new Cavalier. Something about the front seat passenger set alarm bells ringing. While the driver was calm, even chatty, the passenger kept his eyes fixed firmly ahead of him and didn't say a word. Later on, experience would let me identify this reaction as fear through guilt, but at the time I was merely aware of a feeling that something was 'not right'. On the other hand, the casual helpfulness of the driver did much to allay my suspicions. When I asked him for his details, he gave them freely and they matched those on the police database as the vehicle's owner. When I asked him if he minded opening his boot, he agreed readily and taking the keys out of the ignition, quickly unlocked it.

Alarm bells tinkled. A single yellow marigold washing up glove and a crowbar lay in an otherwise empty boot. The combination of these two items could be considered 'going equipped', but they also had purely legal and mundane uses. More to the point, excluding three twenty pence pieces in the car's ashtray, there were no coins anywhere in the vehicle. Once more the driver's charm and confidence were winning me over.

I consulted John, who was absolutely no help. When I told him about the jemmy and glove in the boot he shrugged and told me it was my call. If I wanted to arrest them, that was fine by him and if I decided not to, that was also fine.

Returning to the Cavalier and its occupants, I asked some further questions – where had they been and where were they heading?

'We've come down from the smoke to take out two girls we met at a gig in London last week. Nice girls – not the sort to drop their knickers on a first date if you know what I mean.' He winked at me. 'We've had a nice meal, taken them home to Cowley and now we're off back home ourselves.'

'This is an odd way back to the M40.' I observed.

'Tell me about it. Sherlock here has got us well and truly lost!' The driver nodded his head towards his silent passenger, who managed a weak smile in my direction.

I had done all the checks I could think of. The driver and passenger had come back as 'no trace' on the database, although they had no ID on them that could confirm the names and date of births they'd given me. When I told them they could go, the passenger visibly relaxed into his seat. As I climbed back into the transit, they started their engine and pulled slowly away.

Then it hit me, the reasons for those alarm bells. I told John to reignite the blues; I was going to arrest them after all.

'What's changed your mind?' John asked

'They're not dressed for dinner,' I replied.

'What?' He was confused.

'If these two have really come all the way from London to take two girls out to dinner, they would have been wearing something smarter than jeans, muddy trainers and sweatshirts! And it's virtually impossible to get lost trying to get from Oxford or Cowley to London – all roads lead to the M40 and are signposted accordingly.'

As the blue lights went on, the Cavalier immediately pulled over – perhaps my hunch was wrong after all. I got out and in an apologetic tone arrested both men. The passenger turned pale and looked as though he was about to throw up, but the driver remained calm,

'Well, officer, I can assure you that we're innocent of everything except getting lost, but I understand you have a job to do. I wish there were more coppers like you where I live in London. I've been hit twice in as many months by burglars myself.'

I was relieved that the custody sergeant at Cowley seemed satisfied with my reasons for arresting the pair, and after they were searched and put into separate cells, John dropped me off at their car, which I drove back to Cowley nick. I booked it and its meagre contents into the crime property register and completed a statement of arrest for Cowley CID, before John and I returned to St Aldates for a much-delayed meal break.

The next night, as soon as we'd finished briefing, I rang the custody office at Cowley to see what had happened to my two might-be burglars. I was both surprised and relieved to hear that they were still in custody. Scenes of crime had been able to match a small piece of paint on the jemmy in the boot with the forced window frame of the sports and social club. Their footprints were all over the site, and once these two facts had been pointed out to the passenger, he'd crumpled and told officers where to find the stashed coins.

'Well that seems pleasingly straightforward.' I said to the custody sergeant. 'So how come they're still in custody?'

'Their trainers have left similar footprints at six other high-class burglaries in Boars Hill and Wolvercote. They're being investigated for over a quarter of a million pounds' worth of burglaries, involving antiques, silver and fine art. It was a damn good nick, WPC Foster!'

I was chuffed, and John was overtly complimentary of my efforts to Inspector Cooper, who grimaced and muttered something about 'beginner's luck'.

When the men's fingerprints came back, they showed they had both been using aliases, and they were also wanted by the Metpol for similar offences in London. Why the hell they had decided to target premises as small as Garsington Sports and Social Club I'll never know – but I'm glad they did.

CHAPTER 15

The Ins and Outs of Sex

After three years of uniform shift work, I thought it was time to celebrate my recent divorce. I decided that my new personal status should be matched by a new professional one, so I applied for the Women's Specialist Unit. Euphemistically known as the 'Rape & Pillage Squad', the WSU was viewed by all as a female back-door into CID.

At this time women were still not encouraged to attempt any specialisation, so the setting up of the WSU offered a rare chance for females to undertake plain-clothes work. Even in the late Eighties female officers needed this trade entrance if they wanted a chance at entering the hallowed halls of non-uniform work (before being given the opportunity to bang their heads against the glass ceiling inside). Senior officers always declared that CID wasn't a promotion, but offending detective constables were always 'busted back to uniform' and uniformed offenders could kiss goodbye to CID for years after being disciplined.

As its name suggests, the WSU was a clear breach of equal opportunity legislation as men could not join the unit. It had been created as a knee-jerk reaction to a controversial 1982 Thames Valley Police fly-on-the-wall documentary, in which a detective constable and his sergeant had given a convicted prostitute a savagely hard time on camera regarding an allegation of rape. The public outrage following the programme was to bring about the start of a fundamental change in the way the police handled rape cases.

With the WSU my next goal, I applied for the 'indecency course'. It was a standing joke that Thames Valley whoopsies needed to be taught how to be indecent. The three-week training covered the various elements of sexual deviation that constituted criminal offences. It also covered the problems inherent in bringing a successful prosecution for rape – the easiest of offences to allege and the hardest to prove.

If a victim didn't resist the assault, as recommended by the Home Office as the best way of preventing the attack becoming a murder, an offender who admitted to having sex with the victim could claim it was 'consensual' and so make any physical evidence irrelevant. The most life-shattering of crimes could often boil down to the victim's word against the offender's, and not many courts were willing to convict on this alone.

The complex question of 'true consent' was another area of theory clouded by assumptions and emotion. In theory, a woman who agrees to go back to a man's home or hotel room for a drink is consenting only to the drink, but the prevailing attitude of the male-dominated justice system was that she was asking for it; just like wearing short skirts or low-cut blouses was asking for it. Some members of the justice system still hold this view but they hide it better.

Another legal technicality was the definition of 'penetration'. At the time I was wading through these muddied waters, there was no offence of male rape; penetration was restricted to penis in vagina. Therefore, the sadist who used something other than his penis to penetrate the vagina, or penetrated an anus – although he caused as much emotional damage and usually far more physical damage – was actually guilty of the lesser offence of indecent assault. And these variations were not uncommon. For the truth is that rape is not about sex; it's about power. If a man just wanted sex, even anal sex, he could pay for it. But many rapists get a twisted satisfaction from the power they wield over their victims, including the power involved in what gets put where. In rape, sex is a means not an end.

My first rape victim looked particularly small and fragile. Her tortured body made the shallowest of bumps under the hospital bed's thin green cover. Six hours earlier she'd been grabbed in the street and pulled into some bushes by a stranger. He'd forced her to perform oral sex at knife point, before he thrust a broken glass bottle inside her. She needed over 70 internal and external stitches.

As I interviewed this woman, she talked about the crime in such calm detail that you'd think she was giving me a statement about a minor traffic accident. But her eyes were dead as well as dry, her tone was flat and her body had a stillness to it that reminded me of the morgue. In 1988 post-traumatic stress disorder had only just appeared on the clinical horizon and was still unrecognised and far from understood by most professionals.

Several weeks later I was taking a statement from a victim of a relatively minor indecent assault. A passing jogger had momentarily groped the woman's breast over her jumper. As she tried to describe the man, her shoulders became hunched as she began to drown in a rising panic. Her whole body broke out in hives and she began to shake uncontrollably. I called for an ambulance, which rushed her to hospital suffering from clinical shock.

Although we'd be taught the ins and outs of sex-related law, I would once more find myself leaving training equipped with only the theory. Dealing with the emotion of such crimes was left to experience, and the first thing experience taught me was that no two people would react in the same way to such physical and mental invasions of their lives – invasions that robbed these women of so much more than their dignity.

'Right, girls!' Sergeant Lewis strode into the classroom with the usual roll-up hanging from his bearded mouth. He had a gleam in his eye, 'Tuesday of week two means bestiality!' His smile tipped his roll-up into a mini-erection.

We'd started to play a game with Sergeant Lewis and his roll-ups. Every time he was about to light up, one of us would raise our hand to ask a question or make a comment that would interrupt the flick of his cheap plastic lighter. The class ran a daily book on how long we could delay first ignition.

Sergeant Lewis scanned the women sitting behind the desks in front of him. Seating himself on the corner of his own desk, he fished for his lighter in a trouser pocket made shiny from such expeditions. As it came into sight my hand shot up.

'What's bestiality?' I asked.

'You tell me, WPC Clements.' (I had reverted to my maiden name.) He knew I always read ahead, but the roll-up remained unlit as he asked the class, 'Anyone here had any professional dealings with this particular offence?'

Rachel, a quiet unassuming girl from the Welsh valleys, slowly raised her hand and Sergeant Lewis was forced to catch the unlit fag as it dropped from his open mouth. During the first week she'd sat in silence at the back of the classroom, making no contributions and asking no questions. I had the distinct impression she was embarrassed by the content of the course and I couldn't imagine her actually dealing with any of it in real life.

Recovering his equilibrium, Sergeant Lewis asked, 'So what *bestiality* has occurred in Thame, WPC Steel?'

Thame is a small mid-Oxfordshire market town and his tone rang with a confidence that he would be able to dismiss Rachel's example with a patronising smile.

'Well, Sarge, I was early-turn Station Duty Officer when this woman phones up in a right state shouting, "Some bastard's fucked my cat." I thought she was trying to report a traffic accident, but she was being literal, like.'

'So what did you do?' Sergeant Lewis was having better luck at stifling his laughter than the rest of the class.

'Well the cat had to be destroyed,' – that killed the mood – 'and apparently it was a Persian Blue or something, quite valuable like, about two hundred quid it was, so I recorded it as criminal damage.' The sergeant looked bemused, so Rachel expanded. 'Well you know – property that's damaged beyond repair...' her voice trailed off as she realised she was instructing an instructor.

Sergeant Lewis placed the roll-up back in his mouth. 'Anyone else?' he asked, but with less confidence in his voice.

'I've arrested someone for bestiality, Sarge.' My declaration brought raised eyebrows from the others in a way that suggested they weren't altogether surprised. The lighter was once more lowered, unused.

'You have?' He sounded wary.

'Yep – I saw one of our regular dossers french-kissing his dog in the middle of Westgate Shopping Centre, so I arrested him for bestiality.'

'Really?'

'Yeah, but the bloody custody sergeant downgraded it to drunk and disorderly as the dog wouldn't make a complaint.' The laugher was reignited.

'Seriously,' he brought us quickly to heel, 'that's one of the main problems with this type of offence, a lack of complaint and a lack of witnesses. And, more importantly, people who are prepared to take part in this sort of sick activity pose as serious a threat to the human population as they do the rest of the animal kingdom.'

It is often assumed that sexual deviants lead totally deviant lives, but even after several years on the WSU I was reluctant to form an opinion, never mind issue a statement on the matter. When people talk of sexual deviation, some include everything outside the bounds of the missionary position within a heterosexual marriage bed. Some include common sexual practices carried out in uncommon places, or with inappropriate people, and others consider that anything goes as long as all parties are consenting. Sadomasochists break the law every time they break each other's skin and what is deviation to one culture is daily life in another.

In different times and places throughout history, homosexuality and incest have been considered not only the norm, but in some cases desirable. Incest, in particular, was used as a tool for the preservation of noble and royal bloodlines and all cultures, including our own, have married off young girls as soon as they could bear children. Nine-year-olds were as available for sex in Georgian England as they are in Thailand today.

I only dealt with two cases that I would call 'odd'. The first occurred when I was still a probationer and occasionally dealing with the out-of-hours bodies that arrived at St Aldates mortuary.

When a 30-year-old man was dropped off by the Co-Op (funeral services not supermarket), I was forced to call in reinforcements in the shape of Daniel and Bob. The body was dressed in a wetsuit (no flippers), and instead of a snorkel and goggles he was sporting a full-faced gas mask. The industrial-strength glue in the respirator was probably the cause of death, but hey, I'm no pathologist. Can you imagine trying to get a dead body out of a wet suit? Even with three of us it was a struggle. Our efforts were eventually rewarded with a sight that brought actual tears to Daniel and Bob's eyes.

'Jesus!' said Daniel.

'Fuck me!' said Bob.

In the Eighties, body piercing was generally restricted to earrings in ears and safety-pins in noses. This man had both his nipples pierced with gold hoops and a smaller hoop had been used to pierce the end of his penis; a fairly heavy gold chain connected all three hoops. We all agreed to leave this jewellery in situ as relevant to the post-mortem. If anyone wanted to rob this particular body they would be welcome to their haul.

The second odd case occurred one week after I joined the WSU, and involved a visit to a mid-terrace house in Cowley. My job was to interview twelve-year-old twin sisters about the suspicious death of their father. They'd discovered his body on an iron bed frame, which had been bolted to the wall of the spare bedroom at an angle of forty-five degrees to the floor. The daughters had found their father handcuffed to the frame at both his wrists and ankles and the studded leather collar around his neck had been his only item of clothing.

The girls were obviously upset by their father's death but seemed unabashed by the manner of it. They explained that mum and dad were in the habit of 'playing' by tying dad to this frame and leaving him to what their mother called, 'sexually stew'. Mum would return to the room later to dish up dessert.

The girls had been staying with grandparents that weekend and both parents had been out on the booze, drinking heavily into the early hours of Sunday morning. They had gone back to the pub as soon as it had reopened and when they were forced to return home at lunchtime closing, dad had suggested 'going to bed'. When Scenes of Crime examined the wear marks on the studded collar, it appeared that mum, in her drunken state, had fastened the collar two holes tighter than usual. Leaving her husband to 'stew', she'd fallen asleep on the sofa downstairs and when woken around six by her friend and neighbour, had gone straight back out to the pub, her husband totally forgotten.

When the girls arrived home, they'd run upstairs to find their dad as dead as the proverbial dodo and their mum still in the pub. They'd sensibly dialled 999. The cause of their father's death was recorded as affixation and the Coroner's Court returned a verdict of 'misadventure'.

When I was posted to Banbury WSU, it became too far to travel from Abingdon, so I sold my studio flat and upgraded to a three-bedroom end-of-terrace; two lodgers helping with the increased mortgage. The three of us rubbed along well enough, enjoying evenings in front of the telly with copious amounts of wine and takeaway pizza. It was far better than marriage as there was no emotional expectation. I had a brief fairly on/off affair with another shift member, but my horse occupied nearly all my off-duty time.

Matt, one of the lodgers, asked if an old school-friend called Zac could stay the weekend and would I be around to let him in, as he would be arriving around four and Matt didn't finish work until five. When the doorbell rang at four on the dot, I opened the door with a smile that instantly disappeared when I saw a black man standing on my doorstep. He was enough of a gentleman to ignore this reflex response and he replaced my lost smile with his own,

'Hi I'm Zac – I can come back later if it's not convenient.'

'Of course it's convenient, Zac. Come on in and I'll put the kettle on.' I was aware I was probably overcompensating with my 'hail fellow, well met' tone, but my racist response had both baffled and scared me. I had dreamt about Marlon James in my bed but this was the first black person to actually set foot in my home, and my initial reaction to Zac threw me completely. We had a great weekend and I learned an unexpected life lesson about prejudice that would stand me in good stead in the coming years.

One of my first jobs on Banbury WSU was to be part of a team tasked with sifting through three hundred hardcore porn videos seized in a raid. A bank of four small monitors was set up in a small darkened room, producing an appropriate sense of seediness, and a team of CID and WSU officers took it in turns to watch the videos, four at a time on fast-forward.

If anything 'legally obscene' appeared, we watched at normal speed and recorded the content on a template which listing every imaginable (although *I'd* never imagined some of them) form of sexual deviation. You put a tick under the appropriate heading with the video exhibit number and, using the inbuilt clock on the monitor, the relevant timing. These sheets were then attached to the individual tapes so that magistrates, judges and any other interested party didn't have to sit through this mind-numbingly boring 'entertainment'. Instead, they were given the luxury of accessing the relevant obscenities quickly and efficiently, bypassing silly plots, atrocious acting and the appalling tinkle-piano music;

not to mention avoiding the red eyes and sense of depression that had quickly settled over the police viewers.

Some of the headings on the checklist sounded medical and a few more established practices had even earned themselves proper Latin names. Because of the already extensive nature of these headings, the one that said 'Other' intrigued me and, in an effort to bring some focus to the whole grisly process and help me stay relatively sane, I became determined to put a tick in this particular column. I eventually got my chance with video one-hundred-and-seventy-six.

When the DS saw my isolated tick I had to show him the extract that had merited such splendid isolation; it involved the star of this particular epic inserting a very large and very alive eel into her private parts. When the DS queried why I hadn't ticked the bestiality column, I had my response ready,

'Well, strictly speaking, Sarge, they're fish, and fish are fish – not beasts.'

He didn't allow my tick to stand.

All these videos had come from one private source and the collection was both chronologically extensive and physically varied. I started to track the career of one particular 'actress' who first appeared in grainy early and fairly mundane adult group sex scenes. As her looks and body deteriorated, animals replaced her human partners, including a Shetland stallion, which steadfastly ignored all the actress's best efforts to turn him on as he continued to munch his way through a hay-net. Eventually, she was reduced to working with inanimate objects, bringing a whole new meaning to the words internal phone call.

Cataloguing these videos was the most unrewarding job I ever undertook in the police. I'd been asked if I was prepared to do it and, unlike most of the male detectives, I was not keen. But saying no was not a real option; this was another of those times when 'bottle' was being tested. Watching this woman's slow degrading fall, seeing eyes that had once flashed with passion, real or invented, turn to eyes that were dead and empty, devoid of all humanity, left me feeling more nauseous than any of the individual acts of depravity I'd been required to evidence. Rather than the images, it is a memory of deep sadness that has stayed with me over the decades.

At the end of every day's viewing, I dealt with the depressing sadness by heading straight for the local stables and Mulberry. He was my new pride and joy, an impressive black gelding whose powerful movement regularly beat the stable owner's own horse in competition. Mulberry had an uncomplicated nature that was always on my side. The understanding gentleness in his eye always made everything alright again.

CHAPTER 16

Baby Sitters

'Come on down honey and talk to the nice police lady.' The American accent was shouted up the stairs of a United States Air Force house in Upper Heyford.

'I understand Kirsten is just eleven?' My question filled in the conspicuous silence.

'Yeah that's right.' The mother leant on the bannister. 'Hon, I won't tell you again, get your tail down here – now!'

This was my first solo case involving a child, and it was not the tone I expected between a mother and the victim of a sexual assault. A loud thump was followed by a slammed door and the girl descended the open-plan wooden stairs with a swagger that would have put Jane Russell to shame. Kirsten's air of sexual confidence was accompanied by breasts that made mine feel positively inadequate. Her mother had obviously seen my expression many times before.

'I know, frightening isn't it? She started her periods when she was nine.'

Kirsten had 'allegedly' (I was already putting mental quote marks around the word), been indecently assaulted by a sixteen-year-old English babysitter named Kevin. Kirsten's parents had arrived home to find the pair sitting on the living-room floor, partially clothed and playing a game of strip poker.

The girl might be some sort of biological wonder, I told myself, but whatever she looks like she still only has eleven years of life behind her. So with this fact in mind, I talked to the daughter while her mum went to make a cup of tea.

'Hi Kirsten, I'm here to find out what happened last night when Kevin was babysitting. Is that okay with you?

'Sure.' The reply was relaxed.

Right, follow the prescribed steps and build up the child's confidence – although I already felt one step behind on that one.

'How do you like school, Kirsten?'

'It's okay.'

'What are your favourite subjects?'

'English and science – why?' The irrelevance of my questions was not lost on the eleven-year-old, but I persevered.

'So, who's your best friend?'

'Well, Stacey was, but not anymore.'

'Why's that?'

'Well, she's telling everyone I gave Kevin a blowjob and I didn't.'

I repeated the word slowly. 'Blowjob?'

'Yeah, as if!' When Kirsten noticed the stunned look frozen to my face, she added, 'You do know what a blowjob is, right?'

'I'm fairly certain I do,' I replied, struggling to recover control of the situation, 'but you tell me what you think it is.'

She did; and it was at this point that I began to feel a little sorry for Kevin, who had obviously been playing poker well out of his league. It emerged that not only had Kirsten engineered the whole game in order to stay up late, but when they couldn't find her parents' playing cards, it was she who suggested marking up some baseball cards instead so that they could 'get on with the game'. Reading between the lines, I realised that Kevin had tried throughout the evening to negotiate a more conservative approach, but he'd been outmanoeuvred at every turn. Kirsten did confirm, however, that he had point-blank refused to kiss or touch her.

At the end of the interview, I found myself advising Kirsten's mum to only employ female babysitters and later that morning I enjoyed consoling Kevin's distraught parents with the release of their son; turning tears of anguish and shame into tears of relief and gratitude.

Not all child abuse is sexual. Children can be physically abused by either proactive assaults, or inactive neglect. I dealt with a 'non-accidental' broken leg on a two-year-old, and a four-year-old boy taken into care because he was forty per cent underweight, lice ridden and had not been seen by a medically qualified person since he was six months old.

Every day failed children become failing parents, often while still children themselves. They do not have the necessary (indeed any) life skills to pass on. But some go further in their failure and actively tell their kids, on a daily basis, just how useless they are. Memorable comments I've heard from parents to their kids include: 'The sky's not pink! [referring to a picture brought home by a proud four-year-old] Are you thick or what?' And 'Play the trumpet! He couldn't even play dead – more's the pity.' Chuck in frequent use of the F-word and you quickly get the picture. This is why I was so surprised by my only case of pure mental abuse.

It was around nine-thirty on a Saturday night when Control called me and asked me to phone Emma, an ex-WPC who was married to an Oxford-based sergeant.

'Hi Em, what's up?'

'Chris, sorry to bother you, but I checked with Charlie and he said you were on call.'

'He's right, what can I do for you?'

'I'm babysitting for this couple Charlie and I met last week at a golfing dinner. He's a professor at one of the colleges and she's old money, a stay-at-home wife, roughly twenty years his junior. They've got a five-year-old daughter called Natalie who she dotes on. They live in Boars Hill…'

'Nice, one of those big houses *with room for a pony.*'

'Yeah, the house is gorgeous, but I need you to come and see something that is far from gorgeous. It involves their six-year-old son.'

'What's up with him?'

'I need you to come and see for yourself Chris. Charlie's on his way, but this is definitely a WSU job.'

Charlie and I arrived at the same time, and Emma opened the impressive front door as we got out of the plain CID vehicles used for such callouts. She immediately led us up the imposing spiral stone staircase with a swirling mahogany banister and proceeded to quickly show us the five bedrooms on the first floor, including three ensuites and a very large family bathroom. The master suite was impressive and the door right next to it opened into the daughter's sumptuous bedroom.

The little girl was fast asleep in the middle of a mini four-poster bed. The drapes around the bed were made of pink silk, which matched both the curtains and the wallcovering. Charlie remained at the door, but Emma tip-toed over to the wardrobes that took up an entire wall of the large room. Signalling me over, she opened one of the doors to reveal a whole line of little Dior dresses, beautifully displayed on padded-silk hangers. Below them was a line of cute, but obviously very expensive shoes. The child's numerous toys were neatly stacked but still overflowed from the large bay window-seat, and by Natalie's bed was a night-light that took my breath away. It had the shape and intricate beauty of a Fabergé egg. Tip-toeing back across the thick pile of the cream carpet, I quietly closed the bedroom door.

Emma whispered, 'I'd be happy to give up all the designer trimmings for a little girl like the one asleep in there.'

I was aware she and Charlie had been trying for a baby of their own for some time.

The other three bedrooms were adult guest suites. There was no sign of the little boy.

'So where's the son?' I asked.

Emma pointed to the end of the landing, 'When we were at the dinner, the wife showed me a lovely photo of Natalie. I asked her if she had any other children and she admitted Natalie had a brother a year older, but she sort of clammed up and changed the subject. I assumed the boy was in the doghouse for something – go take a look at his kennel.'

Emma pointed to where two steps led up to a green baize door, indicating the start of the old servant's quarters. Pulling the door open I saw a narrow uncarpeted staircase and as I switched on the light I could see three further doors at the top, which opened off a small square landing. Turning to Emma I asked, 'What's the son name?'

Emma shrugged, 'It's awful, but I don't know. I don't think she ever used his name. When I got here at eight she said the children were in bed and wouldn't need checking on. I was to make myself comfortable and help myself to anything in the fridge. So I played with their Sky for about hour and then I came upstairs – for a snoop at the décor as much as checking on the kids.'

We left Charlie at the foot of the stairs; we didn't want his uniform frightening the boy. Emma followed me up. Opening the first door I found a typical attic room full of odds and sods, the unwanted stuff accumulated in every person's life. As I backed out, Emma was pointing at the opposite door. When I opened it the reason for my presence became clear. The dusty illumination from the landing light fell across a six-year-old boy lying on a bare mattress, which in turn was lying on bare floorboards. He was curled up fast asleep under a single rough-wool blanket. The room was cold and smelt musty and someone had sellotaped a sheet of newspaper over the one small, round window.

I was as shocked as Emma had been, but unlike Emma I turned on the light. The single unshaded bulb let out a weak forty-watt glow, which only emphasised the dingy emptiness of the small room. The shadows contained no toys or books; nothing apart from the mattress, the boy, and an old pine chest of draws. The light woke him and he sat up rubbing his eyes, which seemed over-large and owl-like, blinking out from a narrow, pale, serious face.

'Hello', I said, 'I'm sorry I've woken you, but my friend here is babysitting for your mummy and daddy and we just wanted to check you were okay.'

The boy looked at us blankly.

'I'm sorry, I've forgotten your name,' Emma lied.

'Timothy, Tim,' came the quiet reply.

'Do you always sleep here?' I asked. Tim nodded. 'Where are all your toys? He pulled out a rather battered and semi-nude action man from under his blanket. 'Is that your only toy?' I had to concentrate hard on keeping the anger from my voice. Tim shook his head and reaching under his blanket once more he produced a handful of grey mush.

I held out my hand and he gave it to me without question. I got the distinct impression that Tim was used to doing as he was asked without question. On inspection it became evident that the grey mush had once been a cloth teddy-bear, the sort given to newborns. I gave the mush-teddy back to Tim and asked, 'How do you fancy coming downstairs for some milk and biscuits?'

The boy nodded solemnly.

As we reached the bottom of the attic stairs, Charlie, who had removed his tunic, epaulettes and tie, knelt down and said, 'Hello Tim.' He'd obviously crept up the stairs to listen. 'My name's Charlie and I'm Emma's husband. While the girls here get you some milk and cookies, is it okay if I take a look in your bedroom, too?'

Tim nodded. With his cold left hand in mine and his right still clutching the mush-teddy, he seemed completely unfazed by so many strangers.

Experience was teaching me that abused pre-school and new-to-school children often accepted the innate sadness of their lives for what it was – they had nothing else to compare it with. It wasn't until they were established and confident in school and visited friends in their homes, that they realised their own home life seemed odd or different.

Often it was inappropriate touching or sexually explicit language in the classroom and playground that rang alarm bells to possible abuse taking place at home. Other early warning signs revolved around poor physical condition or injuries that came to light when the child changed for PE.

Back at Boars Hill, the sergeant's fury was barely contained when he came downstairs. The shocking difference between Tim's room and his sister's had been a slap in the face to all of us, but Charlie was vocal, 'The bitch! The total bitch!' he kept whispering through clenched teeth, placing all the responsibility onto the mother.

Once we'd given Tim his milk and biscuits, Emma went to the station to write up her statement and Charlie and I took Tim into the overstuffed but warm lounge. He looked tiny and out of place.

I got on with my job, 'Tim, Charlie and I need to check you over, like when you go to the doctors. Can you take off your top for me?'

Again the boy just nodded his assent and pulled off his Spiderman pyjama top so that I could examine his small white chest and back. 'That's great. Pop your top back on and then can you pull down your bottoms for me?' The question was casual and the mute response was just as casual, as Tim pulled down the red pyjama bottoms. He was well-fed and clean and I could see no obvious injuries or old bruises in any of the usual places.

Charlie was in no way placated. 'Get onto Control, I want a Scenes of Crime Officer out here to take photos and I want social services called out – we need to get this kid to a place of safety!'

Leading the bristling sergeant into the hallway I closed the lounge door.

'Tim's not actually in 'physical' danger,' I pointed out, 'and we've already established that he's been sleeping in that room for as long as he can remember. If you pluck him from it now, in the middle of the night, and drop him into the frightening chaos that is a children's home, you could do more damage in one night than his parents have managed in six years.' Charlie clenched his jaw to bite back a response. 'Instead,' I suggested, 'let's put him to bed in one of the guest rooms and wait for his so-called parents to return.'

It was one in the morning when we heard a car pull up outside the house and we were both standing in the hall as the professor and his wife came in. Charlie had purposely replaced his uniform, including his cap, and on seeing the uniform the usual panic crossed both parents faces as they uttered in unison, 'What's happened, is Natalie alright?'

'Natalie's fine,' Charlie's voice was as hard as steel, 'and, if you're at all interested, so is Tim.'

A look of utter bemusement crossed their faces. Not anger, indignation, embarrassment or shame – just bemusement; they clearly had no idea of what Charlie was getting at.

'We've put Tim to bed in one of the guest rooms.' My statement was delivered as a challenge.

The mother raised an eyebrow, 'Why?'

Charlie threw his hands in the air and turned away in disgust.

I addressed her husband, 'Any ideas?' I asked with open sarcasm. He shrugged. 'Seriously! You both consider its okay to keep Natalie in the lap of luxury and Tim in the attic!'

The start of my sentence was shouted and I had to force myself to finish through a clenched-teeth whisper.

Still nothing: no explanation, excuse, reason or mitigation – absolutely nothing.

Charlie clenched his fists as he stepped into the professor's personal space and eyeballed him, 'My officer asked you a question, *Professor*'. The title was spat.

'Charlie…' said the professor.

'Right here, right now, it's Sergeant.'

'Sergeant,' he had the grace to blanch at the intended threat from the Charlie's physical encroachment into his world, 'it seems to me that this is a housekeeping matter and, as such, is something you need to take up with my wife.'

'Well?' Charlie spun towards his wife, who was calmly taking off her gloves and coat.

'Sergeant, I am at a loss to know what you are so angry about. What exactly is the issue?'

It was my turn to try and impact on the 'what's-the-problem-world' these two apparently intelligent people were inhabiting,

'The *issue* is that you and your husband appear to be committing an offence of serious and premeditated mental cruelty towards your six-year-old son. This *issue* is contrary to Section 1 of the Children and Young Persons Act of 1933 – for which you and your husband could receive five years' imprisonment – that is the nature of *this issue*.'

For the first time the mother looked worried. 'You can't be serious. If I were sent to prison who would look after Natalie?'

'For God's sake!' Charlie exploded, 'I've a good mind to arrest you both now, and Natalie and Tim can go into care – tonight!'

This threat worked.

'Look Char…Sergeant, clearly my wife is doing something wrong. What can I do to help move this matter forward?'

The condescension in the professor's tone nearly cost him a bloody and broken nose and Charlie his career. I stepped between the two men.

'Well professor, I'll tell you what you and your wife *will* do. You will give over one of the main bedrooms to Tim and, in the very near future, Tim will be in receipt of the same trimmings to his life that you obviously feel necessary for Natalie's. I will be back here later today with Scenes of Crime to take some photographs…'

'Scenes of Crime?' Again there was a stereo response of bemusement.

'Yes Scenes of Crime – you are committing a crime and I intend to have that fact recorded with photographs. Someone from social services will attend with me and they will no doubt place Tim on the At Risk Register until things improve.' I was relishing the exercise of my legal powers against these two adult delinquents; this is why I had joined the police, to fight for the rights of the unloved and unheard.

'Register?' The mother's lack of comprehension was not receding.

'It's a list that really crap parents get put on!' said Charlie, before storming from the house. I followed, with a last warning to both crap parents.

'If Tim ever sees the inside of that attic again, I will move heaven and earth to ensure that you two see the inside of a cell. Do I make myself clear?' They looked at me with the same blankness that had crossed their son's face earlier.

Over the next few days I returned regularly to the house with social services, who continued to explain in words of one syllable the unfairness of Tim's situation. Social workers had initially thought along the same lines as me – perhaps Tim had been adopted because the couple couldn't have children of their own. As in many cases, with the stress of childlessness removed, the parents then conceive naturally. But this was not the case, Tim was their biological son. The professor had to be taken upstairs to the attic and shown Tim's old room. He'd been totally unaware of where his son had been sleeping for the last five years and seemed bored with having this domestic incident thrust to the forefront of his academic mind.

His wife made more of the right noises and eventually admitted she had been unfair to Tim, but I had the distinct feeling she was playing the game to protect the existing relationship with her daughter, rather than wanting to create a new one with her son. Although Tim instantly gained the appearance of acceptance within the family, I doubt it ever turned to love. It took months of family therapy for this couple to fully understand that they would not be allowed to merely put aside an unwanted son once their longed-for daughter had finally arrived....

Each of us in the WSU took turns to provide divisional on-call cover. As most sexual attacks happen at night it could end up being a pretty busy week. I'd been on the unit just over a month and this was my first week of providing out-of-hours cover. I'd endured five fairly sleepless nights, not from any actual call-outs, but from the possibility of somehow missing one and I was waking at regular intervals to check my bleeper.

It was just before 1am on Sunday when my phone began to ring in a very persistent manner. I was still pushing my way up from a short period of deep sleep when I picked up the handset.

'Good morning, Ma'am.' A bad American accent entered my fuzzy brain. 'I'm Special Agent Brown...'

'And I'm the Queen of Sheba.' I slammed the handset back down. Bloody control room, you'd think they'd have better things to do.

The phone reignited.

'What?'

'It's Special Agent Brown again, Ma'am — we appear to have been disconnected.' This time the authenticity of the American accent penetrated.

'Sorry, who?'

'Special Agent Brown, Ma'am, I'm with the Special Investigation Unit at USAF Upper Heyford. We have a situation that requires your attendance.'

'Okay, Mr Brown...

'Special Agent, Ma'am.'

'Sorry, Special Agent Brown.' I was now sitting up and concentrating. 'Two things, no, make that three. How did you get this number? What "situation" is it that we have? And please stop calling me Ma'am.'

'I take it you're not WPC Hayward?

'Correct. I'm Chris, Chris Clements. I'm on call this week. How did you get this number?'

'I worked with Jacki on a job several weeks ago and this is one of the contact numbers on our files.'

'So, what's the situation?'

'We've had an attempted rape of a local girl by one of our service personnel – can I call you Chris or should it be WPC Clements?"

'Chris is fine. Where's the girl now?'

'At our medical facility on the base, can you meet me there?'

'Yeah, let the main gate know I'm coming.'

I knew my way around USAF Heyford very well. When the Americans had bombed Libya the previous year, I'd spent two weeks doing twelve-hour days on gate-duty. The US military had no jurisdiction on the main road that ran through the middle of their base and during this period of heightened security, uniform bobbies had been called in to stop and search any vehicles on that particular piece of tarmac.

Having shown my warrant card at the main gate, I drove straight round to the base hospital and was met at the entrance by a six foot blond, blue-eyed American that could only have been Special Agent Benjamin Brown; he was a definite upside to being dragged from my warm bed. Ben filled me in.

Laura was a nineteen-year-old from Bicester who had been at the enlisted men's club – a regular Friday and Saturday night haunt for many local ladies. The drinks were cheap, the men plentiful and it was slightly easier to get inside this military base than many of the nightclubs in Oxford.

Laura and her friends had met a couple of airmen in a Bicester pub who had driven the girls back to the base and signed them into the club. Laura had got talking to a man called Jimmy, who appeared to be a charmer. Having worked their way through the usual routine of drinks, shouted conversation, fast and slow dances, Laura had been quite happy to get some fresh air with Jimmy.

She was far less happy about being pushed behind a large wheelie bin and shoved up against the wall with a switchblade held to her throat. Laura had made her unhappiness clear by kneeing Jimmy swiftly and hard in the best place possible; a reflex reaction on her part that produced an equally quick reflex on his. While he curled forward, moaning and clutching his privates, Laura ran back inside the club and raised the alarm with bar staff. Unfortunately Jimmy's recovery had been relatively quick, and by the time they reached the alley Jimmy had vanished.

Speaking to Laura in the emergency room, she seemed surprised by her own actions. She didn't consider herself a brave person and the after-effects of the adrenalin she'd produced were now causing her to shake. The adrenalin had also acted like strong black coffee and any effects of consumed alcohol were now gone; Laura was weepy but perfectly sober. The only medical treatment she had required was a single taped-stitch to the small wound left in her throat by the point of the blade and some warm drinks for the shock.

The bar staff had called the base police and Ben had dispatched officers to patrol the roads between the club and the barracks, but no one fitting Jimmy's description had been spotted. As a last resort he wanted me and Laura to return to the club when it turned out at 2am. Ten minutes later the three of us were standing opposite the main entrance as the clubbers poured noisily out. Ben had put other agents inside, covering all emergency exits and preventing anyone from taking a shortcut home. About half the club had filed through the main doors when Laura pointed at a large man in his mid-twenties who was now sporting a blue and white baseball jacket.

'That's him! That's the bastard!' She shouted.

Jimmy heard her too and started to run, but Ben leapt forward pulling a handgun from a concealed holster and, in true American cop-show style, he adopted a two-handed grip and shouted, 'Armed police! Freeze!'

The reactions these three words produced was a startling illustration of the difference between American and English and male and female responses to a gun being drawn in public. All the American men, including Jimmy, stopped dead and silently raised their hands; all the English women dived to the floor screaming.

Jimmy was arrested and transported to the SIU offices, while I returned with Laura to the hospital to take a formal statement. We went back to the hospital to avoid 'cross-contamination' – the further transference of any physical evidence between suspect and victim via third parties, such as arresting and interviewing officers. Such standard precautions proved unnecessary however, as Jimmy was still in possession of the switchblade and, when told of the small but telling wound it had left and the likely matching blood trace on the blade's tip, he made a full confession.

American military personnel can be tried in a British civilian court or by American court martial. Jurisdiction was always given to the States in these circumstances for two very good reasons; it saved the British taxpayer enormous trial and detention costs and the American forces internal justice system was both quick and severe. Jimmy was given three years in a military prison which, both here and in the US, make Parkhurst look like Pontins. In addition, military personnel don't get time off for good behaviour; such behaviour being a given. At the end of his three years, Jimmy would be dishonourably discharged from the airforce without back-pay or pension. In the British justice system he would have received around eighteen months and with time spent on remand and time off for good behaviour, Jimmy would have been out in six.

CHAPTER 17

Sons and Daughters

In instances of child abuse, the mother's boyfriend was often the offender, and the thing that angered me most about such cases was that many mothers would side with their lover against their child. The mother may only have known the man for six weeks or six months, but too often she was prepared to take his word against her child's.

Maybe it was because she couldn't let herself believe that her partner found her child more sexually attractive than herself and, deep down, although she believed her child, she just couldn't handle the truth and complete denial was the easier option. Whatever the twisted logic of their thinking, I dealt with many cases where mothers decried their daughters as lying sluts and threw them out of their home – refusing further contact until the boyfriend eventually moved on. Daughters abused by their fathers could still love them. They had an amazingly mature ability, at all ages, to separate the person from the act and be able to still love the person while living in fear of the act.

A boyfriend's physical abuse of children was often based on the presumption that they 'needed it' because the child's natural father was too lazy to care or simply not around. They saw it as their role to instil some much-needed discipline while the mother looked on, grateful to have a man in her life again. The pure selfishness of these women never ceased to amaze me; as did the levels of tolerance and forgiveness usually shown by their children.

Long before professional counselling became standard practice, a well-managed disclosure interview could actually help a child cope with the consequences of their abuse. The little girl who turned her back the first time we talked, would often walk back to me the following day with a quiet purpose-fulness – she had more things to get off her chest.

This lightness of step in children leaving disclosure interviews, compared to the heaviness of their tread as they entered, was one of the most rewarding aspects of my sixteen years' service. It was my job to transfer the weight of the world from their small shoulders to mine and I was glad to do it. But I was still wet behind the ears when I found myself in a side ward at Horton General Hospital, talking to the back of a thirteen-year-old girl who had seated herself in the farthest corner of the room, while a nurse sat quietly in the opposite corner. This was my first disclosure interview involving more than inappropriate touching.

We had got into these positions gradually. I had originally placed the girl's chair close to one side of mine, but as the interview progressed in depth and detail, the girl had got up and pulled her chair backwards, away from me and into the farthest corner. It was obvious she did not want to talk about the abuse and she underlined this fact when I'd asked her to sit down again. She had done so, but facing the wall with her back towards me. Allowing her the comfort of no eye contact I continued to ask the open questions used by police in all interviews.

5WH (what, where, who, when, why and how) had been part of basic training, and I was now using it to maximise the information obtained, while minimising suggestive answers from this vulnerable witness. It takes more than a simple yes or no to answer a 5WH question; 'What did he say?' encourages a fuller answer than 'Did he say anything?'

The girl's first line of defence obviously hadn't worked; I was still there and still asking questions. So she tried a second tack which, subsequent experience showed me, was an intuitive self-defence mechanism in many child abuse victims. She started to swear, dropping the F-word into her replies, before turning to monitor my reactions. If I looked or sounded shocked, or rebuked her use of such language, by her rules she'd win and she'd no longer feel obliged to tell me anything. If I could be shocked I couldn't be trusted – because what she had to tell me would shock the socks off most adults.

The interview had been arranged because of the teenager's sexually explicit behaviour while in hospital. She'd been admitted to the children's ward with non-specific stomach pains, a common symptom of sexual abuse. When the doctor had started to examine her, she had quickly placed herself in an extremely sexually provocative position. By touching her stomach the doctor had triggered a Pavlovian-reaction and the child had remained frozen in that grotesque pose while medical staff looked on aghast.

When police interview anyone under seventeen, they must by law have an 'appropriate adult' present to represent the interests of the child. Usually this would be a parent, but in suspected abuse cases, parents became the least appropriate people. In the 1980s any suitable adult in any suitable setting would do – this was well before we conducted joint interviews with a social worker in specialised video-linked rooms. These were extremely low-tech, laborious interviews involving the recording of every question and answer by hand. Unfortunately, the nurse randomly selected by her line manager to act as the appropriate adult was so stunned by what the girl told me on the first day, that she didn't make it back for the second. She'd called in sick with stress and it was now the ward-sister herself sitting pale-faced in the corner of the room.

I felt guilty that I'd spent no time preparing the nurse for what she had subsequently heard. As my first police encounter with a small child (Sergeant J's wailing toddler) had shown, I lack any maternal instinct. I've never wanted children and always argued I had better things to spend my time and money on – horses mainly. This lack of parental sensibility actually served me well on the WSU. It seemed to radiate from me and allowed abused children to talk openly to me; sensing that my lack of parental emotion meant they could trust me to listen without becoming openly angry or tearful. But obviously not everyone felt the same way as me, including the nurse who had now called in sick. Being a fellow professional and a nurse to boot, I had quite arrogantly and wrongly assumed that she would cope with the type of information coming her way.

I had learned a valuable lesson. Starting with the Sister and with all future 'appropriate adults', I made sure I gave them as much advanced warning and advice as I could about the often-distressing nature of this type of disclosure. My advice included asking them to control all their reactions, both audible – gasps, and involuntary exclamations – and non-audible body-language such as folded arms, eyes wide with horror or screwed tight against the images. Anything showing shock or disapproval could shut a child down as dramatically as the offender himself walking into the room; and it would take very little to shut down an abused child.

Offenders may well have told them that if they did tell

anyone, one of three things would happen. They'd not be believed and thought of as a liar for the rest of their lives; they'd be put into care; or they (the offender) would come back and 'get them'. Such threats were taken seriously by these small victims, and in one particularly nasty case the offender had forced his five-year-old stepdaughter to watch him drown her pet kitten in the toilet of the family's bathroom. This reinforced the threat so effectively that his victim remained catatonic in her silence, and although we could protect the child by fulfilling another of the abuser's threats and placing her in care, we could not produce a prosecution case and he was left free to abuse other children.

Overt sympathy and false promises were also things to be avoided. The more matter-of-fact and unemotional I could remain, the easier it was for the child to deal with their own feelings during disclosure. I learnt quickly to never make promises regarding things over which I had no personal control. It was never 'going to be alright'. Too many other people and outside factors were involved: it would be far from alright if they ended up in a children's home because their mother called them a lying slut and threw them out, and it would be far from alright if the father they still loved was sent to jail because of what they told me.

Instead, I would always thank the child for trusting me enough to tell me what had happened to them and if I believed them (which I did in ninety-nine percent of cases), I told them so. There were only one or two cases where I omitted this declaration of confidence, and that was because I believed the mother was coaching her children to lie in order to deny fathers access during malicious divorce proceedings. I would also state clearly and repeatedly that what had happened to them was not their fault and that they should not feel responsible in any way for what had happened and what might happen to the offender – not that this had much impact at the time.

CHAPTER 18

Breaking Patterns – Not Bones

As the panda screeched to a halt behind the ambulance's open doors, the blue lights of the two vehicles melded into a disco effect that lit up a dusky summer evening on a council estate in Banbury. This type of silent rave was the nearest I got to the drug-fuelled party action of the late Eighties: the constant drone of rave music and its ecstasy-driven dancing completely underwhelmed me.

'I'll kill the bastard!' The man screaming at the medics was being held back from chasing his quarry into the back of the ambulance.

One of the two bobbies went to the rear of the ambulance and winced at the badly beaten pulp that had once been a face, while his colleague stood in front of the screaming man being restrained by neighbours.

'What's going on?' He had to shout to make himself heard.

'I'll tell you what's going on.' The man spat his fury at the officer. 'That bastard – the one in there,' he tried once more to lunge at the ambulance, 'that waste of skin, that fucking excuse for a human being has interfered with my six-year-old daughter!'

'So you've beaten the shit out of him.' The bobby's statement held no condemnation – his own daughter was five.

'Yes – now let me finish the job!'

When the ambulance drew away with its twos and blues

blazing, the neighbours felt it safe enough to release their friend; who pulled his T-shirt straight as he stood tall and defiant.

'I'd have killed that bastard if some do-gooder hadn't called you lot.' The heat had vanished from his voice and been replaced by a cold edge that implied, if the man in the ambulance lived at all, he would never be allowed to live on this estate again.

The officers took names and addresses and returned to the station. It didn't occur to either of them to arrest the father of a molested child and if the idea of checking on the status of the beaten man crossed their minds – they decided against it. If he wanted to make a complaint the hospital would contact Control. If he died the hospital would contact Control and it would be a matter for CID; either way these lazy excuses for coppers had avoided a prolonged interruption of their meal break. Fortunately, the probationer on desk duty at Banbury in the small hours of the next morning was still chasing arrests, still proving himself.

The beaten man was John and in the early hours of the following morning he discharged himself from Horton General Hospital and went straight to the police station. He didn't want to make a complaint of assault which, after the blood had been wiped away, comprised: two black eyes needing stitching, a badly broken nose, three missing teeth, several broken ribs and bruised kidneys – diagnosed by ultrasound and blood in his urine. John dragged himself to the station because he was concerned about the allegations being made against him and he wanted to assure the police of his innocence.

'What allegations are these, then?' the probationer asked.

'Well, Geoff reckons I touched up little Samantha, his

daughter.'

'Why would he reckon that?'

'She told him I did.'

'Why would she say that?'

'I did touch her legs, but only to wash off some mud; nothing else. I'm not some bloody perv.'

'How old is little Samantha?'

'Six.'

The probationer didn't agree with John about him not being a perv and promptly arrested him on 'suspicion of indecent assault on a girl under twelve' – a serious arrestable offence under the relatively new Police and Criminal Evidence Act of 1984.

Known as PACE, this was a radical and far-reaching piece of legislation brought in to protect the rights of individuals who came into contact with the police. It replaced the old Judge's Rules and set down strict parameters under which the police (including Metpol) could stop and search, arrest, detain and interview suspects.

When I first joined, under the old Judge's Rules it was not unusual for prisoners to be arrested on a Friday and left to 'sweat' in the cells over a weekend. CID considered it good practice for the arresting detective to be the only person who had contact with his prisoner. If their prisoner wanted anything: food, drink, a fag, exercise, access to a solicitor, it was all down to the say-so of the arresting officer, and prisoners arrested for serious offences were not often given something for nothing.

My teenage brother was once arrested when working in a bank as a junior clerk. He had been framed by his line manager for a fraud that she was committing. I remember him telling me how disconcerted he was when they'd removed his laces and belt and how he'd spent the time counting the individual bricks that made up the walls of his cell. I have never forgotten the fact that innocent people get arrested, and that having the power to physically restrict a person's movements and actions is something that should never be taken lightly.

The probationer's gut instinct was to be proved correct regarding John. But the instinctive reaction to child abusers once more kicked in, and John's physical beating by the girl's father was now replaced by a mental hammering from the police. Under PACE, there was usually only twenty-four hours to process and charge a prisoner or set them free – this would be the longest day of John's life.

By eleven that morning I'd interviewed Samantha, recording 'our talk' by writing out the very simple questions and her usually monosyllabic answers.

'Can you show me where John touched you, Samantha?' The little girl pointed to her crotch. 'And what do you call that place?'

'My pee-pee.'

'What part of his body did John use to touch your pee-pee?' Sam raised her hand and gave it a gentle wave.

The anger of her indignant parents bubbled and spat on the point of eruption, unintentionally shutting down their child with the implied guilt caused by their rage. Sam knew something was wrong and as she was the centre of all this fury-filled adult activity she felt that it must have been something she did that was provoking it. So, with downcast eyes and a fading voice, she tried to protect herself from the adult anger washing around her by slowly curling into a ball on her mother's lap and hiding her face in her mother's chest; subconsciously trying to minimise the impact she was having on the world.

'Sam?' She refused to look at me. 'Sam, you've been very brave talking to me. Can I ask you one more question?' I took the stillness of the buried head as a yes.

'Did John's fingers go inside your pee-pee?'

Samantha shook her head vigorously and I wrote down a simple 'no' on the form.

Sam's parents, like most in this situation, saw their daughter's withdrawal from the people around her as symptomatic of the abuse, rather than a possible reaction to their own anger. It was to be another two years before Douglas Hurd, the then Home Secretary, opened TVP's first designated rape suite. It was a nondescript semi-detached house in Headington with a fully equipped medical examination room and a pleasant bathroom where, once examined, the victims could scrub away the physical signs of their abuse with heavily scented bubble bath or shower gel. The house also had a video-suite that enabled trained officers and social workers to conduct interviews in a room free from the negative vibrations of the indignant and furious.

Sam had also been examined by the police surgeon but with no major conclusions. She did have some redness at the top of her legs, but so general in pattern and nature as to be of little evidential use. Her hymen was intact.

By eleven that morning, Jacki and I had also spoken to the other children present at the time of Sam's alleged assault and had photocopied her birth certificate as proof of age. Jacki was my regular partner on the unit. She was short and slim with permed brown hair that had the texture and shine of wire wool and her experience on the job acted as an effective sedative whenever Banbury CID wound me up too tight.

Our job done, Jacki and I then began the frustrating process of trying to get a CID officer interested enough to interview John and take on the remainder of the case. This was always a thankless task. In the majority of these cases, after conducting the interviews and completing reams of paperwork, there would be a NFA (no further action) decision due to a lack of *credible* evidence.

It was my work with Banbury CID that so soured my view of the department for most of my career. My level of frustration with them had seen me descend into childish name-calling, referring to them as the crawling insect department or clowns in disguise. In later years it was felt necessary to post me (kicking and screaming) to Newbury as an acting detective sergeant. I was going for promotion to inspector and my lack of formal CID work was seen as a gap that needed to be filled. Although the Newbury CID office was much better than the Banbury office, there were still some egos bigger than the effectiveness of the individuals they belonged to.

Rather than work at finding any evidence, Banbury CID took the view that if the case was likely to be NFA'd, why waste time on investigating it. The lone female detective on the team was just as bad, but for different reasons. She was desperate to avoid being seen as a handy extension to WSU, 'an expert' on whom all the male detectives could dump the sexual offence stuff on. So Jacki and I regularly found ourselves unsuccessfully touting for business like two prostitutes. When we got no takers we'd be forced to make the female DS allocate the case to a detective. Yes, this particular team of chauvinists was led by a female, but one who took so much pride in being 'one of the lads', and had worked so hard at her masculine bravado, that what had once been a matter of show had now become innate.

The problem lay just as much with the system as with the individual. WSU officers were never considered part of CID and were purposely not CID trained – back-door immigration into the department by women had to be controlled. So we were not trained to interview offenders for what were serious offences; we were only allowed to deal with the victims. Senior officers also argued that not only had 'that documentary' shown just how insensitive male detectives were, as most offenders were men it made sense to keep them away from female victims. One of several major flaws in this policy was that the interviewing detective would not have spoken directly to the victim, and so the detectives got no real feel for the case and were restricted to working from sanitised written statements.

As usual no one in the office expressed any interest, let alone enthusiasm, in taking on this latest case. The only effect of my pointing out that the PACE clock had less than four hours to run, was to empty the office as each defective (sorry, detective) remembered urgent casework elsewhere. When the one remaining DC said he'd interview John, my sigh was not one of relief. Neville was an old sweat whose usual lack of enthusiasm was matched only by his lack of ability – but at least he was volunteering this time.

I shouldn't have held my breath. The interview lasted exactly twelve minutes, short even by Neville's standards. As Jacki and I read through the scrawled record of interview we could not believe our eyes. The original script for Z-Cars contained more incisive questioning than Neville's interview; which basically asked the same question three times: 'Did you do it?' 'You did do it, didn't you?' and 'Why did you do it?' All variations had been easily answered in the negative by the prisoner.

When I tackled the DS about the interview (she had been out of the office all morning on enquiries) she went ballistic.

'Fucking Neville? Neville did this interview?' she turned to said detective, who was hiding behind an opened newspaper. 'Neville, backyard – now!'

It turned out she was not concerned about the quality of the interview but the fact that Neville had been the one to conduct it. John was Neville's informant.

Jacki and I were so incensed by this serious breach of protocol that in an effort to calm us down and keep the matter within the office, the DS agreed that Jacki and I could reinterview John ourselves; she also had the excuse that the office was still empty of other detectives. There was now only one hour left on the PACE clock.

My first impression of John was to stay with me for the rest of my life. As I opened the cell door he was curled up in a foetal position at one end of the hard wooden bench, which should have had a plastic covered mattress on it. An image of little Samantha curled into her mother's lap flashed through my mind. John was crying silently – probably from sheer pain and self-pity – his tear-streaked face was a raw mess. His broken ribs caused him to groan as he struggled to sit up.

'John, my name is WPC Clements and this is WPC Hayward. We've been sent to try and sort this mess out, okay?' John nodded.

I may have had no maternal instinct but I feel animal pain keenly, and John's eyes held the look of desperation I had once seen in a fox as it was torn apart by a pack of hounds during the first and only time I ever went hunting.

'Do you want a drink and some painkillers?' I asked.

His reply was muttered through dry cracked lips that were still stained with yesterday's blood. 'I had a cup of water an hour ago. I can't have any more for another hour and the sergeant says that police can't hand out drugs.'

For the second time in under an hour I was furious. PACE states that prisoners should be given food at least every four hours and a hot drink every two, but water should be given when requested or needed. Although the sergeant could not authorise painkillers the police surgeon could, and he should have been called when John was first arrested as there was an obvious question mark over his fitness to be detained. PACE was being used to punish rather than protect.

Ignoring the custody sergeant's stormy face, I fetched John two cups of water, a coffee, a mattress and a blanket and, ignoring the rules, I gave him two of my own paracetamol, while Jacki insisted that the police surgeon was called. John was so relieved to be treated as a human being that, twenty-five minutes into our subsequent interview, he admitted the indecent assault on Samantha.

As the three of us sat in the small windowless interview room, Jacki and I chiselled away, brick by brick, at the wall of self-preservation that John (like Sam) had been forced to build. Under the harsh fluorescent light our even tone and non-judgmental questions had loosened the mortar that had been laid when his jailer had spat in John's tea, dropped his hot meal onto the cold cell floor and refused him a mattress, a blanket or even loo paper. The foundation to John's wall had been laid during a previous arrest, when other officers had treated him like dirt on their boots, with one or two wiping said boots on his torso. John knew his confession would mean prison and he decided he wanted to tell us more. If he was going inside he had other offences he wanted taken into con-sideration; but he would only talk to us. The DS and DI were both highly irritated by this turn of events, but they had no choice – it was let the girlies carry on or give up on some important detections.

We obtained authority for John's detention to be extended, and over the next twelve hours Jacki and I became his jailers, reverting to pre-PACE ways of doing things. We insisted on carrying out the hourly checks, refraining from banging on the door at each check which allowed John to get some sleep. Such banging was excused by its perpetrators as being PACE approved, in that, by waking the prisoner they were doing their duty in ensuring that he was still breathing. The fact that this could be done by quietly unlocking the cell door and checking that the rib-cage was going up and down had been ignored; John had been effectively deprived of sleep. We also ensured that hot meals and spit-free tea were delivered by us and that John had water, loo paper and as many painkillers as had been authorised by the police surgeon.

During our interviews John confessed to three further and far more serious sexual assaults, including the rape of girls under twelve. These offences covered the surrounding counties of Buckinghamshire and Warwickshire, as well as Oxfordshire, and John had already been arrested for one of these offences but released without charge due to a lack of evidence.

When a child is raped the evidence was brutally clear for all to see, but the majority of child sexual abuse involves inappropriate touching and rubbing, which at most might leave some inconclusive reddening of the skin. The offender might also have forced the child to perform sexual acts on them, which again would leave little physical evidence on the victim – although the mental harm would last for decades. DNA had been discovered the year I joined but it was not used forensically until a murder case in 1988; so you were usually left to rely on the confession of the offender for any successful prosecution.

Like John, many sexual offenders subconsciously want to be caught. They know what they're doing is evil, but like a drug addict or an alcoholic, they need help to stop. Paedophiles need to reach that place where they can admit their problem, receive the help necessary to overcome it and so, most importantly, prevent them reoffending. The raw emotion and anger against child abusers is understandable and once in prison, child molesters (like bent coppers) were segregated from other prisoners. But such sanctimonious anger from police officers was not only unprofessional, it was seriously counter-productive. Breaking bones, metaphorical or real, only served to build up and reinforce the barriers between the perpetrators and the place they need to be in order to admit such terrible offending. A muttered comment while passing the cell door, an extra notch tighter on the hand-cuffs, a refusal of anything above the absolute minimum required by PACE, might make the officer feel better, but these actions shut down a suspect and helped prevent the protection of the vulnerable.

Many paedophiles were themselves abused as children and it was this early transference of abuse that often acted as an alarm bell to the outside world. The pre-school child who had teddies doing 'weird' things to each other, and the seven-year-old who touched his playmates in ways that weren't playful, were all signals that abuse might be taking place. Certainly the majority of wife-beaters I dealt with were beaten as children, or saw their mothers beaten. This is not a popular connection to make amongst some professionals, who balk against this idea being used as an excuse – as do I. But I always saw their own abuse as mitigation and a way to get through to 'that place' where offenders like John needed to be – in prison.

CHAPTER 19

Guns and Teddy Bears

It was a mild September afternoon, around four, and I was on my way to an address in the back streets of Banbury to conduct a welfare check on a nine-year-old called Colin. The boy's neighbour had contacted the police as she had witnessed Jason, his mother's boyfriend, hit Colin on several occasions. The last time he'd backhanded the young boy so hard he'd been knocked to the ground.

The double-glazed front door had a red rose inserted into each of its two narrow glass panels and it was answered by a pretty dyed-blonde in her early thirties. She was wearing a rather skimpy pink nylon piece of clothing I was hard pressed to name, black suspenders and stockings and diamante-covered stilettos.

'Hello.' I held my warrant card up for her inspection. She squinted at it and then reached behind the front door for a coat, which she put on and hugged to her slender frame.

'What's going on?' asked a deep male voice, and a bear of a body appeared at the door.

'Jason?' I again held up my warrant card for the low-lidded eyes to inspect. 'I've come about Colin.'

'What's the little bastard done now?' The heavy jaw clenched, while the woman slipped back under an arm that had been placed on the door-jamb to bar entry. She disappeared upstairs.

'Perhaps I can come inside?' My eyes indicated the twitching net curtain next door, and Jason dropped his arm and stepped aside. The front door opened directly into the lounge. It was a surprisingly clean and tidy space, not the dirty mess I had come to associate with physical abuse. There were some houses I visited where you felt the need to wipe your feet on the way out. Not only was the house clean but someone was obviously very keen on DIY — although the décor was unusual. The carpet was white shag-pile, a throwback to the Seventies, which clashed with the cream of the faux-leather three-piece-suite. On the boldly patterned wallpaper, instead of the usual school photos of children, there were full-length colour portraits of the woman who had answered the door. They showed her in various states of provocative, though not obscenely posed, undress.

The lounge also contained another set of open-tread wooden stairs, which the woman now descended wearing a lilac shell-suit. The high heels had been replaced by pink kitten-heel slippers, again adorned with diamante. She saw me looking at the photos and blushed, but Jason was defiant.

'Great, aren't they? Took them myself.'

'Sorry, I didn't catch your name?' I moved my eyes from the photos to the real thing.

'Jade.' Her voice was flat. 'I'm Colin's mum — what's he done now?'

'Nothing I'm aware of. Does he get into trouble?'

'He… misses his Dad…' Jade was interrupted by a belligerent Jason.

'If his dad'd bothered to discipline him when he was here we wouldn't be getting visits from the police now.'

'About that,' I seized the opportunity, 'do you discipline Colin?' I asked the bristling hunk of testosterone.

'Of course.'

'How?'

'When I need to, I whack the little tyke.' Jason's tone was matter of fact.

'Where?'

'Wherever he happens to be at the time he's being a git.'

'No, I mean where on his body do you *whack* him?'

'On his bum and legs – mainly. I'm not one of those cunts who hit kids out of hand,' he declared. 'I only discipline him when it's called for and it's always with an open-hand. My dad used his belt on me, regularly, and it did me no harm.'

I begged to differ but held my tongue. 'And how often, roughly, *is it called for?*'

Jason shrugged and lit a cigarette.

'Tea?' Jade broke the building silence.

'Is Colin in?'

'Not yet, he does drama club at school on Tuesdays, he should be back soon.' Jade's voice contained just a hint of pride.

'Regular little drama queen, your Colin,' observed Jason, leaning back in one of the armchairs and taking a long drag.

'Tea would be nice,' I said and looked at the sofa.

Jason raised his fag, giving me permission to sit.

From the sofa I could see into the kitchen at the rear of the property. It, too, had been opened up and worked on. I could also see a young girl on her knees, defrosting a large American-style fridge-freezer. The girl didn't stop working or look at me once during my thirty-minute visit. Jade came back with two china mugs of tea, which she passed to me and Jason.

I nodded towards the kitchen. 'Your daughter?'

'Yes, that's our Lizzie. She's twelve.'

Nothing more was forthcoming.

During the wait for Colin, both Jade and Jason extolled the virtues of good parenting, which included setting boundaries and discipline. They were highly critical of the parents, especially single ones, who let their kids 'run amok' around Banbury and they explained that both Lizzie and Colin had daily chores to do in return for pocket money. All very laudable I thought, but by now I knew their neighbour had been right to call us.

I passed a comment on how nice the house looked and was immediately offered an enthusiastic grand tour of the tiny property. I accepted with the same degree of eagerness with which it had been offered; it was a useful way of assessing the type of home life a child enjoyed or endured. The house was a three-bed mid-terrace. Upstairs, fashionable floral Austrian blinds in pastel colours matched both the curtains and bed-linen; but Jason's DIY had created an incongruous master bedroom. He had somehow sunk a large water-filled double mattress into the floor and had surrounded it with a padded edge of Barbie-pink fake fur. The stool to the dressing table stood at the foot of the bed and a TV and video had been installed underneath its matching pink fur seat. The other item of questionable taste was a life-sized photo of Jade in a gold plastic frame; it had pride of place on the wall above the centre of the bed. She was dressed in underwear so skimpy that it made Ann Summers look like Nora Batty. As we completed the tour, the front door opened and in walked Colin.

Jason started on him immediately, 'Do you know who this is?' he asked accusingly, pointing at me. 'She's a policewoman and she's here because of you!'

The import of such a statement, delivered in such a way, would have cowed most nine-year-olds; although from Jason's description I had been half expecting an over-confident trainee lout. But Colin was neither cowed nor confrontational. He walked straight up to me, smiled, and held out his hand.

'Pleased to meet you,' he said.

Jade and Jason were standing behind me and my eye caught their glares reflected in the hall mirror. Jade's was an open-eyed warning to Colin, but Jason's was one of pure hostility, the heat of which I could feel on the nape of my neck.

'And I'm pleased to meet you, Colin,' I shook the proffered hand, 'would you like to show me all the animals that Jason tells me you look after?'

'Okay.'

He led the way through the kitchen, past his still-kneeling sister and into the back garden. Well, it may once have been a garden but the long narrow space now resembled an excerpt from 'The Good Life'. It was divided into various muddy pens with chickens, rabbits and guinea pigs, a small aviary and a concrete pond full of green water too dark to spot any fish.

'Goodness,' I exclaimed, 'this lot must keep you busy.'

'They do. Jason makes me clean out all the pens every day. It takes over an hour if I do it properly.'

'And do you always do it properly?' I asked, with a conspiratorial smile.

'I have to – Jason checks.'

My smile faded. 'He sounds quite strict.' Colin nodded agreement. I came to the point of my visit, 'Colin, does Jason ever hit you?'

'Only when I deserve it.'

'What do you do to deserve it?'

'If I don't do my chores properly or if I give him lip, I suppose.'

'Is that often?'

'Not really.'

'Whereabouts does he smack you?' Colin pointed to his backside and calves. 'Has Jason ever hit you around the head?'

'Once – but I'd back-chatted him.' The defence of Jason seemed automatic.

'Someone told me that they've seen him knock you to the ground. Do you remember that happening?'

'Sort of, but I actually slipped as he smacked me.'

I asked Colin if he minded if I checked him for any marks and he immediately pulled up his school jumper and shirt to expose a thin pale torso. He turned around slowly, and without being asked, rolled up his sleeves and rolled down his knee high socks, exposing his arms and legs to scrutiny.

'That's great, Colin, thanks. Does Jason ever use anything to smack you with?'

'Just his hand.'

'Okay.' I sat down on an old wooden bench, grey-green with age, and patted the spare place next to me. 'Come and sit here a mo... do you miss your Dad?' Colin's eyes immediately welled up and he bit his lip as he nodded assent. 'How often do you get to see him?'

'Not often... he's got a drink problem... it's why Mum made him leave.'

'Oh I see. That must be hard for you.' Colin's response was to wipe away a tear with his forearm.

'How do you like school?' We both needed me to change the subject.

'It's good!' He immediately brightened up, as though the retuning of emotions was something he had been forced to practise.

'And do you have a favourite teacher at school?'

Colin though for a moment before replying, 'Mr Jones.

He's nice. He does PE and drama.'

'Well, Colin, I want you to do me a favour. If you ever feel especially sad, or Jason gets too strict, for example if he ever hits you around the head again, will you go and talk to Mr Jones about it?'

'Okay.'

I also gave Colin my card and told him to keep it safe. If he ever wanted to talk to me about anything that had upset him he could ring the number on it and speak directly to me, or he could go to the police station and give the policeman behind the desk the card and he'd go and find me. I stood, and Colin jumped up and once more put out his hand. I shook it solemnly before he turned away to start his chores.

Jason saw me out. I thanked him for his tea and time and said what a great kid I thought Colin was. He just grunted and as the door closed I heard him yell, 'Colin! Get in here.' I knew Jason would grill him over what was said, but I also knew that Jason would now have to be a lot more circumspect about his punishment of the boy. While waiting for Colin I'd explained to both Jason and Jade that we were under a duty to investigate all complaints involving children and that I would log my visit to them. If I ever had occasion to visit them again, for a similar reason, they could be assured my approach would be far more formal. Even I could not have guessed at just how formal, and indeed dramatic, that visit would be.

Fate was to play a large part in my next meeting with Colin and Lizzie. Four months later, three apparently unconnected things happened within two days of each other. First, Jacki had a call from her brother, a self-employed mechanic with a local workshop. He wanted her to visit him at work ASAP, but he wouldn't say why – only that he thought it was a police matter, but he didn't want uniform swarming all over the place. I was as intrigued as Jacki.

Her brother closed and locked the workshop doors before leading us over to an old Range Rover he was working on. Opening the front passenger door and then the glove compartment, he stepped back. Illuminated within the large compartment, lying on a thick bed of assorted condoms, was a large jar of vaseline and a small handgun.

'Who's the owner?' I asked.

'A brick-shithouse of a bloke called Jason. Don't know his surname but he's a big bugger – easily six three and broad. Got jet black hair and a beard.'

'I'll do a PNC on the car,' Jacki said, and sure enough the Police National Computer revealed that it was registered to the address I had visited for the welfare check on Colin. A further PNC, using an approximate date of birth for Jason, brought back no matches. We decided to do nothing immediately; he may well have had a licence for the gun and we needed to be sure of our ground.

I was first into the office the next morning and as usual turned on the answer-machine. There was a worried message from Mr Jones, Colin's teacher. Colin had been taken out of school with no notification or warning. The message said he'd tried ringing Jade but another woman had answered the phone. She'd told him that she'd recently bought the house and had moved in over the previous weekend; as far as she knew the previous family were now in rented accommodation on an estate the other side of Banbury, pending a move to Wales. She did have a forwarding address but she didn't feel she should give it out to just anyone.

I rang Mr Jones back and assured him I would follow this up as a matter of urgency, but before I could make a start the

Guns and Teddy Bears

DI walked in and threw a videotape onto my desk.

'Take a butchers at this, see what you think. It's been handed in by *a concerned member of the public*,' the DI often spoke in italics 'who's part of a homemade porno ring that circulates videos of each other *in action* – Reader's Wives in 3D so to speak. Only this particular video crosses the *concerned-person's* line. It's pretty standard group sex stuff, but there's a very young girl involved.'

I pushed the tape into the small TV and video kept in the office, and as the snowfall of blank tape slowly dissolved into moving images, four grunting adults faded into view. I immediately recognised the pink fake-fur. Five minutes into the video, Jade left the room and returned holding Lizzie by her wrist. The girl was then encouraged to 'join in the fun'. She was clearly not having fun and ran from the room after only a few minutes. Jade looked like she was about to follow her, but Jason told her mother to 'leave the frigid bitch alone' and the group continued without the frightened twelve-year-old.

'What do you think?' The DI asked. 'She's obviously underage, but how the hell we're supposed to identify her God only knows.'

'I know. Me and God, like that.' I said, crossing the first two fingers of my right hand.

The DI looked blank.

'The blonde woman is called Jade. She's the mother of the young girl who's called Lizzie. Lizzie is twelve. The big bloke with the beard is called Jason and he drives a white Range Rover, the glove compartment of which contains a small handgun.'

'Fuck me. Is any of that fact or just *female intuition*?'

'Is what female intuition?' Jacki wandered in and took off her coat.

I explained the latest development in the Jason and Jade saga and she confirmed to the DI that not only was I dealing in hard facts, but that these facts were fast becoming extremely serious.

'I've spoken to firearms and described the gun. If it's an imitation it's a good one. Unsurprisingly, he doesn't have a licence for it.'

That afternoon we held an emergency case conference with the school and social services. Once the extent of our concern for both Lizzie and Colin had been established and the non-police agencies had left, we were joined by an inspector from the tactical firearms team. I was secretly hoping to see Smokey again, but was told he was now on the southern team.

I'd visited the new owner of Jason and Jade's house and got their forwarding details and I'd already done a recce of this new address; confirming Jason's Range Rover was parked outside. The plan was to arrest Jason and Jade for indecent assault on Lizzie and remove both children to the care of social services; but the question of firearms created a whole new aspect to the planning.

It was decided that armed police would force entry into the house at dawn, when everyone should be safely segregated in their own bedrooms. Plans of the three-bedroom house had been obtained from the council and the probable location of Jason and Jade in the main bedroom was identified at the back of the house. Overnight, passing surveillance of the address suggested that at least one other couple were asleep inside and so we assumed that both children were likely to be in the smallest bedroom at the front.

Bang! At five precisely, the red wood of the front door splintered as a support group officer opened it with 'the key', a large metal cylinder similar to those used for putting in fence posts. He then stood back as the firearms team rushed in. I followed four sets of booted feet as they thundered up the stairs shouting 'Armed police!' over and over. Dressed in black bulletproof riot gear and full-faced helmets, they kicked open the doors of each bedroom and the bathroom, while three more stayed downstairs to cover the living areas. As I'd reached the top of the stairs I caught a glimpse of Jason and Jade sitting up in bed clutching a duvet to their naked bodies. Jade was screaming and Jason was following the shouted orders to keep his hands on his head. I was also aware of another couple in the next room undergoing the same wake-up call, but my only concern was Colin and Lizzie.

Following the last of the four armed officers, I made straight for the front bedroom, and as soon as he shouted 'Clear!' I popped out from behind his bulk like a comic afterthought, and grinned at the two children. Leaving the officer and his assault rifle standing on the landing, I closed the door against the continued shouting and screaming. Two pale faces stared up at me in open-mouthed silence, and I became aware of the false smile still fixed on my face.

'Hi Colin, do you remember me?' My voice was tight with false jollity. He nodded but didn't say anything. 'What about you Lizzie, do you remember my visit to your old house?' She, too, nodded but didn't speak. 'Well,' I coughed and forced my tone back to a more normal register, 'all these men are police officers, like me, and they are here to take your mum and Jason down to the police station to ask them some questions.' Both children blinked but still didn't speak. They were remarkably calm in fact and neither seemed overly concerned about the fate of Jason or their mother.

'How about some breakfast?' I asked with more fake heartiness. 'Do you like McDonald's?'

Colin's eyes lit up. 'Really? McDonald's for breakfast? Yippee!'

Lizzie smiled at her younger brother's reaction to this unexpected treat.

'I don't think either of you will be back here tonight – so could you both get dressed for me and then pack up some of your favourite clothes?'

'Okey dokey!' Colin jumped down from the top bunk-bed and started to bounce around the tiny room like Tigger on speed.

'Should he take some toys?' Lizzie's voice was childlike, but her eyes told me she knew exactly what was going on. They possessed the world-weary look of a forty-year-old and at that moment I hated Jason; but I hated Jade more. It took about fifteen minutes to get Colin organised; Lizzie was brilliant, packing a range of sensible clothes and some of her brother's smaller toys.

'What about Albert?' Colin's voice was suddenly full of concern.

'No, not Albert, he's too big. I've packed little bear.' Lizzie was firm.

'Albert?' I queried.

Lizzie indicated a giant bright yellow teddy bear, squatting in the corner of the small room and half hidden by discarded clothing. Albert instantly reminded me of my training school bear – they could have been cousins.

'How long will we be away?' she asked.

'I don't know, Lizzie. It could be a very long time.' I lowered my voice. 'I need to speak to you about a videotape I've been given. It shows you with your mum and Jason and two other adults. Do you know the one I mean?'

'Yes.' Her voice went flat. 'The other grown-ups are next door.' She indicated the second bedroom with a nod of her head.

I slipped out and fetched Jacki from the room where she'd been supervising Jade getting dressed. I told her what Lizzie had said and she handed the now-dressed and arrested Jade to an armed officer, before joining the uniformed WPC supervising the dressing of the other female. I could hear the satisfaction in Jacki's voice as she arrested both the unidentified man and woman on suspicion of indecent assault on a girl under thirteen. I stared at the couple, long and hard; they were definitely the other two grunting adults on the tape. But it would be Jacki sitting in on the interviews of both females; my job was to interview Lizzie and, in the following days, Colin.

Iris Goodacre was high up in social services, but the nature of this raid had brought her out into the chilly early morning. Iris was a big woman with a heart to scale; she liked to keep her large hands involved in grassroots work and she met us outside McDonald's. We had a breakfast full of fat, e-numbers and enforced bonhomie, but I could see Lizzie's mind was elsewhere. I left Iris playing with Colin, who was on his second milkshake, and drove Lizzie to the new rape suite in Headington.

We still hadn't reached the stage of conducting joint interviews with social services, so for the rest of the day I interviewed Lizzie alone, regarding what turned out to be almost daily sexual shenanigans. We stopped for lunch and watched a bit of TV, but Lizzie wanted to talk, so I let her, recording everything on videotape from a camera set high on the wall in the lounge.

The video with Lizzie had got mixed up with Jason's

commercial stock. She was quick to assure me it was the only time she had ever been actively involved in her mother's line of work. With the exception of the seized video, Colin and Lizzie had not been directly involved with Jason's homegrown porn industry, but they were certainly victims of it.

Lizzie described how she and Colin could be sitting at the dining table doing their homework when, under Jason's artistic Polaroid-snapping direction, Jade and Julie (the other arrested female) would lie down on the white shag-pile and start performing sex acts on each other, just feet away from the children. Apparently any domestic chore could suddenly be turned into the set of a porn movie. One afternoon Jade was cooking the children's tea when the second male from the seized video came into the kitchen dressed in just a tool-belt, and started having sex with Jade over the sink; Jason filming this action on a large camcorder. Colin and Lizzie just moved quietly out of the way, retreating to their bedrooms, their tea forgotten.

At the conclusion of a very long day, I drove Lizzie to the local children's home. As we drew up, Colin rushed out to meet us. He had obviously just had a bath and was wearing a brand new dressing-gown over his own pyjamas. His face was still glowing from the hot water but I also detected an inner glow. Grabbing my hand he pulled me into the large converted house, talking excitedly about how great it all was. 'Do you know I'm going to get one pound fifty a week pocket money without having to do any chores!' Could life get any better? his tone and eyes seemed to say.

Lizzie smiled indulgently, but her eyes were full of worry. Iris met us and showed us upstairs. Lizzie relaxed a little when she realised that the home was made up of individual bedrooms, rather than her imagined Victorian-workhouse dormitories, and she was relieved to find she'd be sharing a room with Colin. When Iris took Colin back downstairs to help with tea, Lizzie stopped her unpacking and turned to me.

'So what happens now?'

'In all probability all four adults will be charged. I'll be surprised if Jason and your mum don't get sent to prison for a short time.'

All of Lizzie's resolve and forced maturity dissolved, and for the first time that day she began to cry. I sat next to her on the bed and just held her as she shed tears for her mother, herself, Colin and the sheer overwhelming sadness of her life.

'Lizzie, none of this is your fault – you must remember and believe that.' I held her away from me and made her look into my eyes. 'But what your mum and Jason have done is very serious and you and Colin need to be protected from them.'

She nodded understanding, but gulped, 'I still love her.'

'Of course you do, Lizzie, and when you're a little older you will be free to choose what sort of contact you have with your mum. This is not the end, but for a little while things will need to be different – you understand this?'

We heard Colin running back up the stairs yelling, 'Lizzie you'll never guess what! They've got a pet rabbit!'

Lizzie looked at me, nodded once and scrubbing the tears from her eyes she went to find a bathroom.

Iris asked me if there was any chance of getting the rest of the children's belongings from the house in Banbury and I agreed to make a return visit. I went via the office so I could get an update from Jacki, who decided to come with me to the house. Jacki had spent the day co-interviewing Jade and Julie. She confirmed that they were mid-range prostitutes and Jason was their pimp. He would take them to people's homes or hotel rooms and then wait for them to conclude business. The gun was an imitation that he carried to frighten reluctant payers. When the women weren't engaged with clients, they'd perform lesbian acts for Jason's Polaroid and camcorder, which he then sold on.

Both women had started by denying any inappropriate behaviour. Showing them the video had produced sighs of resignation and a confession but not, according to Jacki, one iota of remorse. At least the video evidence and confessions meant that neither Lizzie nor Colin would have to attend court.

On our return to the house we both had more time to look around. The whole of the stairwell and upstairs walls displayed framed erotic pictures of Jade, Julie, and Jade with Julie. 'What a cow,' was Jacki's succinct assessment of the mother. Re-entering the kid's bedroom I carefully packed all their remaining clothes into a large suitcase Jacki had found on top of the wardrobe in Jade's room. As I was dragging the stuffed case back down the stairs, Jacki came in through the front door.

'What are you doing with that?' she asked, pointing at Albert whose paw was in my other hand.

'It's for Colin.' I knew I sounded defensive.

'You're as soft as shit, you.' she said. 'Bloody social services should be doing all this – we've been on duty for over 15 hours already.'

'Yeah, well, they're great kids and I want to make everything as normal as possible as quickly as possible.'

'Judging by all the crap that was found here this morning, I doubt either kid would know *normal* if it jumped up and bit them.'

'All the more reason to get their own stuff back to them.'

'Are you really planning to take that bear to Homelea? The

other kids will tease the hell out of him.'

'No, they won't. Anyway, Lizzie asked me to fetch it for him and she knows her brother best.'

'Your call,' Jacki shrugged, 'but don't blame me if he's got a black eye next time you visit.'

I thought about Jacki's comment and when I arrived back at Homelea I intended to leave the bear belted in the front passenger seat and seek Iris's advice on this important matter. However, Colin must have been watching for me as he once more ran out in his new slippers and dressing gown.

'Brilliant!' he shouted. 'You've brought Albert.' And he raced around to the passenger door to free his best friend from police custody.

Jade and Jason got three years and their friends eighteen 18 months. I'd been present when they were charged; Jason and Jade had not even asked where Lizzie and Colin were. It was their friends who broke down in tears when the custody sergeant refused them all bail, but the tears were for their two dogs, which had also been taken into care, by the RSPCA.

Sometime later, Iris showed me a magazine article that made me fizz with rage. Throughout my dealings with Jade she'd never showed her children any consideration, never mind compassion or love. But while in Holloway she'd been interviewed by a journalist who was writing an article on mothers who sexually abuse their own children. Jade had attempted to defend the indefensible. She claimed that Lizzie had had a bad time with a boyfriend and that she had just tried to give her daughter a more positive sexual experience. The fact that her daughter was only twelve and had never had a boyfriend was not mentioned in the article.

Iris consoled me. 'This blatant lying and twisting of the truth will mean Jade will continue to be refused access to her children, even after her release.'

Something told me that Jade probably wouldn't care, but I wondered how much Lizzie would.

Iris had also written to the DI expressing her department's formal thanks for a job 'exceptionally well done', regarding the interviews of Lizzie and Colin. The letter was thrown onto my desk by the inspector,

'What I can't get my head around,' he declared, 'is that you can get something like this off someone like Iris Goodacre, but you manage to rub the rest of the office up the wrong way on an almost daily basis!'

I left the WSU shortly after this case. It hadn't upset me; rather it highlighted how boring the work had become. I know how awful that sounds, when you say it out loud; bored with other people's misery. It wasn't compassion fatigue, my heart still felt compassion for the woman or child sitting in front of me, but my mind was now continually wandering elsewhere. The real police work involved in Lizzie and Colin's case had served to underline the monotony of most people's offending. I was spending more time in case conferences than in the interview room or rape suite and my work was reduced to the recording of people putting things (usually fingers) where they shouldn't. My statements had become templates; you could change the name and date but everything else remained more or less the same.

So back to uniform I went, and from the start things livened up no end.

CHAPTER 20

More Domestics,
More Disputes

I was single-crewed, covering a notorious estate in Banbury, when I was sent to a violent domestic. An ex-husband was breaching a court injunction banning him from the ex-marital home.

I have often felt some sympathy towards these men. The law did not treat fathers with the same equity it treated mothers. I have known many cases where the wife and mother has had an affair, kicked the husband out of the marital home, moved her new lover in and made it virtually impossible for the father to spend time with his own children − while all the time expecting him to continue paying the mortgage and maintenance. If the cheated-on father objected to this state of affairs, he was often arrested, taken to court and had an injunction slapped on him − judicial salt in the marital wound.

This, however, was not the case at this well-known address. Phil was a violent drunk who had beaten both his wife and young son, and this particular injunction was all that stood between them and repeated hospitalisation. Control was already sending back-up and the good news was that the neighbour, who had phoned in the complaint, had also confirmed the mother and child were safe with her. So, on my arrival I had the luxury of staying in the panda until back-up arrived − age and experience were at last kicking in.

I watched Phil kung-fu kicking his former front door. He

was roaring drunk. No way was I going to risk bodily harm to save a bit of double-glazed plastic. As I heard the approaching blues and twos, I also heard the sound of breaking glass – Phil had managed to kick out the panel in the upper half of the door and had cut himself badly in the process. He was now hopping around the small lawn holding his right leg with both hands.

I asked Control for an ambulance and, as Gary and Dave arrived, I got out of the panda and we converged on Phil, who had fallen onto his back. When we came into view his adrenalin quickly kicked back in and he leapt to his feet, ready once more to take on the world. Fortunately, although drunks are often violent, they're rarely quick. As Gary and I faced Phil, Dave darted behind him and, grabbing both his arms, forced him back onto the grass, face down. He held Phil still while Gary put on the cuffs and I sat across Phil's bleeding but still-kicking leg. Gary then held his good leg still while I examined the cut to the other. It was deep and the spurting blood showed Phil had probably nicked an artery.

I shouted above Phil's flow of obscenities, 'Dave, turn him over!' I then rammed my fist into Phil's groin, leaning hard on the femoral artery. 'Where's that fucking ambulance?' I shouted, as Gary struggled to control the good leg, which was still attempting to kick hell out of me; meanwhile Dave had Phil in a neck-lock to prevent him head-butting Gary. When the ambulance arrived it continued to take all three of us to hold Phil down, while the medics applied a proper tourniquet and dressed the wound more effectively.

'You're not taking me to no fucking hospital', was Phil's response to our joint efforts. 'I ain't going in no fucking ambulance. Leave me a-fucking-lone you bastards.'

'We can't treat anyone against their will,' said one of the

medics. 'What the hell are we going to do?'

'Phil, you're under arrest for breaching your injunction, and criminal damage,' I said. 'Now, you're badly injured and we're going to get you to the hospital one way or another. Do you want to do it the easy way or the hard way?'

'Hard way? I'll show you hard you fucking bitch!' and he started to struggle again.

'Right,' I said, 'let's get him in the back of the panda. Dave, you get in first and then Gary and I will feed his head and shoulders towards you. Gary, if you can kneel over from the front passenger seat and keep his legs under control and some pressure on the dressing, I'll drive.' When neither lad argued I felt a fleeting glow of satisfaction – perhaps I could make sergeant.

Dave was such a big bloke, the back of a panda didn't afford him much room at the best of times, never mind being forced to share the tiny space with a fighting ball of drunken fury. I asked the ambulance crew to follow us to hospital – Phil was losing so much blood that he might well pass out and then they'd be able to treat him; an unconscious body can't raise objections. The medics agreed, but Phil was still struggling when we arrived at A&E five minutes later. We managed to pull him out of the car and carry him bodily into Horton General.

The duty doctor examined the wound while we continued to hold down the struggling Phil and he confirmed that it was as bad as it looked and would need internal as well as external stitches. However, Phil was still telling everyone to leave him the fuck alone and threatened to 'do the fucking doctor if he came anywhere near his fucking leg with a fucking needle'. The doctor confirmed that he could do no more while Phil was refusing treatment, especially in such an unambiguous way, so he re-bandaged the wound with plenty of padding and pressure and we carried Phil back out to the panda. It took us nearly ten more minutes to reload him, before unloading him again at the custody suite.

Hearing the commotion in the backyard, the custody sergeant opened the door, took one look at the blood already seeping through Phil's bandage and shouted,

'What are you lot thinking? That man needs hospital!'

'Been there, done that,' I retorted as we continued to unload Phil. 'He's refused treatment, so the hospital can't do any more for him.'

'What if he dies from blood loss?' The sergeant was not happy.

'Apparently that's his legal prerogative.'

'Better bring him in then. I suppose you'll want your solicitor, Phil?'

'Course I want my fucking solicitor, he'll sort you fucking bastards out – police fucking brutality, that's what this fucking is!'

Although the verbal assaults continued unabated from Phil, the physical ones were getting noticeably weaker. Dave, Gary and I looked at each other and I went next door to phone for an ambulance. He couldn't stay conscious for much longer. Phil's bloody-mindedness and adrenalin kept him going long enough to be booked in, have his property removed and speak briefly to his solicitor. But as he was telling his brief what a 'bunch of fucking bastards' we all were, his voice began to fade and he slid gently down the custody wall to the floor, with the handset still in his hand. He slipped into unconsciousness just as the ambulance arrived. While the custody sergeant explained to the solicitor the sudden disappearance of his client, I reacquainted myself with the two medics who had treated Phil earlier. As he was my prisoner, I had to accompany the now still and silent Phil back to the hospital for his stitches.

The same doctor was awaiting our arrival with a needle threaded and ready to go. It took over an hour to treat Phil, including matching his blood type and getting several replacement units of the precious stuff back inside him. Fortunately, he remained unconscious throughout, but when the anaesthetic wore off and the new blood kicked in, Phil was back with a vengeance,

'What have you fucking bastards done to my fucking leg?'

Once more I had to call for back-up to get Phil back to the station. But this time Dave and Gary were prepared, having swapped the panda for the transit. On our return the custody sergeant had already sent for the police surgeon to certify Phil's 'fitness to detain' and hopefully give him some sedatives. We finished off the interrupted booking-in procedure and Phil then limped quietly into his cell.

I asked him if he'd like a cup of tea and he gave me a sullen nod. When I returned to his cell a few minutes later, he'd removed his bandage and was sat on the bench trying to unpick the stitches with his fingers. Luckily, the stitches were tiny and his fingers fat and nail-less, so what he was doing must have been painful but was not going to be effective.

For six months between 1989 and 1990, the ambulance service went on strike and I had every sympathy for their fight. They were being appallingly paid for their vital work and insulted by Health Secretary Kenneth Clarke, who accused them of being 'glorified drivers'.

On the run-up to the strike, a telex was circulated to all affected police areas, asking for volunteers to cover ambulance work on an overtime basis. The telex stated that the following qualifications were 'desirable' for those wishing to take on this work: a current first aid certificate or *an interest* in this type of work. As overtime was paid at time-and-a-half, everyone was *interested*; many officers had taken on big mortgages during the miners' strike and were now feeling the pinch.

Although my mortgage wasn't huge, inflation was running at above four per cent and I, too, needed the extra money. But I was torn between helping those needing to get to hospital and feeling a bit of a scab. I ended up salving my conscience by donating a third of my ambulance-overtime to the ambulance strike fund.

In place of a high-tech ambulance we were given an old benched transit van, a canvas-and-pole stretcher and some grubby-looking custody blankets, before we were released onto the unsuspecting public. I found myself crewed with Gary for much of the strike. He was slightly shorter than me but that didn't stop me appreciating his penetrating grey eyes and we had a brief fling. But I was uncomfortable dating a shift member; things could quickly become complicated and when they did, the WPC rarely came out of it well. So our affair ended before the strike did.

Our very first job was a call from the local GP to help an old lady who'd fallen and broken her hip; the message stated we should try and arrive within two hours. Gary wanted to take his meal break first, but I said no; if it was my Nan with a broken hip I'd want her in hospital not lying on her lounge floor. When we arrived at the house Gary had the decency to look guilty – the woman was in obvious pain. As we inexpertly lifted her onto our unsupported stretcher and her broken hip wobbled, she bit back screams of agony. The GP had given her nothing for the pain and lifting the stretcher over various obstacles in the cluttered lounge, I silently cursed his lack of consideration, which I felt bordered on malpractice.

In the transit we had to place the stretcher on the ridged-metal floor, and the pain was now so bad that the woman began projectile vomiting. The only thing I could do during our slow journey to A&E was to hold up a blanket as a screen against the vomit, which exploded every time our old transit negotiated a speed hump. I spent the journey silently cursing both the ambulance men for their strike and Maggie Thatcher for causing it.

Once at the hospital we were met by a senior nurse, whose face assumed a look of horror at the barbaric way in which this patient had been forced to travel. But her horror produced a supply of new blankets and cardboard vomit bowls.

On leaving the hospital, the first thing Gary and I did was return to the station and smuggle a wipe-clean mattress from custody, which we squeezed onto the floor of the transit. When the bench legs got in the way, I went to the canteen and persuaded Muriel, the cook, to loan me a large sharp knife. Much to Gary's consternation I then hacked into the parts of the mattress near the bench legs and so managed to get it to lie flat.

'You'll get done for criminal damage when the sarge sees this,' said Gary with genuine concern.

'Tell someone who gives a fuck!' I was still furious at the pain I had been forced to inflict and witness. 'The fucking government got us into this fucking mess, so the fucking government can fork out for a new fucking mattress!'

Our next job was a sports injury at the local football club. The transit, with its single blue light flashing, a parody of the real thing, was guided into the ground by a troop of scouts. As I climbed out of the front passenger seat I tried to emit a sense of confidence. 'Any of you lot got your first-aid badge?' I quipped. Several eager hands shot up, but when I saw the player's leg my smile faded. Gary too looked appalled and I wondered what would happen if we both threw up in unison. The footballer had broken his fibula, or was it his tibia? Whatever the bone, I knew it was broken because it had pierced his skin and the jagged end pointed upwards, a brilliant white against the mud and blood that covered the rest of his leg.

The man's grim silence spurred me on to be brave and professional, as I quickly twisted a large sling into a rough donut-shape and placed it gingerly over the protruding bone. Gary and I then tied his ankles and knees securely together with two more slings, before we got him to shuffle onto our rubbish stretcher. As four of his teammates lifted it up, Gary and I got into the back of the transit and guided it onto the newly converted mattress.

Because there was no room to sit near enough to have access to the wound, I found myself lying on my stomach along one of the benches in order to hold the donut gently in place as Gary drove slowly back over the rutted field. I remember looking back once or twice during the short journey to see large, silent tears rolling down the pale face at the other end of the transit floor. The words 'Fucking Thatcher' rolled like a mantra through my brain as I counted the slow minutes it took Gary to once more pull up at A&E.

Over the next few months our first-aid improved drastically – it had to – but I felt overwhelming relief when the strike ended.

The last job I did in Banbury as a uniformed WPC was also with Gary. We were en route to 'a violent domestic' in progress at the old people's home next door to the police station. Walking across the dried grass and open shrubbery that divided the two buildings, we were shown into the communal dining room by an agitated warden and we both burst into unprofessional laughter.

Two of the residents, Fred and Reg, who were eighty-two and eighty-four respectively, were stood facing each other across one of the small square dining tables. Each was pointing an ordinary table-knife at the other. Between wheezes (at one point Fred actually got out his inhaler and took a puff), they were shouting threats such as,

'Come on then if you think you're hard enough.'

'I could have you for breakfast, you piece of dog shit!'

Reg, the more verbally aggressive one, was hampered by needing the support of a walking frame, so Fred was able to keep shuffling around the table to keep out of his reach. Mind you, if he'd let go of the table, chances are Fred, too, would have fallen over. Suppressing my mirth as best I could, I turned to the warden and asked what the fight was over.

'Her,' she replied, pointing at a frail lady who was easily in her nineties. She sat proudly looking on as these two toy-boys fought over the right to sit next to her on the next minibus excursion into town, a mile away. Having removed their knives and all other ancillary cutlery from the table, we made them sit down and draw cards. It was agreed that ace-high would win the fair maiden.

It was around this time that my own romantic life was reignited. I started dating Mike; a married man and a fellow livery owner at the stables were I kept Mulberry. He was also a divisional commander in the Fire Service, with his office situated just across the car park from the police station.

Born in Birmingham, Mike's looks belonged to the Mediterranean; he'd tan in a passing patch of sunlight and had jet-black hair with a matching moustache. His eyes were the deepest brown with flecks of gold. We would regularly go out on hacks together, and it was on one of these that we shared our first kiss. Mike was the first man I could communicate with as an intellectual equal. I also found his rank very sexy; he was a powerful man within the Fire Service who wore his power with convivial ease. When I discussed work with him it was in a kind of emergency-service shorthand, and if I'd had a bad day he would either talk things through without judgment, or just let me be. He was also a man who had no expectation of me giving up my career to provide him with an heir – he already had two.

Mike and his wife had a fairly open marriage; she even encouraged the affair as it left her free to follow her own. However, when Mike and I got more serious, she turned nasty and one night Mike appeared on my doorstep with a bin-liner full of clothes and an upright piano. He moved in. It was not planned. Like my marriage to Brian, it just sort of happened, but I didn't mind. I would never be head-over-heels in love, but our relationship was slow-burning and satisfying; Mike became the nearest thing I ever got to a human soulmate.

CHAPTER 21

Life's Still a Riot

During basic training I'd been warned that female officers were their own worst enemy when it came to a career in the police; they kept leaving to have babies so no one took them seriously for specialisation or promotion. In the1980s the average career expectancy of female and ethnic officers was just four years, as opposed to the twenty-six (medical pension payable), or thirty-year careers of most white male officers. The statistical existence of this four-year rule meant that each of my probationer reviews and subsequent interviews was started with the same question – and it was always a male doing the asking.

'So WPC Foster/Clements, when are you planning to start a family?'

For the seven years I remained between husbands the question altered slightly to, 'When are you planning to re-marry?'

It was 1989, nearly five years to the day that I'd joined Thames Valley Police, when I found myself once more sitting opposite three very senior offices at headquarters. The same long, highly polished table still separated the made-its from the wannabes, but this time I was embarking on my first promotion board. I'd recently put in a formal request to be married and the first of two chief superintendents opened the interview with, 'So, PC Clements,' (the W had recently been dropped. Like our male colleagues we were now just police constables, as opposed to women first and police officers second. This change in title was not yet mirrored by a real change in attitude, and many forces added a tell-tale digit to female collar numbers so that those compiling duty sheets could still tell the men from the women). The chief-super continued, 'What about family?'

'They're in Somerset, Sir.'

'No, I mean when are you planning to start a family?'

'Thank you, Sir.'

'For what?' Sir was bemused.

'For winning me ten pounds... Sir.' His raised eyebrow asked the unvoiced question, and I could see I now had the undivided attention of the third member of the panel – the assistant chief constable.

'Ten pounds?' The ACC was intrigued.

'Yes, Sir, I bet the ten members of my shift a pound each that the first question I would be asked would be the same as I've been asked in every interview since joining – when I was planning to start a family.'

'Ah.' He looked suitably embarrassed.

My dander was up; polite, but up. 'I will answer as I have always answered, Sir. I've never had, I do not presently have, nor will I ever have, any intention of starting a family. Therefore, any financial commitment you make to my training will be amply repaid by a long and hopefully *fruitful* career.'

The ACC smiled at this rebuff, but his superintendents wore looks of reproach; they did not appreciate being faced down in front of their leader. I answered the questions that followed with an easy confidence, thriving as always on the pressure interviews created. At its conclusion the ACC asked me to mark myself out of ten for my performance on the board.

'Ten, Sir' I smiled, 'after all, it's a nice round number.'

He obviously agreed. I was promoted to sergeant on my first attempt.

Mike was now my fiancé. His divorce had been far harder than mine as he had two sons aged eleven and fourteen. He was waiting for me in the car park at headquarters and, as I walked towards him, stripping off my number one tunic, he produced a battery-operated fluffy pink pig, which he set off across the roof of his estate car. Its snuffling, snorting and twirling tail was a perfect end to a really good day. Looking back now, I wonder if he'd brought it on the assumption I'd need cheering up rather than as a celebration of my success – but that is an ungenerous (and perhaps rather paranoid) thought.

However, many female officers did not possess the defiance or resilience necessary to combat the constant undermining of their careers, and after a varying number of knockbacks they would often end up marrying a colleague and starting a family – thereby fulfilling the chicken and egg scenario that was the four-year rule. There was a lone exception to this rule when I first joined the job. She was the only WPS at the station who had joined after the Police Woman's Department was disbanded in 1976. Vicky was viewed as a dyke by the men and an emotional wreck by the women, but on one crossover shift I spent some time in her company. I learned she was an abused alcoholic struggling to get over what happened to her in her probation.

Like me, she had started on nights, but in the early hours of her first shift several of 'the lads' had put her through an initiation ceremony that constituted a clear criminal offence. Dragging her into the parade room, they had pulled open her shirt, pulled up her bra and rubber-stamped both her breasts with a Thames Valley Police property-store stamp. This was a serious sexual assault in anyone's eyes, except the shift and the shift supervisors – who refused to see it as anything other than 'a bit of fun'. Vicky had wanted to be a police officer her whole life and, on the surface, she shrugged off the assault. But it left strong emotional scars that she dealt with through alcohol and a series of unstable relationships.

I had been 'acting sergeant' for nearly a year when I was officially promoted to the rank. At the time I was seconded to the Home Office as a trainer at HMS Ganges in Suffolk – a regional centre for probationer training.

Immediately preceding this posting I had undergone fourteen weeks of hell at CPU, the Central Planning Unit in Harrogate, where we learnt about learning; the new-fangled student-centred type. The Police Training Facilitation course was run by inspectors who, having themselves undergone some sort of psychoanalytical process, were then released onto the would-be police trainers to wreak a mental havoc of their own.

The teaching of law by rote and the sitting of exams had been replaced with 'student-centered facilitation'. Instructors were now called trainers and they sent students away in small groups to find out about relevant laws for themselves. Students would then return to the classroom and give the rest of the class a visual-aid-heavy lesson on the subject. Trainers would allow the other students to ask questions and give feedback on their classmate's performance, before filling in any gaps or correcting mistakes.

It seemed to me that the trainers' course used self and peer feedback to dismantle a person's mental stability by creating a situation that encouraged self-doubt and self-loathing. Grown men and women were in tears on a weekly, if not daily basis and, as you can imagine, I railed and fought against this oppressive system of self-destruction. It was therefore suggested I was not up to the job, but I knew better.

During the last two weeks of training, we were sent out into live classrooms of real probationers, to put into practice what we had been taught so badly. I blossomed: top-box ticks all round. The technical tools we'd been taught: braining-storming, working in pairs, in cross-over and buzz groups, followed by self, peer and trainer feedback (always in that order), worked without any of the tears and tantrums thought necessary by CPU. There was just straightforward communication and a lot of laughter – the soft, round, good sort, not the judgmental, brittle-edged CPU kind. Lessons remained centred around the students, but in a supportive rather than destructive way. My students were never set up to fail like the trainers had been.

In every regional training centre, every fourteen weeks each pair of trainers were allocated up to twenty-five new recruits, ranging in age from eighteen to over forty. Shortly after my formal promotion I was paired with Sergeant Siobhan McCabe from Hertfordshire. It was the first time that the centre's management team had dared put two female trainers together and this 'experiment' had already caused raised eyebrows.

Ignoring the doomsday predictions of the odd dinosaur, Shevy and I were really looking forward to working together. We got on well, had the same sense of humour and made an effective 'good-cop bad-cop' duo when it came to discipline and welfare matters. I was tall, slim, with spiky hair and a hard stare that made me good at playing bad cop. Shevy was shorter, rounder, with soft curls and a big smile, whose natural default setting was good cop. But we both shared the same reaction to some of the recruits in our first class.

There was a higher than usual proportion of ex-squaddies amongst this intake, two of whom were over forty and had themselves held positions of ranks. On the first morning, as this group of ex-servicemen filed into the classroom, I watched their faces fall and harden, and heard their loud banter fade into silence as they realised that both their trainers were female. These squaddies obviously felt short-changed and made no attempt to hide their feelings as they milled about the room, glowering expressions now replacing previously excited animation.

Shevy and I came out of the glass-walled office and stared back. 'Sit down, gentlemen.' My command was delivered with an edge, which Shevy instinctively tried to soften.

'You too, ladies.' she smiled at the female recruits huddled near the door.

As Shevy and I watched the squaddies reluctantly take their seats, I continued to stare at them. I even inclined my head, slightly but overtly, and looked them up and down; appraising their physical appearance in much the same way I would look at a horse I was considering buying. The ex-servicemen stood out a mile with their number-one haircuts, boots already bulled (given a military high-gloss shine) and the meticulously ironed creases down the front of their shirts. Sitting with red-faced scowls, tattooed-arms crossed and anger flashing from eyes that bore into Shevy and me, they openly balked at the stripe-wearing females standing in front of them.

As we took our seats, it felt as though they were hoping their open hostility would make us run from the classroom in tears, pleading with the course inspector to give us back our male partners. But Siobhan and I did not cry, run or plead; instead we began to experience a quiet rage. We were, after all, in a position where we could squash these alpha-egos as easily as a tigress walking on ants. I had an appetite for the upcoming battle.

As Shevy and I kicked off the opening exercises, the atmosphere remained sullen, like lead-heavy air compressing into a thunderstorm. Something was going to break, but Shev and I were determined it would not be us. That afternoon, as the class lined up for its first life-saving session in the pool, we couldn't let the matter drop; the irritation the squaddies had created had to be scratched, exorcised, dealt with.

So Shevy and I walked up and down the poolside, casting our eyes down to the row of costumed male butts arrayed for our inspection. In stage whispers, we awarded marks out of ten for the tightness of each tush. Non-squaddies, too, suffered the fallout of our anger, but as I looked at the pale shoulders of the innocent, hunched in embarrassment, I viewed their discomfort as acceptable collateral damage – all was still not fair in sex equality.

I knew at the time that this response was less than professional, and it was the only time I ever indulged in sexual harassment – but by God I enjoyed the buzz. Of course it wasn't ever about sex; it was all about the power. Shevy and I had been given a rare opportunity in the wielding of so much control over so many mature males and, unlike Shevy, I revelled in the wielding.

The next morning, our elected class leader (who had replaced the nominated drill-pig), PC Matt Ash, asked to speak to Shevy and me in private.

'What's the problem, PC Ash?' My tone was hard, inflexible and emphasised his rank.

'Well, Sergeant,' Matt was standing to attention, I had not told him to stand at ease or asked him to sit, 'some of the lads are a bit worried.'

'About what?'

I wasn't going to give him an easy ride. My rage at their sexist behaviour had been cooled in the swimming pool, when I'd seen my payback written clearly in the discomfort on their faces, but it had not been entirely quenched.

Matt was not a man to beat about the bush. 'They are concerned that you and Sergeant McCabe appear more interested in the size and shape of their asses than any ability they may possess as police officers.'

'Welcome to our world, PC Ash.' My smile was almost a sneer. 'Sergeant McCabe and I have suffered that feeling for most of our careers.' I heard Shevy fidget at my side and could sense her reddening.

'Well then, Sergeant, with all due respect, you should know better.'

I sighed, and leaning against the edge of my office desk I studied my own bulled toecaps. Enough was enough. The buzz had been enjoyable but it was not acceptable and would not be repeated. I looked back up with a genuine smile on my face, 'You're quite right of course, Matt.' I indicated a chair, 'take a pew.'

Shevy and I talked through the issue with Matt, who quickly acknowledged that he and his fellow squaddies had not acted with the respect due our rank when they'd entered the classroom twenty-four hours earlier. While Shevy and I were willing to earn respect over time as individual supervisors, we were not prepared to have the sergeant's stripes dismissed out of hand because they were being worn by a female.

The conversation was continued with the rest of the class and in eight hours we reached a state of cooperation that would normally take an average class two weeks. We used the concerns raised to address important issues such as: the misuse of power, sexual harassment, behaviour breeding behaviour, the power of non-verbal communication and an individual's responsibility to address negative situations positively.

I then used Matt and Pete, another of the scowling-squaddies, to illustrate to the class how easy it was to abuse power. Telling Matt to stand with his back to Pete, I instructed them to get as close as possible. They were both clearly uncomfortable with this invasion of their personal space, but when I told Matt to bend down and touch his toes he visibly balked at the instruction. I merely repeated it.

'PC Ash, touch your toes!' and he did; both him and Pete turning bright red.

'Alright,' I relented, 'you can both sit down. So, why did I do that?'

'Revenge?' I loved Matt's honesty.

'No, it wasn't revenge – but if you didn't want to do it, why did you?'

'Because you told us to and you're a sergeant.'

'Did I *order* you to do it, Matt?'

He thought for a moment. 'No, you didn't.'

'So why did you do it?' He looked confused. 'You're right of course, it was because of these,' I said, tapping the metal chevrons on my lapels, 'When you're in uniform people will do things you tell them to just because of your uniform. If you tell someone to open the boot of their car they will probably do it without question, which is fine, but you need to be careful what you ask people to do *voluntarily*, because if you don't have the legal power to ask that question you could find yourself in very muddied waters.'

'Like if I was to make a complaint to the camp commandant?' Matt smiled at me.

'Exactly, Matt, but I chose you and Pete because I know you're big enough to see the point of the exercise.'

In less than twenty-four hours, without really trying too hard, Siobhan and I had totally undermined twelve male probationers: but by the end of the first ten weeks our class had bonded so well and achieved so much, that Siobhan and I were allowed to remain as partners for another four intakes.

The female recruits in this first class were a mixed bunch, too. One was gay, out and proud; while one was so far back in the closet she held a Narnian passport. A third was quickly nicknamed Mary Poppins; she was a goody two-shoes who never broke the law and loved Doris Day. I learnt valuable lessons from all three of these women.

On the first morning, when the scowling thundercloud of short-change still hung over the classroom, we ran a get-to-know-you exercise. The squaddies had herded together in the first half of the semi-circle of seats that now replaced the lines of desks, and I instructed this half to pair up with someone from the second half of the semi-circle. Using 5WH, they were to interview that person about how and why they came to be sitting in this classroom.

Matt was paired with Michelle, the lesbian officer who had been to Vegas to get married. She had also argued for, and been given, a police house. His introduction of her to the class was surprisingly subtle.

'This is Michelle. She's 23 and married to Rachel.'

Silence gripped the room. I don't think anyone could have told you what came after Matt's opening sentence. Some of the men turned red and looked at their shoes, others looked disappointed, while one or two of the good-looking ones eyed her as they might assess an upcoming assault course.

Nina also turned bright red. Nina was from Narnia. Because she did not wish to exit the closet, her home life remained a mystery that unfortunately brought a false ring to anything she said about it. She was caught out once or twice when she couldn't keep track of what she'd already told the class about her activities the previous weekend. Her classmates subconsciously lost trust in her and that was an important part of course life. This, in turn, made her not trust them and the situation quickly spiralled downwards.

Shevy and I tried to talk to her about being 'out of sync' with the class, but because she was not ready to openly acknowledge her sexuality, the group dynamic was too pressurised and after three weeks she resigned. Michelle confirmed that Nina was gay and in a long-term relationship, and she reassured Shevy and I that we'd done all that we could. I'm not so sure. I know that if I'd then had the equality training that I was to receive later, I might have been of more use to Nina.

Michelle however thrived, becoming Matt's unofficial number two. The confidence she needed to be openly gay in the police service at this time, carried through into everything she did. In class she rarely took things at face value. Shevy and I would set up practical scenarios that deliberately led the probationers down blind alleys, but Michelle rarely took the bait. She listened rather than assumed, she asked rather than told and she was as effective in the bar as she was the classroom.

'So, Michelle, how goes it?' It was her mid-term tutorial.

'Great, Sarge. Really enjoying it.'

'Any problems with the lads?'

'Nothing I can't handle. Got the usual bullshit about not having had a real man out of the way on the first night and they've behaved themselves ever since. Matt's been great.'

'And things alright at home, with Rachel?'

'Yeah, she's fine – looking forward to the dining-in and passing-out parade.'

'Good for her,' I said.

'Good for you,' I thought, as I imagined the looks on the faces of some managers as Michelle and her wife twirled around the dance floor together. But Michelle would not care, her classmates would not care, and Shevy and I just appreciated her ground-breaking confidence.

But not everyone was as inclusive towards gay colleagues as my class, and a gay female inspector regularly had offensive items such as used condoms and hard porn deposited in her pigeonhole. I became aware of this harassment only because I once found her crying in the staff loos. I told her to report the matter but, between embarrassed smiles, she told me that she was fairly certain that one of our bosses was the perpetrator.

Like Michelle, female recruit Mary Poppins also oozed confidence; but it was a 1950s housewife sort – born from sweet naivety and a trouble-free small-town upbringing. This clash of character and chosen career was to bring great humour to the classroom when Shevy opened another first-day exercise.

'Put your hand up if you have never broken the law.'

With the exception of two of the ex-squaddies everyone raised their hand.

'That includes any juvenile cautions,' I added, three more hands went down, 'and any undetected shoplifting as a kid.'

Five more hands went down.

'It also includes parking tickets and speeding fines,' Shevy chipped in.

The last hands went down – all except Mary's. She sat in solitary splendour, her right arm raised high and straight.

'So, Mary, you've never broken a speed limit?' I clarified.

'No, Sergeant.'

'Not even a thirty-mile an hour one?'

'Especially not a thirty one – they're all important but that's the *most* important.' Mary's observation was not as irritating as it sounded.

'It's true, Sarge.' Matt confirmed. 'I followed her here on Sunday, thirty miles an hour the whole way, the whole eight miles from the A-road.'

The class was to take note of Matt's observations and there was always a rush on Friday afternoon to get out of the front gates before Mary Poppins and her little red Ford Fiesta. But Miss Poppins' open enthusiasm for knowledge, for new experiences and for life in general, quickly endeared her to the class.

In the first week we covered the Town and Police Clauses Act, and in particular obscene language.

'So who can tell me the two words that will always constitute an offence under this legislation?' I asked.

Everyone's hand shot up, eager to swear at the sergeant; everyone's, that is, except Mary's. Knowing she'd have the answer, I zoomed in on her closed, quiet face.

'Mary! Can you please give me one of the words?'

'I'd rather not, Sergeant.'

'Why?'

'Well I wasn't brought up to be a potty mouth.'

The rest of the class roared with laughter but I didn't join in. Mary had tensed into an ethereal-ramrod, pale and sweating but determined not to give in.

'The thing is, Mary, there are certain times in this job when you will have to use these words and use them publicly. Can anyone think of one?'

'In court, Sarge,' Matt jumped in 'if someone uses them in their reply to caution, you'll have to stand in the witness box and repeat their reply to the court.'

'A good example, Matt. So, Mary – let's have one of them.'

Mary took a deep breath but the 'fu' sound was strangled to death behind clenched teeth. Shuffling to edge of her seat she tried again. 'Fu … fu.' Again the sound died. By now the whole class was leaning forward in their own chairs, willing Mary to get the word out into the open. Sensing this support, Mary gripped the edge of her seat and made one final effort. 'Fu … fu … cunt!' The word exploded from her delicate mouth with the force of projectile vomit and the whole class burst into a rolling laughter that bounced from the walls and met itself coming back. Mary joined in, utter relief washing the tension from her body as she leant back in her chair; it had been a difficult birth.

'So, Matt.' I fought to regain control, 'what's the second word?'

'Fuck knows, Sarge.'

Mary continued to develop her own unique policing style. At the end of ten weeks the recruits were sent back to their forces to be tutored for two weeks on the streets, before returning to the training centre for two more weeks' consolidation on their real-life experiences. Exams had been replaced with continual assessment via PDP's (personal development profiles) and, according to Mary's, her two weeks on the streets had been as much of an eye-opener for her tutor as it had been for Mary.

On day one, Mary and her tutor were on foot patrol when they came across a stationary bus with its hazard lights flashing. This was a signal that the driver was having problems and as Mary and her tutor boarded the bus they could hear legally obscene language floating down from the top deck. Before her tutor could stop her, Mary had flown up the stairs and marched to the rear of the bus, where a skinhead was sitting with his booted feet resting on the upholstered seats.

By the time the tutor's head emerged from the stairwell, Mary had apparently swept the lad's feet from the seat with the immortal words, 'What would your mother say if she heard that potty mouth?' Mary then assaulted the skinhead by clipping him round his studded ear and ordering, 'Off this bus now! People don't want to hear that kind of language!' The tutor watched mesmerised as the youth walked sullenly towards him, head down. He got off the bus without a word; stunned by his confrontation with Doris Day in uniform.

Public order training was now a prerequisite for new recruits, and at the end of the second period of training the whole intake at HMS Ganges underwent a simulated large-scale public order exercise, with the newest intake acting as the rioters. Ganges was an excellent location for this sort of exercise, as there were many large derelict buildings surviving from its days as a naval-cadet training establishment.

I was acting as the safety officer and I had just supervised the fourteen-week probationers' progress up a staircase. They'd been pelted with wooden blocks, hurled enthusiastically by the new intake. On reaching the top of the stairs, Inspector Jim Boyle had given the probationers a five-minute debriefing and, in order to hear his words of wisdom, the students had raised the visors on their riot helmets – training schools did not run to radio earpieces. As the exercise resumed, I noticed that one of the students had failed to pull his visor back down, and as he made his way along the corridor towards me I yelled at him.

'Simpson, get that fucking visor down!'

But the rioters, only eight feet in front of the officers at this stage, were making too much noise. So I pushed my own visor up to make myself heard as I repeated the shouted order. It was at this exact moment that the rioters saw a break in the shield wall coming towards them, and running at it, they grabbed one of the six-foot plastic shields and threw it backwards like an oversized Frisbee. The edge of it caught me squarely on the bridge of my nose. There was blood everywhere and I only just managed to blow my whistle before I collapsed down the nearest wall into a crouching position, desperately trying not to pass out from the pain. The whistle was a signal for everyone to stand absolutely still.

'Who the fuck's blown that whistle?' Jim's strong Scottish accent flew along the now-silent corridor. Before his recent promotion to course inspector, Jim had replaced Shevy as my class running mate.

'It's Sergeant Clements, Sir!' shouted the rioter nearest to me.

'Why's she blown it?'

'It's probably got something to do with the blood, Sir.' The shouted reply had a sardonic edge to it.

'Christ!' said Jim, as he pushed his way through the probationers and saw me sitting on the floor, pinching my nose against the unceasing flow. 'Right, which one of you wants to practise first-aid?' he asked.

Before I was swamped by an army of both uniform and non-uniformed volunteers, I managed to stand and shake off all offers of help.

'Not bloody likely! I trained you buggers. I know just how bad you are.' I managed to make it, unaided, to the cold tap of the nearest loo.

'Tough lesson?' asked the commandant as I passed him on the stairs.

Having cleaned myself up and stopped the bleeding by plugging both nostrils with wet toilet paper and then cotton wool, I was taken to hospital for an x-ray. The bad news was I had indeed broken my nose, but the good news was that the shield edge had hit cleanly and the break would mend on its own. However, I quickly developed two impressive black eyes, and my peers once more began calling me Chi Chi.

This little incident had taken place on a Thursday afternoon. When Mike came to pick me up on Friday lunchtime his first reaction was expected.

'What the fuck?' He traced the edge of my bruises with the tip of his index finger.

'Accident with a riot shield.' My reassuring smile crinkled the swollen skin around my eyes. His own eyes shifted from the real concern of a fiancé to the mock condemnation of a senior officer.

'So what happened?' His tone was stern, official.

'I was safety officer for the full-scale riot ...'

Mike pretended incredulity. 'Seriously? You as safety officer – whose idea was that?'

I told him what had happened.

'Have your lot heard of health and safety?' he demanded.

'Omelettes and eggs,' I retorted, and gave him my best Paddington Bear stare, but looking like a panda it just made him laugh out loud.

Mike was picking me up because we were spending the weekend in Northumberland; where he was to undergo some informal interviews regarding a possible promotional move to that brigade. The brigade's rather old-fashioned and conservative powers-that-be, had specifically asked that he bring 'his partner' along, for what I presumed would be some informal vetting. His partner now looked as though she had done ten rounds with Mike Tyson, but Mike remained surprisingly philosophical.

'They might as well see the real you,' he winked.

I was to have the last laugh, however. That night we found ourselves in a small out-of-the-way country pub, enjoying a bar meal. I kept getting concerned looks from the locals and when Mike got up to go to the loo, two of the larger ones followed him. Mike was not tall, and they looked like bodyguards protecting some small-time crook off to do a dodgy deal.

Mike had once tried to join the police himself, but had been refused entry by the sergeant at the West Midlands recruitment centre in Birmingham. He'd taken one look at the expectant teenager and declared,

'Sorry son, can't take you on account of your eyes.'

'There's nothing wrong with my eyes,' Mike had declared. 'I've got twenty-twenty vision.'

'That's as maybe,' the sergeant was adamant, 'but they're too close to the ground. Fuck off and join the fire service – they'll take anyone.'

Mike followed this advice and decades later he became a chief fire officer. He also received the Queen's Fire Service Medal for putting out her house fire, as he was the senior officer onsite at the time the fire at Windsor Castle was brought under control. As he handed the site back to the acting chief officer the next morning, he was met by a barrage of national and international media. Exhausted from the most demanding night of his life, he was dragged into the nearest white van, which happened to belong to BBC radio. Asked why the Queen had been allowed to live in a building that did not possess a fire prevention system, Mike's tired reply had been succinct.

'You've heard the expression an Englishman's home is his castle I suppose?'

Mike now found himself facing similarly difficult questions, as he stood at a urinal in a Northumberland pub flanked by two guys who stood head and shoulders above him. 'Do you know how hard it is to pee in those circumstances?' he asked me a few minutes later.

As Mike was being followed into the loo, a third man had come and sat down next to me. 'What's a nice girl like you doing with a git like him?' he asked, indicating Mike's disappearing back.

'Sorry?'

'We don't hold with wife-beating in these parts.'

'Oh you mean these?' I pointed to my forgotten black eyes. 'Mike didn't do this,' I smiled, touched by the concern of a complete stranger.

'So what happened?' The stranger was determined to get a satisfactory explanation.

'You wouldn't believe me if I told you.'

'Try me.'

(I thought, I could have done with you on Banbury CID.) I told him the story and he shook his head in disbelief.

'They shouldn't allow it. It's not right allowing a lass to be hurt like that.'

Mike's inquisitors clearly did not believe him either, and he was 'escorted' back to our table so that I could verify the facts. Who says that chivalry is dead?

Mile wasn't offered the job in Northumberland, but the following spring, Shevy formed part of the guard of honour at our wedding. Four female sergeants in number-one uniforms held aloft four long riot batons decorated with white ribbons. They formed an arch with the four ceremonial silver axes being held aloft by four firefighters in dress uniforms.

There was many things wrong with my second wedding day. My dad had died unexpectedly from a heart attack three weeks before and it was my uncle Eric who walked me up the aisle. A large portion of my mum's family had boycotted the wedding because I'd refused to invite a cousin who had sexually assaulted another relative at a previous family wedding. He'd suffered a serious head injury as a teenager and had no sexual inhibitions, and some of my aunts thought his behaviour should be ignored. My sister-in-law had given birth to her second daughter a month before the wedding and my mother's attention was focused firmly on her new granddaughter rather than her daughter; added to which, two of the male guard of honour weren't on speaking terms.

But none of this mattered because Mike was there, and my future life with him was all I really cared about. This time I'd got it right, this time it wasn't about the day, it was about the life that came after the day.

CHAPTER 22

Face Off

My honeymoon period as a new sergeant had come to an end and, after my real honeymoon, I returned to 'active' supervisory life on the streets of Banbury – a busy market town with a rapidly expanding population who worked in shiny new industrial units and lived on yellow-brick housing estates. It was to be a big change from training school as I found myself landed with the shift from hell, the support of another newly promoted sergeant and a graduate entry inspector.

Graduate-entries were recruits who had a university education, which was supposed to propel them to the rank of superintendent within ten years of joining the police. In practice, it meant that after their probation they would spend a further two years working their way through pre-destined specialities such as CID, drug squad and various staff-officer roles, before being moved quickly through the lower ranks. This gave the bad ones just enough time to cause maximum damage before they were moved to the next department, leaving us lesser mortals to clear up the mess.

I remember seeing a postcard pinned to the wall of a regular inspector's office. It carried the printed declaration, *Chaos, Panic and Disaster! My work here is done!.* It had been given a hand-written title – *Graduate Recruits.* I once walked in on this same inspector crying at his desk. His wife had just phoned to tell him that their cat had died. I would have followed that inspector anywhere and done anything for him. He cared about the job, not his career, and he cared about his people. I'm sure there were some excellent graduate-entry officers, but the few I actually worked under never inspired me. They were usually followed by their colleagues in the same way a parent follows a toddler, with a sense of amused curiosity and mild panic.

I had a feeling that Hedgehog would fall into this group. Hedge's nickname related to his very short spiky haircut. He also possessed a first-class honours degree in chemistry from Oxford and his graduate-entry status ensured that he was always picked first. So it was Hedge who was awarded the honour of the first recruit practical training exercise, back at Ryton. He was sent to a 'disturbance' in the training centre's shop and on his arrival was confronted by two instructors, acting as the shopkeeper and a customer. They were in the middle of a very heated argument and I presumed that Hedge was there to make an arrest for 'breach of the peace', a subject we had covered that morning. Hedge, however, didn't seem to grasp this aspect of the scenario and while the rest of the class stood around in a semi-circle watching, he tried to make himself heard.

Lesson one – stamp your authority on the situation. It took Hedge nearly five minutes to achieve this and I suspect it only happened then because the two instructors were getting bored shouting at each other.

Lesson two – establish the facts. Apparently, the customer was trying to return new boots that didn't fit, but because he'd worn them outside and scuffed the soles, the shopkeeper was not prepared to make an exchange or refund on the boots. This took poor Hedge another five minutes to establish and by now a persistent drizzle had settled on the students and the class-instructor, observing from outside the shop.

Lesson three – know the law. The shopkeeper had called the police for assistance in ejecting an argumentative customer and Hedgehog was supposed to ask the man to leave quietly, threatening to arrest him, in order to prevent a breach of the peace, if he didn't. This proved a little too straightforward for our graduate entry.

Hedge first took the side of the shopkeeper and then the customer, before returning to the shopkeeper's view of things. This to-ing and fro-ing kept us going for another ten minutes and, as we approached the twenty-minute mark, the instructor was about to call a halt to proceedings, when Hedge produced his coup de grace.

'What size are the boots?' he asked the instructor-customer.

'Tens, why?'

'Well, I'm a ten,' said Hedge. 'If they fit me, I'll give you a tenner for them.'

In Banbury, my fellow sergeant was an ex-detective who wanted to remain *one of the boys* rather than take on the responsibilities of the rank. Of the eight officers that made up the shift, the two probationers proved to be the most productive and reliable. Of the others, one old sweat had made just one arrest in two years and only then because someone handed themselves in at the front counter and the arrest could not be avoided. Another shift member was seen to drive in the opposite direction to a ten-nine shout on more than one occasion, and when I tackled him about this fact he remained defiant.'I've done my share of rolling around on the ground.' Meanwhile, his best mate on shift was a wife-beater and another officer was having an affair with the wife of a firefighter, which twice resulted in the shift having to break up a fight in the station's car park.

An example of the 'exemplary' police work undertaken by my new shift was the arrest of a husband for a breach of the peace following a violent domestic. He came into custody with tiny little v-shaped wounds all over his face, which from a distance looked like measles. Now, while I accept the fact that domestic offenders are statistically 'he', when the arresting officer gave me the facts surrounding this arrest, I refused the man's detention and instructed the jailer to make him a cup of tea. I then ordered the arresting officers to drive their ex-prisoner home and bring in his wife, Cynthia.

Cynthia was a giantess of a woman; twenty-five stone was a conservative estimate amongst the troops. I knew she was married but I had never seen her hubby, whereas Cynthia had been quite a regular in her day – mostly for assaults on other women after a night of alcohol-fuelled bingo.

Following a report of a violent domestic in the street outside Cynthia's house, my A-Team found Cynthia in a drunken rage, straddling her husband on the pavement and stabbing at his face with a potato peeler. Following stereotypes rather than common sense, the officers had dragged Cynthia off her husband and promptly arrested him – the offence? Being the male in a domestic.

My last memory of Banbury was walking back from my first court appearance as a sergeant. As I made my way back to the duties of the custody block, I was still feeling quietly proud of the large silver chevrons carefully sewn onto the sleeves of my tunic. My self-satisfied musings were interrupted by an old bloke in a carefully mended cloth cap.

'Here,' he said, pointing at my chevrons with his walking stick. 'You're a sergeant!'

'That's right.' The internal smugness leaked through to a

smile.

'But you're a girl.'

'True.' I confirmed. My radio interrupted the old man's astute observations.

'Sergeant Clement-Green can you return to the station immediately, you have an incoming prisoner.'

As the custody sergeant it was my job to assess the initial evidence for each prisoner's arrest, and if I felt it was sufficient I would authorise that prisoner's detention, becoming personally liable for that individual's welfare under PACE. At this time it was also up to the custody sergeant to decide if there was sufficient evidence to charge and what charges would be the most appropriate in the circumstances. I would often have to argue my chosen path, and the question of bail or bail conditions, with defence solicitors. All in all it was a very important and highly responsible job. I pointed to my radio and apologised to the old man.

'Sorry, I have to get back.'

He nodded and waved me on. 'Aye love, you get off – 'spcct that prisoner will be wanting his dinner.'

Mike got his promotion and moved from Oxfordshire to Royal Berkshire Fire and Rescue as their assistant chief officer. I was heartily relieved when TVP obligingly moved me from Banbury to Reading, but I was to find myself jumping out of the frying pan and into the fire.

I'll call my two fellow patrol sergeants Bob and Terry, although I quickly came to regard them as Tom and Jerry. Terry was tall, with a ghostly complexion; his pale, pinched faced was an external expression of an internal nastiness. Bob was gnome-like – he had the beard but was missing the fishing rod. Tom and Jerry spent their time fighting and point-scoring against one another while I was pushed into the role of Spike, the bad-tempered bulldog who'd have a go at both of them given the chance.

It is a hard thing establishing your 'street-cred' with a new shift in a busy city you've not policed before. Just finding the right location on a blue light was difficult enough, without your operational decisions being continually questioned and then surreptitiously cleared with the male sergeants. But I kept my head down and bit my tongue for as long as possible.

Then one day I was approached by several females from the shift, which resulted in Spike breaking free from the leash and going on the rampage. Storming into the sergeant's office I confronted Terry head on. 'I've just been informed that females aren't allowed in response vehicles – is that correct?'

'Yep. No splits in RV's.' Terry didn't even look up from the next week's duty sheets spread across his desk. Bob had the decency to blush, but Terry kept scribbling. I'd never heard the word split before, but I knew it wasn't a compliment.

'Split?' I asked.

Bob grabbed his crotch. 'It's Terry's way of describing the main difference between males and females – a lack of balls – literally and metaphorically.'

I was too new to have noticed that Terry always took it upon himself to do the duty sheets, which specified what patrol car or beat was given to each shift member. Two of the pandas were designated response vehicles; they were not tied to patrolling set areas and their job was to provide immediate back-up to any situation in any part of the city. It was a prestigious posting and one that was apparently only ever filled by males aiming for Support Group.

As Terry got up from behind his desk and started to stroll

towards the noticeboard that displayed the duty sheets, I could feel my face forming into a snarl. I walked slowly up to him and we stood eyeball to eyeball, Terry blandly trying to stare down my fury.

'If anyone's a cunt round here Terry, it's you – you chauvinistic bastard.' I spat the words out as I began to back the lanky git up against some metal filing cabinets. I didn't care about the open door and the officers I could sense loitering outside in the corridor. 'If I ever hear you use that disgusting description again, you'll be at headquarters answering a formal grievance so fast your fucking size twelves won't touch!' Terry stared at me, silently assessing whether he dare call my bluff. He decided against it.

When I'd cooled down a little, I checked the duties of the other shifts, which confirmed they all crewed experienced female officers in their RVs – ours was the only shift that didn't. 'Not on my watch' I thought, and I returned to the fray. As I walked into the canteen, (Terry spent a lot of time in the canteen), he made a pre-emptive statement,

'It's a shift rule, not a station rule. All RV officers have to be PSU trained.'

'That's bollocks. You've crewed male probationers and their tutors in RVs rather than experienced females.' Terry shrugged off my research and continued stuffing his face.

I went in search of the shift inspector. I actually liked Inspector Wilson; he was something of a paradox. George was a gentle man with a hard edge. The hard edge had been honed on Support Group, but CID was his natural habitat; where his soft Irish lilt could charm the birds from the trees and confessions from the hardened criminal. More at home in an interview room than a parade room, he was being forced to sit out a short spell back in uniform before he'd be allowed to return home as a DI.

'Well, Chris, it's not a rule as such, but it's considered best practice.'

'By who?' My question was delivered as a slap and the inspector floundered slightly. I pushed my advantage. 'You do realise that this *shift policy*,' my emphasis redirecting any blame to the shiny new silver pips on his shoulders, 'is a direct breach of equal opportunity legislation?' I wasn't sure that it was, I was yet to undergo Equal Opportunities training, but the inspector was less sure than me.

'Okay, okay. Tell Terry to make sure the whoopsies get their fair share of RV work.'

'The who?' My voice was ice-cold.

'The female officers – now get off your soapbox and make a brew.' He gave me a smile that was genuinely apologetic.

'Make your own fucking tea, Guv. I've got police work to do.'

Terry did as the inspector ordered. The following set of nights he crewed both response vehicles with two women and then sat back in a cloud of self-satisfied smugness, waiting for the wheel to fall off. When it didn't, I tried to persuade him that this 'all or nothing' approach was as stupid as his sexist crewing had been unfair.

'Terry, crewmates, like the shift as a whole, have to work as a team and an effective team needs to balance its assets on individual talents and experience, not just the sex of the officer.' Terry snorted. 'There was a female officer in Oxford, five foot nothing and looked like she'd blow away in a strong wind. But what she lacked in physical presence she more than made up for in quick thinking. While off duty, she managed to bluff a wanted armed robber into taking her on a date and then took some of her workmates along.'

Terry remained unconvinced. 'That sort of crap may work once...'

'It only has to work once ...'

'But when push comes to shove, I'd rather have a van full of blokes than a van full of girlies, it's as simple as that.'

'But how often does push really come to shove, Terry? Christ, now we've got pepper-spray, when push comes to shove we just gas the toe-rags from three feet away!'

Terry was looking out of the office window as I continued with my uphill struggle to convince him of the value of the female officers. It was a battle that raged on and I not sure it was one I ever won with this particular officer.

One bright and sunny Saturday, at the start of the football season, I was scheduled to lead ten of the shift on the policing of a trade union march. As the demonstrators quietly organised themselves and their placards in a meadow by the river Thames, radio traffic highlighted that the rest of the shift was already having problems with the gathering football supporters. It was the annual grudge match between Reading and Swansea and the record of past violence meant all leave and rest days had been cancelled. No one was sure when or why the grudge had started, but some put it down to the ancient English-Welsh feud.

As my protest march set off, the first ten-nine shout went up from just outside the football ground. During a lull in the resulting radio traffic, I queried if I and my officers should abandon the peaceful marchers and make for the football ground instead, but I was ordered to continue escorting the demo until it reached its destination. This took approximately forty minutes, and all the time I was monitoring reported fights in and around the football ground and railway station.

There were further ten-nines and several calls for ambulances. The match itself had already been abandoned. As soon as the majority of marchers had entered Transport House for their rally, I commandeered a passing bus.

Arriving at the ground, I radioed our presence and we were sent straight in. I was told to report to Inspector Wilson at the 'away' end and on entering the ground I saw four mounted officers on the pitch. The noise and excitement ensured that the horses were compensating the groundsmen for the damage their hooves were causing by leaving plenty of free fertiliser. Several dog handlers were being hauled around by their over-excited partners and, in an effort to stop the pitch becoming the venue for a full-scale battle, rows of patrol and PSU officers were standing between the sidelines and stands.

The ten officers in my unit had already fastened the chin straps on their helmets and bowlers, and drawn their batons, but we had no public order gear and, due to the sunshine, were in shirt-sleeves. As we made our way over to our shift inspector, I was surprised to see him just standing, focusing on something on the ground rather than the riot going on around him. He was completely ignoring the shouting fans trying to scale the eight-foot mesh fence that was all that stood between them and their avowed enemy.

Without thinking, I started to push these fans off the top of the fence and back into the stands. The officers behind me followed suit and where a fan was particularly obtuse about getting down off the fence, my baton made contact with their fingers. As I reached the inspector, a great shout went up from the corner nearest to him and the fans surged forward, forming a crush against the chain-link fence.

Grainy, colour-faded telly pictures of Hillsborough flashed

through my mind; the images were reinforced when I saw what Inspector Wilson had been focused on. Two paramedics were working on a Swansea fan lying near the inspector's feet. I recognised one of them as Shane, a lodger at a local farm where I now kept Mulberry.

'Hi, Shay, what's up?' I asked.

Looking up, he took a second to recognise me, then he grinned. 'Bloke's had an epileptic fit.' He ducked as a fifty-pence piece with sharpened corners just missed his unprotected head. 'That lot,' he nodded at the crush of rabid Swansea fans, 'think your lot have killed him.' We then both leant in opposite directions as a half-full can of coke flew between us.

'Right, Guv,' I said, turning to Inspector Wilson. 'What's the plan?'

'Plan?' He looked up and seemed to register the fans for the first time. 'Containment, I suppose. Keep the bastards off the fence. You two,' he pointed at two officers with the luxury of full riot gear and short shields, 'cover these paramedics back to the ambulance.'

I watched Shay and his partner stretcher off the unconscious fan, while two police officers shielded them from the missiles being thrown by his so-called friends. Striding over to the crush at the corner of the fence, I shouted to the fans.

'Your mate's ok. He's had an epileptic fit that's all – he'll be fine.'

If they heard me they didn't seem convinced, and two more started to scale the fence. As their fingers wrapped themselves around the smooth pole at the top, I hit them – hard. Unlike Hillsborough, the crush at the fence was of their own making; the fans had plenty of room to move backwards. As I walked up and down the fence line I continued to mete out the same punishment to any would-be invaders and pretty soon my stretch of fence was clear of climbers. Other officers, however, were a little more reserved in their use of the baton and in these places the fans congregated and started to pull at the fence, rocking it back and forth in an effort to loosen it from its mountings. It was at this point that Gold Command decided to send in the dogs.

'Cry "Havoc", and let slip the dogs of war!' My favourite Shakespearian line came to life in front of my eyes, and my lesson from the Downtown Manhattan night club flooded back. I took care to keep my uniform well clear of their snapping jaws. Gradually, order was restored. Trained shield parties were sent into the terraces to begin clearing them a section at a time and my squad was redeployed to a road junction outside the ground, where we were at last issued with PSU overalls, helmets, gloves and shin-pads. We were then instructed to keep the Swansea fans moving back towards the train station in the town centre, while the home fans were channelled in the opposite direction. As I was pulling down my visor, two Swansea fans walked past, one nursing an injury to his right hand.

'Did you get her number, mate? You could sue you know, get a fortune for a broken finger, you would.'

'Nah, but keep your eyes peeled. If I see her again, I'll break more than her bloody fingers.'

My smile behind the visor was smug.

I eventually got off duty around midnight and when I arrived home, Mike was waiting up.

'Are you alright? I've been worried sick! Why didn't you phone?'

'What do you mean?'

'I saw Shay at the stables. He told me he saw you in the

middle of a full-scale riot at the football.'

'Yeah, I'm knackered. Put the kettle on and I'll fill you in. How's Mulberry?'

One of the great things about being a police officer is that you've never seen it all. I had to wait over six years for my first murder scene. Hard to imagine if you're a fan of Inspector Morse, but murder was not an everyday occurrence, even in Oxford. I'd been a patrol sergeant in Reading for just over a year when I found myself standing over the body of a beautiful young woman. She was lying on her back covered in a vast amount of blood from several stab wounds, but it was her open eyes, staring out at the breaking dawn, that proclaimed her death so clearly – that and the bright red gash that had once been her throat.

Andy had been called out from an early-turn briefing to check on an unconscious drunk. A neighbour, on drawing back her bedroom curtains, had seen the girl lying fast asleep on the tiny patio of an overgrown and neglected back garden, which belonged to the bedsits of the four-storey terrace next door. Gaining no response from any of the doorbells, Andy had gone down the alley running between each pair of properties and had climbed over the locked wooden gate into the relevant garden. He was an experienced officer and he did everything right. After turning the woman over, it was obvious she was well beyond any type of first aid, so he radioed for a supervisor. Then, touching nothing, he'd retraced his steps, unlocked the wooden gate and awaited my arrival.

I followed Andy's example, getting to the body via his initial route and once there quickly formed the same opinion; we had a murder scene to preserve. However, her blood, although already darkening as it dried, was still seeping and wet at the source of some of the wounds. 'She can't have been dead very long,' I said, looking at the pooling blood. 'Given this closed location, my money's on some sort of domestic.' It was a probability rather than a possibility. 'The other person could still be in the building, injured. We'd better check.'

Andy turned pale, but nodded his understanding. I had come a long way in seven years and before undertaking the check, I radioed Control, updating them on the circumstances and ordering the kick-start of the murder circus. Then I slowly pulled opened the door that loomed above the girl's body. It swung open easily. Behind it, a flight of narrow uncarpeted stairs rose at a steep angle to a tiny landing and another door. Using my elbow I pushed on the auto-timer to the single unshaded bulb at the top of the stairs, its dull glow illuminated trails of blood down both walls.

Andy trod exactly where I trod as we both avoided touching the walls. At the top, the second door was also ajar and I slowly pulled it open, using the side of my index finger. There was more blood on the inside panel. Opening the door wider with the edge of my foot, Andy and I flicked open our extendable metal batons and crept into the tiny bedsit. It was fairly obvious that no one could hide in such a small, cluttered space, but it was equally obvious that there had been some sort of fight. Chairs were overturned and surfaces had been swept clear, the contents strewn across the floor. I told Andy to stay put and carefully picked my way across the tiny space to the only other door. Opening it, I found the world's smallest bathroom. It, too, was empty.

Retracing our steps, we made our way back outside as we heard the first sirens. Why people feel obliged to use blues and twos to get to a dead body is beyond me – too much telly I suspect. I'd made a mental note of what looked like the murder weapon, a blood-encrusted bread-knife lying on the kitchen floor beside an overturned chair. What was odd, was the number of smaller knives scattered about the same area and also covered with blood.

CID barely had time to dust off their overtime forms before SOCO (Scene of Crime Officers) and the pathologist had written the job off as a suicide. Apparently, the only blood and fingerprints on all of the knives were those of the girl herself. The angle of the wounds, even that dreadful gash to the throat, showed they were all self-inflicted, and the pattern of the blood splatters confirmed this conclusion. The large smears of blood down either side of the stairwell had been caused when the dying girl had staggered against the bedsit door, which opened out. She'd then fallen down the stairs, gathering enough speed and force as she went that her weight had pushed the second door open and carried her dead body onto the tiny patio. But it was the tiny spots of blood inside a closed kitchen table draw that provided the icing on the SOCO cake, as they pieced together this girl's tragic death.

The woman was being treated for clinical depression and although she'd tried several times in the past to take her own life, there were no institutional beds available and she was being cared for in the community. She had started this last, successful, attempt by trying to cut her wrists with one of the smaller vegetable knives, but her cuts were too small and in the wrong direction – horizontal as opposed to the more effective vertical incisions. With her wrists now dripping blood, she had opened a kitchen draw to get the bread-knife and, in a moment of tidiness amidst the chaos that reminded me of Andrew Little's neat rail-side death, she'd closed the draw again before trying to cut her throat with the bread-knife. But its serrated edge had made this gruesome task too difficult, and in an act of final desperation she'd stabbed herself several times with a filleting knife. This thin and deadly blade had eventually pierced her heart. As she fell against the door she'd dropped the knife, before rolling down the stairs and out into the fresh air of the garden... only by then her lungs had ceased working.

What despair this young woman must have felt, and what a violent way to choose to leave it all behind. But as her psychiatrist told the inquest, 'Choice is not something such people feel they have.'

CHAPTER 23

Not All Gay Men Mince

Despite my early stand against Terry's overt type of sexism, I was still blind to the covert. During one early turn the whole shift had been involved in the containment, search for and arrest of a burglar who'd been operating for several weeks on the university campus. It had been an effective team effort and I was glowing with pride in a job well done. I had been the first supervisor on scene and no one had tried to take over or question any of my decisions.

I shouted to Penny to hold the lift. She'd been the arresting officer and we were on our way to the canteen to celebrate with a full-scale fry-up. As the metal doors were sliding shut, a podgy hand appeared and they were once more slid open with a silent authority. The station's senior operational officer joined us, acknowledging our presence with 'Ladies', but keeping his back to us. 'I understand the lads did well this morning.' He addressed the lift doors. 'A good arrest, tell the lads well done.'

The lift doors opened again and the superintendent exited; you could see why he was podgy; we'd gone up one floor.

'Well, that's fucking brilliant!' Penny was furious.

'What?' I was genuinely bewildered by her sudden change in mood.

'That idiot's on my CID board next week and as far as he's concerned women don't exist. Ladies! I'll give him fucking *ladies.* The fact that you organised this morning and I actually made the arrest has totally bypassed that chauvinistic dinosaur!'

'It's only an expression. We're included when he says *lads.*' I wanted to reassure her and return to our celebrations, but Penny would have none of it.

'I don't want to be *included*! I don't want to be *an honorary bloke*! I want to be recognised as the individual I am – the one that actually nicked that burglar this morning!' She had a point, but it was a point I was yet to get to grips with; the subtle art of using language and labels to undermine. In the same way WPC had put my gender before my role for the first five years of my service, the superintendent's use of the words 'lads' allowed him to subconsciously ignore twenty-five per cent of his workforce. And this mattered when one of that twenty-five was sitting before him on any type of specialisation or promotional board.

We had come a long way in the twelve years I'd been with TVP. My original soft, white-topped hat had been replaced with a black bowler that offered the same degree of protection as a helmet. My extra-short truncheon, designed to fit into the issue handbag, had been replaced with a full-sized one when we were given permission to wear trousers on duty; although we still had to put up with baggie crutches for another few years before the trousers were tailored to the female form. All police constables now wore white shirts, not just the girlies and senior officers, and female officers no longer had to try and pick up a police motorcycle if they wanted to join Traffic. Although you could spend a whole career in Traffic without ever getting on a bike, in the past females wanting to join the department would be asked to lift an 1100cc bike that had been left on its side on the ground. Most men would struggle to do this, but it kept the women out of Traffic for many years

Headquarters was building on this equality of equipment by creating an equal opportunities course, designed for the divisional training of every police constable – including detectives. I didn't envy the civilian staff who, like me, had been given the equal opportunity of running these sessions and putting up with the police aggro that was expected. Fully aware of the likely backlash to this compulsory training, headquarters had ordered that the groups should be limited to ten and no group must contain more than two defectives.

I really enjoyed the six months I spent running these sessions. After the course at Sulhamstead, each trainer was left to devise their own package as long as it covered the following subjects: prejudice and discrimination, the five A's (how name-calling can lead to genocide – more of this later), the importance of politically correct language (Terry!), sexism, racism, disability, uniform versus non-uniform and lastly but by no means least, homophobia.

Gay legislation was another area of legal theory that had produced human dilemmas. When homosexuality was decriminalised in 1967, it was done under very strict limitations, referred to as the Pool's Charter (I know!) which stood for: in **P**rivate, **O**ver twenty-one, **O**nly two men involved and both **F**reely consenting. Although this high age limit was subsequently lowered to eighteen, it still meant that if a gay man wanted sex legally, he would have to wait two years longer than his heterosexual counterparts.

Gay women, on the other hand, had no restrictions. Modern myth will tell you that this was because Queen Victoria could not countenance the idea that women would do such dreadful things and she refused to give royal assent to legislation. This is apparently untrue but, whatever the reason,

it was the right result for lesbians, at a time when society felt free
to brutalise gay men. Every time I drove past Reading jail I
was reminded of this brutality, and how that building's hard
labour regime had physically broken the brilliant Oscar
Wilde. But I was still shocked when my mother told me about
my Aunt Joan's experience.

As a young woman in the 1950s, Aunty Joan had found
herself sitting in judgment on a middle-aged homosexual.
She was a reluctant member of the jury that was deciding
the fate of the man, whose only offence was being caught in
a police sting having sex with another male. My aunt had
apparently cried when the judge had sentenced him to six
months. Her tears were also shed for the man's bed-ridden
mother, who had to be moved from her home of sixty years,
where her son had been caring for her. While her son
received beatings from strangers in prison, she died alone
among strangers in a nursing home.

Decades later, mum and dad were running a village post
office and stores in deepest Somerset. Comedian Frankie
Howerd, and his life-partner Dennis, retired to the village
and became quite friendly with my parents. But while dad
was happy to play bridge with Frankie and Dennis, he would
not let my young brother deliver their groceries.

Towards the end of my uniform career, when acting as a
'problem-solving manager' in Pangbourne, I was asked to
visit a woodland car park that was being used by gay men for
lunchtime cottaging. The car park also served a nature
reserve and this mixed use of the same space was causing
conflict.

I followed an intermittent trail of used condoms from the
car park to an underpass of the M4, which is where the

cottaging actually took place, and I was truly horrified. Not by the evidence of sexual activity but by evidence of sexual violence. Men had left graffiti warnings on the walls for others, which including descriptions of men who had assaulted and/or robbed them. Some of the warnings related to gang rape and stabbings, none of which had been reported to the police. Offenders knew that these victims were vulnerable, both physically and legally.

I approached the solving of this particular problem on two fronts. Obtaining sponsorship from the parish council, I put up signs warning that, in order to protect the local badger population (how times change), both the police and members of a local wildlife group regularly patrolled this area with mobile CCTV equipment. We didn't have such equipment but the signs did deter the lunchtime cottaging and a simple metal barrier to the car park, locked each evening, left the badgers as sole occupants of the woods at night.

More importantly, my second line of approach was to contact community health workers, who in turn introduced me to leaders of the gay community. Through them I set up informal non-uniform police clinics in many of the gay bars across Reading and Slough. Although I had blocked gay use of the underpass and woods, I also provided some of the community with a more effective means of reporting homophobic crime, and in a way I tried to make as non-judgemental as the underpass wall. But I knew this was just scratching the surface. Many of the men that cottaged at lunchtime probably did so because they were married with families, and they wouldn't be seen dead inside a gay club. It may have taken a further decade, but I was really pleased when homophobic crime was eventually recognised and treated as a hate crime.

I opened my equal opportunity training sessions by showing a 1960s documentary called 'Brown Eyes, Blue Eyes', in which a primary school teacher in Texas divided her totally white class into two groups by using the colour of their eyes.

Over two days and using blatant discrimination, the teacher encouraged first the brown-eyed children, and then the blue-eyed, to dominate their classmates. Like Nazis forcing Jews to wear the Star of David, the teacher made the blue-eyed children wear blue cloth collars on the first day and the brown-eyed children wear brown collars on the second day. She gave instructions that collar-wearing children could not use the water fountain, could not play on any apparatus in the playground and could not have second helpings at dinner. When a collared-child got a question wrong, it was because of their eye colour, and when a non-collared child got something right, it was because of their eye colour.

The five As of any 'ism' are: *Antilocution*, a posh word for name calling – 'blue eyes' was used in this way within ten minutes of the experiment starting. *Avoidance*, casual segregation – 'blue eyes smell'. *Apartheid*, enforced segregation – blue eyes are not allowed on the climbing frame. *Assault*, physical attack on people and their property – 'He called me 'brown eyes' so I hit him and then some blue-eyes threw my books into the toilet.' Finally, there is *Annihilation* – genocide or the more modern term, ethnic cleansing. In the documentary, it took just over an hour for the name-calling to escalate to the first bloody nose.

Child welfare issues aside, this powerful experiment proved a point: given the right set of circumstances and encouragement, we all have it in us to discriminate. One of the children, a boy called Brian, tried really hard to fight for the rights of the collared-underdogs; but he was a child and easily bullied into submission by the teacher. Those two childhood days clearly traumatised both the child and the re-interviewed adult Brian; but I highlighted his reactions, his willingness to stand up for others, in the hope that his efforts would inspire those in the workshop when it came to dealing with the victims of discrimination.

However, from the police point of view, racism was no longer a lead issue. It was the prospect of openly homosexual police officers that was causing the biggest response in these sessions. Lesbian officers still didn't count as, with the squaddie probationers, they were viewed by most male constables as an erotic-challenge. But an openly homosexual male being allowed to mince down the high street in full uniform was a step too far.

'Stereotyping is stereotypically a bad thing. Not so!' Was my opening gambit to this part of the session. 'Stereotyping is a starting point,' I argued. 'In some areas of police work an instant assessment can still be vital. Is everyone with a gun a danger? No. Is someone pointing a gun at you a danger? Yes.' The important point was not to *not* stereotype, but to know when and why you were doing it.

'So, do all gay men mince?' I asked.

'No, that's a stereotype,' was the general response.

I'd smile, 'It is a stereotype, but stereotypes need to be dealt with.' I thought about my first meeting with Marlon all those years ago. 'So, is this first stereotype a genuine concern? In thirteen years, I've never seen a copper mince.'

'That's because we haven't let them in yet,' would be a commonly voiced misconception.

'Gay men make up ten per cent of the male population,' I'd point out. 'While this percentage is probably far smaller in the police, believe me, we already have gay officers and probably have had since Robert Peel's day.'

This observation invariably brought a few sideways looks from the more senior in service, especially CID. (Yes, I fully acknowledge my continued prejudice against detectives; although I'd argue that 'prejudice' means to pre-judge and my judgment was based on personal experience.)

I'd then go on to tackle the other two homophobic fears that the prospect of gay male police officers always produced amongst their male colleagues; blood and sex. Stereotype number two: all gay men have either HIV or AIDS (we at least knew there was a difference now) or, at the very least, their behaviour meant that they had an increased potential to catch them.

I confronted the issue head on. 'Would you refuse to give mouth-to-mouth to a gay person?'

'How would you know they were gay?' It was usually a female who asked this question.

'My point entirely, but what if the man was in drag?'

'Just because he's in drag, doesn't mean he's gay.' The same person would invariably re-make their point.

'Good! We're getting there. So what if the collapsed man was outside a known gay bar and it's the man's boyfriend asking for your help?' Silence. 'Would anyone here refuse to give this man mouth-to-mouth?' Everyone, even the most defiant heterosexuals, would shake their collective heads. 'So what would you do?' I pushed the point to its conclusion.

'Use the provided resus,' they'd all acknowledged.

These small plastic mouthpieces and latex gloves were now shoved into every police pocket at the start of each shift.

We'd then move on to the third stereotype – gay men can't control their overheated libido.

'I'm not showering with a gay,' was an often-mooted

scenario.

'Has anything ever happened to any of you in any police-related shower in your varied careers to date?' My eyes would sweep the males in the room and I never got a positive response to this question. 'Stereotype three – gay men have no taste.' I'd again sweep the room, eyeing the old sweats and detectives, 'although who'd fancy you lot is beyond me. Despite solidly held views to the contrary, gay men will not leap under a hopping toad for a shag, nor molest the first bum they see in a shower. What would happen if they did?'

'They'd get the shit kicked out of them!' was always the unanimous and considered male response.

'Exactly. While many of you Romeos wouldn't hesitate to hit on any female officer or staff member, if you were gay you'd be at least ninety per cent sure your advances would be reciprocated before you made a move. The consequences of getting it wrong would be life-changing. . .'

'Bloody right, I'd have his balls for breakfast!'

'I wish blokes would be ninety per cent certain of a favourable response before they hit on me,' would be an equally common response from female delegates – usually the pretty ones.

'If you say *no*" do they hear *no*?' I'd asked.

'Yes – in the main.'

'Good, but if it's unwanted you have my permission to rip his balls off and I'm sure one of these gents will tell you how to cook them.'

'I can handle this sort of shit from peers,' was a frequent comment, 'but it's supervisors, usually senior officers that are the worst offenders. We can hardly complain to our line managers about our line management.'

I'd then outline the new grievance procedure, which was

intended to put things right quickly, rather than making a victim out of either party. 'This new system automatically defaults to the rank above the one you've got a problem with. It's my experience that inspectors and above can be roughly divided into three equal-opportunity camps: those who truly believe in the effectiveness of the principles surrounding equality of opportunity, those who don't believe it but still have promotional aspirations and so pay lip-service to it, and those who have gone as far as they are going and feel safe enough to ignore both legal requirements and force policies.'

Removing the name of the officer involved, I would then relate a personal experience. I knew that most people would know who I was talking about and I knew that the officer concerned would have been made quickly aware of my example, but I didn't care.

I'd recently received a pro-forma asking me two simple questions: 'Was I PSU trained?' and 'Did I want to be considered for PSU training?' My answer to both was an emphatic no. I had no desire to run round in a hot flameproof overall while fellow officers lobbed real petrol bombs at me. It was a case of horses for courses and running, of any kind, was still not my type of course.

Knowing that my view of PSU training was a minority one and that male sergeants could wait impatiently for over a year for such training, I was more than a little surprised to find that my negative answers had resulted in dates for two days of training. I queried these dates with support group at headquarters, who confirmed that the supply and demand situation for such training had not altered, but my name had been specifically selected by a certain superintendent from Reading.

Enough was enough. I decided to take him on and I took

the matter up with the chief superintendent. By now, this chief superintendent was aware that I had been selected to train as an equal opportunity adviser, and on seeing the steely glint in my eye and my determination to take this matter to headquarters if necessary, he revoked my PSU training and it was recycled to another, far more enthusiastic, sergeant.

But war had been declared. The superintendent was not best pleased by this reversal and showed his displeasure by blocking an application for annual leave that had already been sanctioned by my inspector. I explained to each group how this was a clear case of victimisation and when the superintendent could not provide me with a good reason for cancelling my leave, he was forced to reinstate it before I once more took the matter further.

I hoped that by sharing these experiences I'd effectively illustrate the new concepts of grievances and victimisation and that it would give weaker people the strength to act and defend themselves. I also didn't mind giving the superintendent a metaphorical poke in the eye – he'd started it.

CHAPTER 24

Fallout (The Saga of Henley Regatta)

Due to his uncanny resemblance to Danger Mouse's sidekick, this superintendent's nickname was Penfold. This didn't seem to bother him; he had a cartoon sketch of the character in police uniform pinned to his office noticeboard. But while he may have looked like the mild-mannered cartoon character, this man was a bully.

When my equal-opportunity workshops ended, he posted me from Reading to Henley. He wanted me out of his station, to punish me for the example I'd made of him, but the reason he gave for the move was that Henley had no female supervisors. Now, although this posting was based purely on gender and therefore discriminatory, I didn't raise any objections.

I lived nearer to Henley than Reading at the time and, unlike Reading, could easily park at this small-town station. I was also looking forward to the additional responsibility of being the only supervisor on duty most of the time. All four shifts shared the one inspector and as the only shift sergeant, the day-to-day policing of the town would be down to me.

Unfortunately, the inspector in charge of Henley at this time was one Ali Dizaei. His hyper-arrogance and total disregard for anyone but himself saw him spend time in prison: twice-tried and twice-convicted of perverting the course of justice and misconduct in public office. I suspect he will probably have spent the majority of his sentence in solitary confinement, due as much to his personality as to the fact he is a corrupt ex-police officer.

When I arrived at Henley, this same detached arrogance kept him chained to his desk, in a state of splendid isolation that left the cleaner spitting into his tea. I saw her do this once, before she knocked on his permanently closed door. She entered on the command of 'enter', placed the spat-in tea on his desk and left without Inspector Dizaei even bothering to look up, never mind say thank you. But there was an equality to Dizaei's arrogance and I, like all the other officers at the station, was treated to the same level of respect and attention as the cleaner.

Fortunately, Inspector Dizaei and I only had to share the small Henley station for a matter of months before his dedicated pursuit of promotion moved him on. As he politicked and blackmailed his way up the ladder, he played the race card with a regularity that became almost boring, but did produce enough material for his own memoir, *Not One of Us: The Trial That Changed Policing In Britain Forever.* Over a decade later, following his unlawful arrest of a man who had a genuine civil dispute against him, the late-night news played the audio-recording Dizaei made to Metpol Control, and showed CCTV of his continuing arrogance in the custody office. I wondered then who else was spitting in his tea.

However, after six months on the job, I did have some sympathy with Dizaei's desire to move from Henley. The small town came alive for one week of the year at the Royal Regatta in early July, but apart from this social event, Henley was a peaceful place with low crime and no real challenges or opportunities for enthusiastic policing.

My initial view of this upper-class market town had been coloured by a weekend of rioting in the mid-Eighties.

Anarchists from all over the country had descended on the Royal Regatta to take out their social anger on the rich residents and visitors. Rolls-Royces were keyed and sprayed with the circled capital A of their cause, as the anarchists, dressed in black with their faces covered, rampaged through the picnic area of the regatta, upsetting the hooray Henrys and Henriettas. In the town centre boutique shops were trashed and dustbins were set alight.

The event had been so well published that the BBC was there to record it all. I had always respected the BBC, but I saw a darker side to their journalism that day. One reporter was seen stirring up the newly arriving anarchists at the train station, directing them towards the town hall, where the main cameras were positioned. He was then telling police about the town hall being a major target for the anarchists and so actively tried to set up a location of mass conflict.

But now my problem was a complete lack of any kind of conflict or disturbance. The superintendent's punishment was coming home to roost: it was one thing to have sole responsibility but there was nothing to be responsible for. On my first set of nights I worried that the shift must be missing something, but we got no calls and when we came on duty the following night no crimes had been reported. Nothing, we'd missed nothing; literally nothing had happened. Then one night the normally silent radio burst into life.

'Ten-nine Henley town centre! Repeat, ten-nine Henley town centre!' The shout was accompanied by the sound of breaking glass and wild barking.

'You alright?' I asked Lenny, the young probationer who was sitting next to me as I switched on the blues and twos.

'Yeah, you?'

'Obviously. So who the fuck's putting up a ten-nine?'

Fallout (The Saga of Henley Regatta)

Due to sickness, annual leave and court commitments, we were the only two on duty, and were returning from a cup of tea with some protection squad officers out in the countryside. A few minutes later we skidded to a halt in the market place, where a dog-van was being beaten to death by a psycho with a baseball bat. He was high on drugs and had come out of nowhere, screaming incoherently and swinging his bat at the windscreen. Both the handler and his dog remained trapped inside, as the beating of their vehicle continued.

Although Lenny and I flicked open our metal batons as we leapt out of the panda, we waited the extra few seconds it took for the first traffic car to arrive before we set about arresting this particular nutter. It needed more than one shot of pepper spray to floor him, and nearly half an hour to calm the poor police dog.

The only other time my adrenalin was needed during my year at Henley, involved royalty and a suspected terrorist incident. A few miles outside of the town was the fairly modest (by Henley standards) home of a royal couple. Although considered 'minor royals', they did warrant full-time armed protection, but I had never been dispatched by Control to this location before.

'Sergeant Clement Green, we have a code red at golf-zulu. Repeat code red at golf zulu.'

'En route.' I flicked on the blues and twos. 'Have you informed the duty inspector and superintendent?'

'Affirmative. The inspector's en route with a PSU and we've launched hotel-quebec zero-one.'

HQ01 was the force helicopter; a code red meant there were intruders on premises and golf-zulu meant the premises belonged to royalty. Approaching the house I slowed down and dipped my headlights; the blues and twos had been turned off as soon as I left town as protocol dictated a silent approach. I was met by the two armed protection officers, guns in hand, and they signalled me over to a car parked on a wide grass verge against the high beech hedge that surrounded the royal abode.

The vehicle was an old Volvo estate registered to an address in Birmingham. It seemed an odd choice for terrorists. The engine was still warm and when I lifted the tail gate there was a strong doggy smell in the empty vehicle, although the boot did contain some old sacking and blue nylon rope. It was three in the morning and the car had not been there at two-thirty when the protection officers had completed their last patrol.

Fortunately, the royals were not in residence and the house had already been checked and confirmed secure, so when the inspector and his officers arrived, it was decided to place a covert cordon around the car and wait to see what happened. An hour later two men appeared. We could hear them before we saw them, their thick Brummie accents breaking through the still night like hammers on an anvil. When they came into view they were carrying something between them in a thick sack. The 'something' was alive. As they opened the boot and placed the struggling sack inside, ten uniform officers, two of them armed, sprang out at the two men and the force helicopter appeared like a gunship over the high beech hedge, firing a spotlight onto them.

'Jesus F Christ!' cried the older one.

'Fuck me!' said the younger one, 'you lot certainly take a bit of poaching seriously.' Both men had raised their hands at the sight of the guns.

'What's in there?' I asked.

A wild sort of snarling was coming from the toddler-sized sack.

'Why don't you take a look-see?' retorted the young, mouthy one.

One of the protection officers raised his gun from the lad's chest to his face. 'Why don't you tell the sergeant what she wants to know?' His suggestion was made with a quiet intensity that made the gun redundant.

'It's a badger!' shouted the older man, worried his son was about to make a bad situation worse.

'A badger?' My face hardened. 'For baiting?'

'No, for breakfast – what do you think?' The lad remained defiant.

If I'd been holding the gun I'm not sure I could have stopped myself from blowing a hole through that smug face. Badgers were caught and taken to flats in inner cities where they were torn to death by pit bulls and other fighting dogs. Large sums of money were gambled on the dogs, and the cruelty involved, to both badger and dogs (which were often seriously injured before the badger died), was beyond my ability to comprehend. As I struggled to contain my anger, the Reading lads handcuffed both men and placed them in the transit.

I waited with the badger, still in the sack but now quietly exhausted, for a vet to come out and check it was okay. She injected the animal through the closed sack, sedating it in order to examine it. Once the badger lay unresponsive, we used the opportunity to take evidential photographs on her mobile, before carrying it back to the nearby woods. There we waited for it to come round and eventually watched it amble, a little drunkenly, back into the wild. I remember spending this time thinking that if I ever won the lottery I would fund a private task force to take on the scum that both ran and attended dogfights and badger-baiting rings. In my anger, I imagined that their punishment would be biblical: an eye for an eye, a savaging for a savaging, a slow death for a slow death. The next day I bought my first lottery ticket.

By the time of my first Henley Regatta, the superintendent and I were securely entrenched in a hate-hate relationship. I had suggested to the new inspector that my shift should perform plain-clothes duty inside the car parks of the regatta as, for the last three years, there had been a spate of thefts among the large crowd and their expensive vehicles. The inspector thought it a good idea and I'd briefed my shift accordingly.

It was a hot day and I made the mistake of entering the police tent to get a cold drink. I was immediately spotted by the superintendent, who was acting as Gold Command. Within minutes of leaving the tent I was told by Control to report to the station inspector; the superintendent did not agree with the inspector and me about the best use of my shift. He demanded we all return to uniform patrol on the streets of Henley and I was personally banned from entering the area of the regatta itself. I shrugged and recalled my shift to break the bad news. Within two hours I had no shift left.

One by one, the superintendent dispatched them all over the division to deal with shoplifters in Reading, vagrants at the railway station (where a Reading PSU was already dealing with the problem), and two missing persons from neighbouring Buckinghamshire. As I was returning from dropping off the last member of my shift, who was to act as an extra jailer in Reading's custody suite, I was dispatched to take a statement from a retailer in Henley regarding some juvenile shoplifting. This was a step too far and other supervisors, who obviously felt the same, told Control that the matter was already being dealt with by an appropriate probationer, and I continued a panda patrol of the main streets of Henley as ordered.

Around six in the evening, I saw two Reading officers arrest a young drunk. They had him subdued on the ground and I heard them call regatta control for transport. When an ETA for the requested transit came back as ten minutes I began to get worried for the officers.

Although they had the drunk under control, they were surrounded by a growing number of his real and would-be friends, who clearly thought the officers should release their pal. I radioed regatta control, informed them of the situation and said I would pick up the officers and their prisoner and rendezvous with the prisoner transit away from the town centre. Control replied that my call sign was not authorised to use the regatta channel and that the officers should wait for the transit. I was furious. The superintendent's pettiness was actually putting officers at risk and ignoring Control I went and picked up the Reading lads and their struggling prisoner.

As we approached a major crossroads, I again radioed regatta control and asked for a meeting point. Again I was told that my call sign would not be acknowledged on the regatta channel. The two Reading officers looked bemused as I asked them to use their call sign and request a rendezvous. When a second drunk stopped our progress by standing in the middle of the road, it was one of the struggling PCs who again had to use their call sign in order to summon assistance for this second drunk.

After eventually transferring the prisoner to the Reading transit, I returned to Henley nick and wrote out a general report addressed to the chief superintendent. In it I stated I wished to pursue a formal grievance against the superintendent. I then drove over to Reading and shoved it under the chief superintendent's locked office door, before making a pocket notebook entry of my actions – I suspected I might need proof of 'good-service' of this complaint.

At nine the following morning, I received a phone call from the superintendent,

'I understand you intend to lodge a formal grievance against me?'

'Yes, Sir.'

'What are the grounds for this grievance?'

'With all due respect, Sir,' I replied, in a completely respect-free tone, 'I do not have to divulge the content of my griev-ance to you, as you are the subject of said grievance.'

'Right, I want to see you immediately regarding a debrief of the regatta!' I could hear the superintendent turning puce on the other end of the phone.

'Well, Sir, as that particular topic is now the subject of a formal grievance, I would only be willing to speak to you about it within the confines of the grievance procedure – which of course means in the presence of the chief superinten-dent. Will the chief-super be present at this debrief?' I relished the tension the calmness of my question was creating.

'Sergeant Clement-Green! I am giving you a direct order to come and see me regarding Henley Regatta. Are you going to disobey that direct order?'

'Yes, Sir.'

'I beg your pardon?' His tone instantly transported me back to Coop's old office, all those years ago in Oxford.

'I do not believe your order to be a legal one, Sir. I'm there-fore not going to speak to you about the regatta outside the forum of a formal grievance procedure.'

My tone was that a mother explaining to her child that they were not going to be allowed sweets immediately before their tea. Before I could offer to travel to Reading to be 'stuck on' (formally notified of disciplinary proceedings against me), the superintendent was yelling down the phone again,

'Right, stay right where you are! I'll be over in ten minutes!' And he slammed down the receiver.

I felt strangely calm. I knew I was in the right, and when the superintendent stormed into my office some twenty minutes later, he was shaking with rage as he sat down opposite me. I had used the time to lower the chair he would be sitting in and raise mine higher. I also had a steaming cup of tea at my elbow to help create a picture of nonchalance.

He pulled out a brand-new pocket notebook and I almost smiled as I looked down at his bent balding head, which was now on a level with the large battered desk. He was scribbling away furiously in bright purple ink.

'Right, Sergeant Clement-Green, I am giving you a direct order to discuss the Henley Regatta with me. Are you refusing to obey that order?'

'I am.' I did not wish to waste his expensive-looking ink with a long-winded response.

He looked at his watch and noted the time in the margin of his new pocket book. 'Right!' he repeated, 'I am now formerly reporting you for the offence of disobeying a lawful order,' and, with the help of the printed caution found at the rear of all notebooks, placed there for those police officers not in the habit of using it regularly, he cautioned me. Looking up once more he glared at me, silently demanding a formal reply.

'Lovely,' I said, taking a sip of my tea. 'Would you like one before you return to Reading?' I raised my mug in a final salute of defiance.

The superintendent recorded my whole response with little stabbing movements, before he jumped up and left the office, slamming the door behind him. The interview had lasted less than four minutes.

At nine-thirty the following morning, my equanimity was somewhat disturbed by a call from the chief superintendent's secretary. She told me to be in his office at noon and to have with me, in writing, the details of my grievance. When I explained to her that under the force grievance procedure I was not required to put anything into writing until level two, she asked me to wait. Within seconds the chief superintendent himself was shouting down the phone at me.

'Sergeant Clement-Green! If I tell you to be in my office at twelve you will be here at twelve, and if I tell you to produce a written report you will bloody well write one! Do I make myself clear, sergeant?'

'Perfectly, Sir.' I whispered, as he, too, slammed down the receiver on me.

Shit! It was one thing for Penfold to shout at you, but the chief superintendent was another ball game altogether. He was God, chief of his own division, ruler of all he surveyed, answerable only to the chief constable. Talk about Davina and Goliath! It was time for reinforcements. I rang the police federation office and was lucky enough to get straight through to John Ryan, the branch secretary. It was his last day at work, but he said he had nothing organised and told me he'd come straight down. 'I fancy going out with a bang!' he declared.

Fine, I thought, as long as you don't take me with you. 'Stay put in Henley, you're not to go anywhere near Reading until I've had a chance to discuss things with you. I'll phone and let him know.'

John then phoned the chief superintendent and informed him that, as I had already formally invoked the grievance procedure, when I was seen by him it would be in John's company. I would therefore not be able to make his office by twelve as John had to travel down from the federation offices in Banbury.

'While you wait, may I suggest that you refresh your memory of force policy regarding grievance procedures, chief superintendent?' John had suggested.

'That'll certainly kill or cure,' I observed, when he told me.

I suppose anyone's last day at work after thirty years would give them a sense of freedom, power too; after all, they'd not be around the next day to deal with any fallout. As we made our way over to Reading, John asked, 'Do you know why he's called you to his office?'

'I'm assuming it's to deal with my grievance.'

He shook his head. 'No. He apparently intends to try and deal with your discipline first.'

I was stunned. Not only did this breach both disciplinary and grievance codes, it was a totally unfair way of dealing with a fair complaint. I remained horrified at this gross breach of procedure as I was kept waiting outside the chief superintendent's office. John had gone in on his own to explain the relevant force policies to the man who should have been upholding them, and as his secretary entered the office with a cup of tea for the boss, I actually heard him say, 'I don't know if I can enact policies that don't allow me to run my own division.' That said it all.

When I eventually entered his lair, I was immediately given 'divisional advice' for disobeying a direct order from the superintendent. Not for refusing to discuss Henley Regatta, which John had reiterated was the subject of a grievance, but for refusing to attend Reading nick to be 'stuck on'.

Leaving aside the blatant untruthfulness of this statement and the unfairness of this decision, 'divisional advice' meant no formal proceedings would follow and no records would be kept. Before I could argue the toss about such 'advice', without drawing breath, he moved on to the question of my grievance.

'What's it going to take to make this situation go away?'

I was so angry at the way I had just been treated, that I looked the still-smouldering chief superintendent straight in the eye, and replied,

'Nothing! There is nothing that you can do or say, 'Sir',' I spat out the title, 'that will *make this go away.* I intend to take this whole matter to headquarters. Someone needs to air the dirty linen about the way this division is being run when it comes to grievances.'

I thought he was going to have a seizure. He turned purple and started to splutter, but John held up his hand and excused us both from the office. Once outside, he tried to reassure me.

'Look, I'll make sure this whole episode is disclosed to the right people at HQ, but right here, right now, you take what you can and run. Understand?'

Reluctantly, I returned to the office. 'I refuse to work under that man's direction again.' I glared at the chief super as our mutual rage clashed in the ether, invisible but potent. 'I want my move to Newbury division, and I want it now!'

Mike and I had recently bought a house in Lambourn, which was as far west as the force went. The superintendent had, unsurprisingly, refused my application for a move.

'Fair enough,' the chief super agreed, 'but it may take some time...

'One week,' I snapped, 'or I will take this matter to head-quarters. I know John has told you that you and the superintendent don't have a leg between you to stand on.'

I walked out of the office without being dismissed and

closed the door firmly behind me. This time there were no
tears and my move was authorised within three days.

It was not long after this that I attended a seminar on how the
force was progressing with its equal opportunity policy. The
assistant chief constable gave the opening address in which he
described how, in general terms, the force was settling successfully into the policies, but that one or two individuals,
often senior in rank, were being shown up as bullies. The
word hit me like a bullet. I had been bullied – there was no
other word for it. Bullied. I had always been a strong, confident person, prepared to raise my head above the parapet,
but a fighter can also be bullied. The assistant chief constable
finished his address with an open invitation,

'If anyone here has been bullied, or knows of someone else
who has been bullied, I will be only too pleased to speak to
them on a formal or informal basis. My secretary has been
told to put through any officer who wishes to speak to me
directly about this matter.'

As soon as I returned to my Newbury office, I put this
open-door policy to the test and telephoned the number the
ACC had put up on the overhead projector which, I noted,
quite a few others had hastily copied down.

'Assistant chief constable's office.' The voice was female
and pleasant.

'This is Sergeant Clement-Green from Newbury. Would it
be possible to arrange an appointment with the ACC?'

'Can you to tell me what it's in connection with?'

Here we go, I thought, instantly sceptical about the open-
door invitation. 'Bullying,' I replied.

'I can put you straight through now if you'd like, Sergeant
Clement-Green, or I could arrange a face-to-face appoint-

ment if you'd prefer?' The offer was gobsmacking.

'Um, well, I'd like a little time to think through the details. How long would I have to wait for an appointment?'

'The ACC could see you for half an hour this Thursday afternoon. Will that be a long enough slot?' she enquired.

'Yes, thank you.' I was impressed.

At three o'clock that Thursday, I was shown into the ACC's office and related the saga of Henley Regatta and the background to it. The ACC listened with an open face that grew steadily more serious, until his jaw became tight and his initial smile of greeting set into a deep frown. His verbal response however gave nothing away.

'Well, Sergeant Clement-Green, can I start by thanking you for your honesty. I have no reason to disbelieve anything you have told me. If I felt the need I could check on your version of events from paper records and control tapes but, as I've said, I don't feel the need.'

'Thank you, Sir.' I felt an echo of the reassurance I hoped I'd managed to give other victims of abuse.

'I am already looking into other matters regarding the superintendent – you are not the first officer to allege bullying by this man.'

Again I felt the same sort of relief I had witnessed on the WSU, when I could tell one victim that they were not alone and that in court it would not just be their word against the offenders.

The ACC continued. 'With regards to the chief superintendent, there are several options for you to consider. Firstly, you can ask me to take the matter no further and that will be the end of it. Or you can leave the matter with me and I will deal with it personally, but informally. However, if you want me to take the matter forward formally, I am also quite happy to do that. I will have the chief superintendent stuck-on and investigated – the investigating officer will be an ACC from another force.'

This honest statement of facts, totally devoid of tonal or facial expression, was a master-class in empowering victims.

'Thank you, Sir.'

Having been given the power, I was happy to hand it straight back.

'I'll leave the matter in your hands. If you feel it necessary, for the good of the force, to deal with the chief superintendent formally, I will supply a statement. If you want to deal with it informally I am happy for that process to take place. I'm confident that neither of us feels the option of doing nothing is a suitable one.'

The ACC smiled and as I closed the door his voice came over the secretary's intercom.

'Gladys, arrange for Reading's chief superintendent to come and see me at his earliest convenience.'

Several months later, the superintendent appeared on the local news. He was at the centre of a high-profile sex discrimination case involving another female officer. Her legal team had contacted me to see how I felt about being a witness and I told them that while I was happy to give evidence against the superintendent, I would not say anything negative against the force as a whole. They didn't come back to me for a statement. The tribunal found in favour of the female officer and I believe the superintendent was forced to take early retirement, although I've been unable to verify this with TVP.

I never found out what happened to the chief superintendent.

CHAPTER 25

Dungeons and Pendragons

Crash. 'Fuck! It's happening!' The tree-dwellers were instantly awake. It was January 9th 1996 and the evictions and tree-felling had just begun in earnest. The Newbury Bypass, or more specifically the Winchester-Preston trunk road, was actually under construction.

A false war had raged on and off since the first eco-warriors and concerned housewives had protested by occupying land in July 1995. Lines had been drawn; on maps, in the mud and in the trees. For nearly three more years the 'Third Battle of Newbury' would rage along this nine-mile stretch of road (the first two battles having occurred during the Civil War). Defenders of the Desmoulin's whorl snail's rights had suffered their last defeat in the High Court, and at a cost of quarter of a million pounds the tiny snail had been moved to a new home which, unlike its last, would have protected status.

Six months earlier I'd been designated as the full-time custody sergeant at Newbury Police Station. Like a military commander, I had organised the logistics and processes for handling hundreds of arrests a day. My goal was to avoid the thousand-pound-an-hour civil damages accrued by Hampshire Police during construction of their section of the bypass. This figure was the hourly rate the civil courts had awarded each protester for any wrongful detention.

Initially most of the bypass arrests were made under the

old common-law of power of preventing a breach of the peace, but as the battle raged and aged, more serious offences occurred: criminal damage, breach of bail conditions and assault. One form of medieval assault used by a minority of protesters began by them collecting their urine in bottles. Like burning oil poured from ancient ramparts, these protesters would then empty the bottles into the faces of the private security guards, climbing up towards their treetop fortresses. The protesters were marking their territory in an extremely unpleasant but effective manner.

The subsequent detention of prisoners was the absolute responsibility of each custody sergeant; under PACE I was legally liable for any unlawfully authorised detentions. Not Thames Valley Police, not the chief constable, not the divisional superintendent or station inspector, but me, Sergeant Clement-Green; I was the one they could sue. I'd been offered grey assurances that this would never happen, but the law was there in black and white for all to see and for all to use.

So I had a vested interest in devising a comprehensive and compensation-free plan to manage the expected mass arrests. It was later estimated that around seven thousand physically protested during the Third Battle of Newbury.

Each arresting officer had a Polaroid taken of themselves with their prisoner at the place of arrest and we soon had a great collection of pictures. They started with big cheesy grins from the officers, standing like big-game hunters next to their prize kill. Some of the protesters even joined in, posing with matching grins or expressions of mock horror; treating the whole battle as some sort of life-sized board game. But as time passed and more arrests were made, both sets of faces became serious and exhausted as they blurred into Us and Them. The arresting officer would fill in an arrest statement with the details of the offence and the prisoner would then be placed in a police van. When the van was full it would be sent to the nearest police station with spare cells and the next van would pull forward. It was a conveyor belt of incarceration.

The nearest police station with capacity might be over thirty miles away and even in a different force area – Hampshire was still not free from the battle of the bypass. From the police point of view, when a protester was bailed thirty miles away from their camp it gave us a theoretical breather as they made their way back. But, like Zulus on the horizon at dawn, there were always other warriors waiting to fill any gap. Because Newbury would always be the first station used, I had organised for the dog kennels to be converted and extended to house prisoners safely, but with the minimum of police supervision; thus releasing foot soldiers back to the battlefield.

Bottom-sized plywood boxes had been built, with a bench at the rear and a grilled door at the front. Each prisoner could stand or sit, shout at their fellow inmates and walk two strides to the door to discuss the politics surrounding their lack of liberty with the sole constable, who walked the line of doors like a private on a lonely and unappreciated patrol.

These 'holding cells' were numbered so that each detainee could be confident they'd be dealt with in turn – we British do so hate queue-jumping. During the day, when their turn arrived, it was me they invariably met for their formal booking-in. I grew to really appreciate the vast array of people that appeared before me: the committed eco-warrior who shed genuine tears as each ancient oak was felled, the veterans of the Greenham Common nuclear protest and the local housewife caught up in an eviction when she'd taken soup to her teenage daughter who had tied herself to a tree.

Then, there were the celebrities: Arthur Uther Pendragon, born John Timothy Rothwell, and Daniel Hooper, who became better known as Swampy, a tunnel-living protester who successfully slowed the bulldozers for a respectable length of time. I recall with semi-awed amusement my first encounter with King Arthur; he was dressed in his druid robes, muddy and battle-worn, but his sword Excalibur shone brightly as he laid its polished blade carefully across the raised custody desk.

'That's an offensive weapon if ever I saw one,' I observed.

'Well that's where you're wrong, Sergeant. It is the sacred symbol of my druid faith.'

'That,' I said, pointing at the glistening blade with my chewed biro, 'was made to kill. Therefore, although beautiful rather than offensive, it is nevertheless a weapon.'

'That's not what a judge has decreed. He agreed with me, that to take a sword from a druid sword-bearer is to leave him symbolically naked.'

'So, what's your proper name?' I continued with the process, determined not to engage in political or religious argument. There were another twenty prisoners to process.

'Arthur Uther Pendragon!'

'Your real name?'

'It is my real name – I had it changed by deed poll on the 11th June, 1986.'

'Fair enough.' I tapped his name into the computer.

'Date and place of birth?'

'5.4.54. England.'

'Address?'

'The Great Hall, Camelot.'

'No Fixed Abode,' I punched into the computer.

This was all part of the game. If I'd accepted Arthur's

address as a bivouac in a camp on the battleground, it would have muddied legal waters. Having said that, some long-term protesters did get their mail delivered to such addresses as: Pixie Village, Babble Brook and Heartbreak Hotel.

'Occupation?'

'Druid.'

'Shouldn't that come under religion?' I queried.

Arthur shrugged.

'How about warrior, for occupation, and druid for religion?' I ventured.

Arthur smiled.

'Any special dietary requirements?'

I expected the standard response of nothing with a face, but Arthur was an unconventional eco-warrior.

'Meat and two veg would be nice – I'm starving.'

'That'll make a change for the canteen,' I said, 'they're sick of doing baked beans on toast.'

'If I have to have toast, make sure it's white – none of that brown crap.'

'Right you are, Mr Pendragon. Now, about this sword...'

'I need it with me.'

'Well, that's not going to happen. I have to put you in a cell with at least two other people and I can't let you go in armed. I will, however, keep the sword in my possession until the court's ready for you. That way you'll know no one will mess with it, deal?'

'Deal.' Romantic hero that he was, Arthur was also a pragmatist.

'If our court says you can have it back, then so be it.'

The court did give Arthur Uther Pendragon the right to bear his sword in public.

Other eco-warriors described him as 'fluffy but firm',

because Arthur's first line of attack was always to disarm by charm. While some thought this made him fluffy, he would take no shit and he won several skirmishes by using the law against itself. For example, he always pleaded guilty and he always demanded to be sent to prison for his persistent breaches of the conditions of the 'sausage' bail.

The sausage referred to the shape of the area on a map that encapsulated the nine-mile stretch of the bypass. On first arrest, detainees were cautioned if they agreed to stay out of the sausage's nine-mile exclusion zone. This cautioning system allowed individuals, like the soup-bearing mother and her tree-hugging daughter, a get-out-of-jail-free card. They had done their bit and could return to their work and school life without any sort of criminal record.

Professional protesters accepted the first caution so that they could return to do battle the same day. These people were therefore put before the court on their next arrest and the magistrate would make the Newbury-sausage part of their court-bail conditions. It was his breach of his bail that saw Arthur remanded to prison on more than one occasion, but he didn't mind prison; it was what he wanted – part of his great plan. Arthur wanted to get all the protesters remanded. He wanted the Newbury sausage to jam up the penal system and this tactic became known as the Camelot Pact.

Sometimes this game-plan worked and sometimes it didn't. Towards the end of the battle, Arthur and eighteen co-protesters were once more before the Newbury magistrate for further breaches of bail. Arthur demanded they all be sent to prison rather than have another 'conditional discharge' thrust unfairly upon them. But the magistrate had got good at the same game. He agreed to Arthur's demands for a custodial sentence and, like Billie all those years before him, Arthur and the protesters were 'detained until the rising of the court' – which followed hot on the heels of the sentence.

At quarter-past-one in the morning on Monday 9th November 1998, the Newbury Bypass was opened in secret. It had cost Thames Valley and Hampshire forces in the region of five million pounds to police, while total costs have been circulated as high as twenty-four million. Arthur went on to win more legal battles – I'm especially proud of his work in opening up public access to Stonehenge – but Swampy simply vanished into the mists and legends surrounding the history of the Third Battle of Newbury. As far as I'm aware, Thames Valley Police did not have one successful case of unlawful detention made against them.

Epilogue

In 1984 I joined a Police Force, full of militaristic machismo, sexism, racism and homophobia. Sixteen years later I retired from a far more inclusive Police Service, which not only now recognised the diverse elements of the communities they policed, but cared about them, too. When I joined, the memory of WPC Yvonne Fletcher was still raw and I am writing when the memories of PC Nicola Hughes and PC Fiona Bone are even rawer; policewomen have always had equality in being able to die in the service of the public.

But now, looking back, women have also achieved a real equality of opportunity in every other aspect of 'the job'. On telly Juliet Bravo gave way to the formidable DCI Tennison and on the real streets, a slim girl of a sergeant I worked with at HMS Ganges became chief constable of Dorset. Indeed, TVP itself is led by a woman and the only male bastion left, the top job at Metpol, fell in February 2017 to Cressida Dick, a former Thames Valley superintendent educated in Oxford.

I feel privileged to have lived through such dramatic changes; to have known the joys of solo foot patrol around Oxford's historic colleges as the sun rose over the dreaming spires. I loved owning the city in this way; to have had it to myself in the quiet moments and then fought on its pavements in both private battles and a full-scale riot. Policing is always going to be stressful, but it's rarely dull for long. I don't miss the job and I don't envy today's police officers. Handheld computers have replaced typewriters and telex machines and, as with teachers and health workers, social problems have grown while resources have shrunk. Today, community workers find themselves continually being forced to stick plasters over wounds that need stitching and, as with the ambulance strike, I would find that too frustrating.

Looking back on my sixteen years with Thames Valley Police I feel a sense of quiet bemusement that I didn't feel at the time. I have been a part of national issues and the most intimate moments of private lives. How did I pack so much life into my day-to-day living? It wasn't until I sat down to write this book that I realised just how broad my experience had been – at the time I was simply doing a job to the best of my ability. I may have joined the police for the huge pay rise, but I stayed for the buzz.

Yes there were boring days, there were bad and sad days, but each one had the potential to make you realise why life is worth living. Policing taught me to handle life's grey areas with compassion and tolerance; it showed me that good people can do bad things and that the act is not necessarily the person. But, best of all, it made me determined to grab hold of and enjoy each day, because life-changing and life-ending tragedy may be just around the corner. So many memories gathered, so many lives entered and exited. It was totally brilliant.

In August 2000 I retired from the police. Mike was in the process of becoming the chief fire officer of Royal Berkshire Fire and Rescue Service and we no longer needed two incomes. Aged forty, I was free to follow my lifelong passion and I started up my own livery yard, training and competing dressage horses. It was not a question of being disenchanted with the police; it was about having the opportunity to do

Epilogue

something else that I really loved.

Mike and I were together for 17 years, but when he retired we drifted apart. We stayed friends until he found a new woman who wasn't comfortable with our friendship. I have lived alone now for nine years, enjoying every minute of a single but not solitary life. After the divorce I returned to the workplace, drawing on my police experience and working with the previously despised CID as a civilian investigator on various Serious and Organised Crime Teams, including several murder incident rooms. My last job was managing sixty registered sex offenders for Wiltshire Police.

Perhaps it's time to write another memoir.

Also by Mirror Books

Falling Through Fire
Clifford Thompson

The true story of a London firefighter, now journalist, and his involvement in domestic and high-profile disasters across 25 years.

One incident, early in his career, had a profound effect on him that he carries to this day.

In a frank and honest way he recounts his personal experience of the 1988 Clapham train crash, the 1993 bombing of New York's World Trade Centre and the aftermath of the King's Cross fire.

Clifford describes the trauma that firefighters deal with on a daily basis – and reveals that despite facing many horrific situations and experiencing major disasters, he cannot escape the haunting memory of a three-year-old boy dying in his arms after a house fire just days before Christmas.

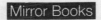

Also by Mirror Books

The Green Bicycle Mystery
Antony M Brown

The first in a unique collection of books. Each tells the story of an unsolved true crime and then invites the reader to decide on the outcome. Beautifully presented with evidence images and maps — perfect for lovers of puzzles, mysteries and crime stories, this new collection of Cold Case Jury books will not only bring a murder story to life — it will make you part of it.

The series begins with the tragic case of Bella Wright: In a lonely lane running through rural Leicestershire in 1919, a solitary bicycle lies on its side, its metal frame catching the glow of the fading evening light.

Next to the bicycle, lying at an angle across the road, is a young woman. She is partly on her back, partly on her left side, with her right hand almost touching the mudguard of the rear wheel. Her legs rest on the roadside verge, where fronds of white cow parsley and pink rosebay rise above luxuriant summer foliage. On her head sits a wide-brimmed hat, daintily finished with a ribbon and bow. She is dressed in a pastel blouse and long skirt underneath a light raincoat. The blood-flecked coat begins the story...

Also by Mirror Books

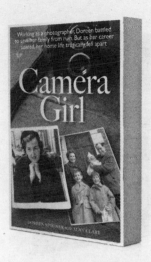

Camera Girl
Doreen Spooner with Alan Clark

The true story of a woman coping with a tragic end to the love of her life, alongside a daily fight to establish herself and support her children.

A moving and inspiring memoir of Doreen Spooner – a woman ahead of her time. Struggling to hold her head high through the disintegration of the family she loves through alcoholism, she began a career as Fleet Street's first female photographer.

While the passionate affair and family life she'd always dreamed of fell apart, Doreen walked into the frantic world of a national newspaper. Determined to save her family from crippling debt, her work captured the Swinging Sixties through political scandals, glamorous stars and cultural icons, while her homelife spiralled further out of control.

The two sides of this book take you through a touching and emotional love story, coupled with a hugely enjoyable portrait of post-war Britain.

Also by Mirror Books

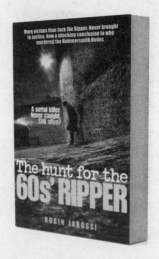

The Hunt for the 60s' Ripper
Robin Jarossi

While 60s London was being hailed as the world's most fashionably vibrant capital, a darker, more terrifying reality was unfolding on the streets. During the early hours a serial killer was stalking prostitutes then dumping their naked bodies. When London was famed for its music, groundbreaking movies and Carnaby Street vibe, the reality included a huge street prostitution scene, a violent world that filled the magistrate's courts.

Seven, possibly eight, women fell victim – making this killer more prolific than Jack the Ripper, 77 years previously. His grim spree sparked the biggest police manhunt in history. But why did such a massive hunt fail? And why has such a traumatic case been largely forgotten today?

With shocking conclusions, one detective makes an astonishing new claim. Including secret police papers, crime reconstructions, links to figures from the vicious world of the Kray twins and the Profumo Affair, this case exposes the depraved underbelly of British society in the Swinging Sixties. An evocative and thought-provoking reinvestigation into perhaps the most shocking unsolved mass murder in modern British history.

Mirror Books

Also by Mirror Books

1963 - A Slice of Bread and Jam
Tommy Rhattigan

Tommy lives at the heart of a large Irish family in derelict Hulme in Manchester, ruled by an abusive, alcoholic father and a negligent mother. Alongside his siblings he begs (or steals) a few pennies to bring home to avoid a beating, while looking for a little adventure of his own along the way.

His foul-mouthed and chaotic family may be deeply flawed, but amongst the violence, grinding poverty and distinct lack of hygiene and morality lies a strong sense of loyalty and, above all, survival.

During this single year – before his family implodes and his world changes for ever – Tommy almost falls foul of the welfare officers, nuns, police – and Myra Hindley and Ian Brady.

An adventurous, fun, dark and moving true story of the only life young Tommy knew.

Also by Mirror Books

Death at Wolf's Nick
Diane Janes

In January 1931, on a lonely stretch of Northumberland moorland known as Wolf's Nick, flames rose up into the night sky. Evelyn Foster, a young taxi driver, lay near her burning car, engulfed in flames, praying for a passing vehicle.

With her last breath, she described her attacker: a mysterious man with a bowler hat who had asked her to drive him to the next village, then attacked her and left her to die. Local police attempted to track down Evelyn's killer – while others questioned the circumstances, Evelyn's character and if there was even a man at all…

Professional crime writer and lecturer Diane Janes gained unprecedented access to Evelyn's case files. Through her evocative description, gift for storytelling and detailed factual narrative, Diane takes the reader back to the scene of the crime, painting a vivid description of village life in the 1930s.

Central to this tragic tale, is a daughter, sister and friend who lost her life in an horrific way – and the name of her murderer, revealed for the first time…